# PROGRESS IN EDUCATION
## VOLUME II

# PROGRESS IN EDUCATION
## VOLUME II

R. NATA (EDITOR)

**Nova Science Publishers, Inc.**
*Huntington, NY*

KH

| | |
|---|---|
| **Senior Editors:** | Susan Boriotti and Donna Dennis |
| **Office Manager:** | Annette Hellinger |
| **Graphics:** | Wanda Serrano |
| **Information Editor:** | Tatiana Shohov |
| **Book Production:** | Cathy DeGregory, Kay Seymour, Lynette Van Helden and Jennifer Vogt |
| **Circulation:** | Ave Maria Gonzalez, Ron Hedges and Andre Tillman |

*Library of Congress Cataloging-in-Publication Data*
*Available Upon Request*

ISBN 1-56072-934-1

Copyright © 2001 by Nova Science Publishers, Inc.
227 Main Street, Suite 100
Huntington, New York 11743
Tele. 631-424-6682      Fax 631-425-5933
e-mail: Novascience@earthlink.net
Web Site: http://www.nexusworld.com/nova

*Printed in the United States of America*

11/22/04

# CONTENTS

# PREFACE

Education, it seems, is one of those areas of human endeavor, which is constantly either the subject of proposals for reform or actually being reformed. This state of ferment is no doubt due to education's intimate connection to contemporary life and mankind's desire for self-betterment at least in the area of knowledge acquistion. Recent reports have shown the earning gap to be widening even more between college-education individuals and those not obtaining higher education, which has triggered a new surge in education reform proposals and initiatives.

This book presents state-of-the-art analyses of the some important ideas and programs in education.

*Chapter 1*

# Impact of Proficiency Testing:
# A Collaborative Evaluation

### *Robert DeBard and Patricia K. Kubow*
School of Leadership and Policy Studies
Partnerships for Community Action
Bowling Green State University

## ACKNOWLEDGEMENTS

This project would not have been completed without the cooperation of many individuals. The grant provided by the Partnerships for Community Action program of Bowling Green State University provided for printing, material and travel costs, but the considerable human resources needed to conduct such a study had to be contributed by representatives from both the Perrysburg Schools and Bowling Green State University. The end result exemplifies the intention of and spirit behind the initiative of BGSU President Dr. Sidney Ribeau in establishing the Partnerships for Community Action program.

The researchers wish to thank the students, faculty, staff members and parents who participated in the focus groups whose thoughtful reflection helped us formulate the salient issues that were ultimately to be included in the research instrument. The viability of this study depended on gaining the input of those impacted by proficiency testing rather than presupposing what should be important to them. The qualitative transcripts generated from these focus groups confirm that the research instrument truly reflects the concerns of the various constituents.

It was anticipated that a major expenditure would be required to pay for the transcription of the focus group sessions. Through the willingness of the College of Education and Human Development and its former dean, Dr. Les Sternberg, the transcription was completed as a contribution to this project by the Word Processing Center of the College.

Ms. Judith Maxey, Word Process Supervisor, and Ms. Sherry Haskins, Word Process Specialist, were diligent in their willingness to transcribe the 27 different focus groups tapes presented to them.

The review of the survey instrument involved administrative staff members from the Perrysburg Schools. Throughout the process of this project, Dr. John Crecelius has been most helpful in coordinating the participation of Perrysburg. The contributions of Dr. Rona Simon, Dr. John Pertner, Mr. Terry Teopas helped refine the survey down to a number that was judged to be feasible for the various constituent groups.

The Office of Institutional Research at BGSU contributed significantly to this project. Ms. Jie Wu, Institutional Research Analyst with the Office of Institutional Research, generated the final instrument. Her continuous cooperation in loading data on SPSS was invaluable to the successful completion of this study. It was Dr. William Knight, Director of Institutional Research, whose expertise with SPSS and patience in helping us generate the necessary reports to analyze the extensive data generated through this study, who represented the best example of how University expertise can benefit PCA projects.

## STATEMENT OF PURPOSE

The purpose of this project was to collaborate with Perrysburg Schools to construct and administer a survey based on the perceptions of those constituencies within the school district affected by proficiency testing of elementary and secondary students in Ohio. The goal was to give voice to concerns, needs, and challenges of various constituencies impacted by proficiency testing so as to reaffirm testing processes that are effective as well as to suggest improvement in areas that are perceived as needing improvement in order to better achieve the desired outcomes of such testing within the district.

The survey was constructed through a series of focus groups of students, teachers, administrators, and parents/community members designed to ascertain the salient issues that need to be evaluated if the impact of this public policy is to be better understood and implemented effectively for the benefit of education in the district. The eventual survey instrument's content, length, and language were constructed through collaboration with representatives of Perrysburg Schools. The cooperation between the school district constituencies and university representatives offers an exemplary example of how the resources of a community can merge with the expertise of the University to form a partnership to implement community action to improve the educational process so vital to community progress.

# STUDY FINDINGS BY CONSTITUENT GROUPS

In the pages that follow, the findings of the proficiency testing study are organized according to the five constituent groups involved. These groups and the number surveyed include: teachers (203), support and administrative staff (33), elementary students (884), secondary students (1167), and community/parents (129). A summary list of thematic responses, general comments, an item analysis, and a table of results are provided.

# THEMATIC RESPONSES

## Teachers

*Impact on Student Learning Behavior*
    Motivation
    Increased Anxiety
    Test Taking Skills
    pressure
    Apply Knowledge           = Eight Items
    Think Critically
    Reading Comprehension
    Apply Information

*Impact on Professional Job Environment*
    Stress
    School Climate
    Workload
    Held Accountable
    Morale
    Comfort
    Fostered Collaboration       = Ten Items
    Imposed on District
    Raising tThe Bar
    Unreliable for Teacher Evaluation

*Impact on Curriculum*
    Alignment of Curriculum with Proficiencies
    Teaching to the Test
    Identify Curricular Weaknesses
    Align Curriculum Between Grades
    Emphasis on Math and Science
    Add-On
    Educational Outcomes
    Learning Outcomes             = Eleven Items
    Curriculum Constriction
    Creative Teaching
    Student Creativity

*Impact on Response to Student Learning Needs*
    Helped with Academic Problems
    Learning Difficulties
    Results Arrive Too Late
    Single Test             = Six Items
    Developmentally Appropriate
    Self-Esteem

*Community Relations*
    Parental Involvement
    Increased Competition
    Public Support           = Five Items
    Appease Public
    Measure Learning

## TEACHERS

## General Comments:

*Impact on Students' Learning Behavior*

Teachers are very concerned about the impact proficiency testing has had on students' learning behavior. Teachers reported that proficiency testing has resulted in the increased anxiety students feel toward school and that such testing places too much pressure on students. The teachers were divided as to whether proficiency testing has helped motivate students to take their studies more seriously. Less than half of the teachers are convinced that proficiency testing has helped students' test taking skills. Even fewer perceive that proficiency testing has helped students' ability to think critically or has increased students' ability to apply knowledge. Rather, the majority of teachers believe that proficiencies test a student's reading comprehension more than a student's knowledge in a particular subject area. Although most teachers agreed that proficiency testing has helped students apply rather than just recall information, more females than males are convinced of this benefit of proficiency testing. Overall, elementary teachers, as opposed to secondary teachers, felt more strongly that proficiency testing has had a negative impact on students' behavior and their learning environment.

*Impact on Professional Job Environment*

There is no question that proficiency testing has impacted teachers' job environment. Just as teachers expressed concern about the pressure proficiency testing has placed on students, teachers have experienced excess stress in their job and an increased workload as a result of proficiency testing. Moreover, they feel that proficiency testing has resulted in teachers being held accountable for results but are adamant that proficiency tests are not a reliable way to evaluate teacher performance.

An overwhelming number of teachers felt that proficiency testing has been imposed upon the school district rather than policy makers seeking input from the district. This imposition of policy upon teachers, without having input in the decision making processes affecting their own work lives and that of their students', was of greatest concern to teachers. Teachers also believed that proficiency testing has resulted in a constant "raising of the bar" by state officials.

Only a little over half of the teachers reported that proficiency testing has become more comfortable for them as they have gained experience. Teachers are also divided as to whether proficiency testing has fostered more collaboration among teachers. Very few are convinced that proficiency testing has improved school climate, with the majority of teachers expressing that proficiency testing has adversely impacted morale among faculty and staff. Overall, elementary teachers reported more adverse impacts than did secondary teachers, as evidenced by stronger agreement among elementary teachers that proficiency testing has resulted in more stress, an increased workload, and lowered morale.

*Impact on Curriculum*

Teachers overwhelmingly agree that proficiency testing has resulted in school curriculum being aligned to fit the proficiencies and that a major impact of proficiency testing is that it has forced teachers to teach to the test. The majority of teachers agreed that proficiency testing has resulted in having to teach nine months of curriculum in six months; however, this sense of curriculum constriction is felt more keenly by elementary teachers than by secondary teachers. Most teachers believed that proficiency testing has helped the school system align curriculum between grade levels, has helped educators identify curricular weaknesses, and has made educators more conscious of educational outcomes. Less than half of the teachers expressed that proficiency testing has been treated as an add-on rather than a regular part of the school year. Although there is agreement that proficiency testing has placed greater emphasis on math and science curricula, fewer teachers believe that proficiency testing has helped the education system focus on learning outcomes rather than just curricular inputs. In relation to teacher and student creativity, a majority of teachers believe that proficiency testing does not allow for creative teaching activities and that proficiencies have tended to stifle student creativity in the classroom. Overall, elementary teachers more than secondary teachers are feeling the impact on curriculum as a result of the proficiency-testing mandate.

*Impact on Student Learning Needs*

Teachers are convinced that proficiency testing has not increased students' self-esteem and that it places too much emphasis on a single test. Elementary teachers expressed the strongest conviction that proficiency testing puts too much credence in one test. Moreover, teachers believe that proficiency testing is overwhelming for students with learning difficulties and that the test results arrive too late for successful intervention response. Only a slight majority reported that proficiency testing has helped educators identify academic problems of individual students. Relatively few teachers feel that proficiency testing is developmentally-appropriate for the ages of students who take them. Those teachers with four to ten years of experience were more convinced than others about the developmental inappropriateness of proficiency tests.

*Community Relations*

Teachers expressed that a result of proficiency testing has been increased competition among school districts. Most teachers are convinced that proficiency testing is used more to appease public concern about education rather than to improve it, and teachers are divided as to whether proficiency testing results have actually increased public support for the Perrysburg School District. Although parental involvement has been hypothesized as a positive outcome of proficiency testing, most teachers disagree that it has encouraged more parental participation. Overall, the vast majority of teachers disagreed that proficiency testing is a valid way to measure students' learning. There was, however, more agreement regarding the validity of proficiency testing as a measure of student learning by high school than by elementary teachers.

## Teacher Findings Listed in Descending Order of Agreement

| Wording of Statement | Heart of Statement | Percentage of Agreement |
|---|---|---|
| (-) | imposed upon district | 96.2 |
| (-) | not reliable way to evaluate teacher performance | 94.4 |
| (+) | curriculum aligned | 94 |
| (-) | increased competition among schools | 92.9 |
| (-) | reading comprehension than knowledge | 90.1 |
| (-) | teach to test | 89.9 |
| (-) | emphasis on a single test | 89.9 |
| (-) | appease public | 87 |
| (-) | overwhelming for students with learning difficulties | 86.7 |
| (-) | increased anxiety | 86 |
| (-) | raising the bar | 82.2 |
| (-) | excess stress | 80.7 |
| (-) | teachers held accountable | 75.4 |
| (-) | increased workload | 75.1 |
| (-) | nine months curriculum in six months | 73.5 |
| (-) | too much pressure on students | 72.4 |
| (-) | results arrive too late | 70.9 |
| (+) | conscious of outcomes | 70.4 |
| (-) | adversely impacted morale | 68 |
| (-) | does not allow creative teaching activities | 64 |
| (+) | aligned curriculum between grades | 63.5 |
| (+) | emphasis on math and science | 63.1 |
| (+) | apply rather than recall information | 62.1 |
| (+) | identify curricular weaknesses | 61.9 |
| (-) | stifles student creativity | 60.6 |
| (+) | focus on learning outcomes | 58.4 |
| (+) | identify academic problems | 57.6 |
| (+) | comfortable with experience | 54.5 |
| (+) | motivate students | 50.8 |
| (+) | more collaboration | 50.3 |
| (+) | increased public support | 50.3 |
| (-) | treated as add-on | 48.7 |
| (+) | test-taking skills | 44.9 |
| (+) | think critically | 38.9 |
| (+) | encourage parental involvement | 36.7 |
| (+) | apply knowledge | 33.2 |
| (+) | developmentally-appropriate | 32.6 |

| (+) | measures student learning | 16.8 |
|-----|---------------------------|------|
| (+) | increased students' self-esteem | 9.5 |
| (+) | improved climate | 8.6 |

## ITEM ANALYSIS OF TEACHERS

### Responses to Survey Statements

***MOTIVATION*** *(Proficiency testing has helped motivate students to take their studies more seriously)*

Teachers were equally divided (50.8%) in relation to whether proficiency testing has helped motivate students to take their studies more seriously. There were differences by gender among teachers in terms of level of disagreement with more than one of four male teachers (26.7% strongly or very strongly) disagreeing with the statement compared to less than one of ten females (9.0%).

***STRESS*** *(Proficiency testing has created excess stress in my job)*

A majority of teachers (80.7%) reported that proficiency testing has created excess stress in their job. There were significant differences among teachers by grade level. With regard to the strength of the agreement, more than eight of ten K-3 teachers (83.3%), 84.2% of fourth grade teachers, 78.6% of fifth grade teachers, 52.9% of sixth grade teachers, 37.5% of seventh grade teachers, 33.3% of eighth grade teachers, and 33% of 9-12 teachers either strongly or very strongly agreed with this survey item.

***ALIGNMENT OF CURRICULUM*** *(Proficiency testing has resulted in school curriculum being aligned to fit proficiencies)*

Teachers (94%) overwhelmingly agree that proficiency testing has resulted in school curriculum being aligned to fit the proficiencies. There is a significant difference for teachers by years employed only because over half of those employed more than 20 years very strongly agreed, while only 19.5% of those with three or less years of experience very strongly agreed. None of the fourth grade teachers disagreed with the survey item. There was a difference by building due to lower percentages by high school (53.1%) and junior high teachers (50%) in the "strongly agree" category compared with the percentages of elementary teachers strongly agreeing from Frank Elementary (100%) and Woodland Elementary (90%).

***TEACHING TO THE TEST*** *(Proficiency testing has forced teachers to teach to the test)*
Almost nine of ten teachers (89.9%) indicated that proficiency testing has forced them to teach to the test. There were significant differences among teachers by building. One hundred percent of teachers at Frank agreed (with 93.3% strongly agreeing with the survey item), compared to 87.7% of agreement among high school teachers (with 47.7% strongly agreeing). At the junior high, 83.3% of teachers agreed, with 44.4% strongly agreeing. At Fort Meigs, 95.5% agreed (with 72.7% strongly agreeing), 90.5% at Toth (with 66.6% strongly agreeing), and 93.3% at Woodland (with 83.3% strongly agreeing). It is clear from these findings that the elementary teachers are feeling teaching to the test more keenly. At the high school, there were significant differences according to subject taught. For example, all of the science teachers agreed (76.5% strongly) that proficiency testing has forced teachers to teach to the test, while only 70% of the writing teachers agreed (and only 25% strongly). More than eight of ten math and citizenship teachers agreed, 81.2% and 85.7% respectively.

***SCHOOL CLIMATE*** *(Proficiency testing has improved school climate)*
This survey item received the lowest percentage of support from teachers, with only 8.6% of teachers agreeing. There was no difference among teachers according to gender, building, or years of experience.

***WORKLOAD*** *(Proficiency testing has increased my workload)*
Three of four teachers (75.1%) reported that proficiency testing has increased their workload. Although there were no differences according to gender, there were differences among teachers at grade levels taught. One hundred percent of fifth grade teachers agreed (85.7%) strongly, 97.2% of K-3 teachers agreed (77.7% strongly), and 79% of fourth grade teachers agreed (but only 52.7% strongly). Although 81.2% of sixth grade teachers agreed, only 25% did so strongly. At the junior high, 73.3% of seventh grade teachers agreed (33.3% strongly), 85% of eighth grade teachers agreed (45% strongly), and only 52.6% of high school teachers agreed (only 20.4% strongly). Furthermore, when only "very strongly agreed" was taken into consideration, 47.4% of fourth grade teachers indicated agreement, and only 5% of eighth and 10.2% of high school teachers did so. According to subject area, a strong majority of math teachers (93.6%), citizenship teachers (85.7%), and science teachers (82.4%) agreed that proficiency testing has increased their workload, while only 63.2% of writing teachers agreed.

***HELPED WITH ACADEMIC PROBLEMS*** *(Proficiency testing has helped us identify academic problems of individual students)*
A slight majority of teachers (57.6%) reported that proficiency testing has helped educators identify academic problems of individual students, although less than one in six (15.2%) did so strongly. There was a significant difference by subject taught, as 85.7% of citizenship teachers agreed, while less than half of science (47%) and exactly 50% of math teachers did so.

***INCREASED ANXIETY*** *(Proficiency testing has helped us identify academic problems of individual students)*

A total of 86% of the teachers agreed that proficiency testing has increased the anxiety students feel toward school. There was a difference, according to building, in the strength of agreement of the survey item. Only 40% of high school and 30.9% of junior high teachers strongly agreed, while 68.2% of Fort Meigs, 62.5% of Frank, 59.1% of Toth, and 73.3% of Woodland strongly agreed. There was also a difference among teachers by grade level taught. Although no fifth grade teachers and only one fourth grade teacher disagreed, 31.3% of sixth grade teachers and eleven high school teachers (18.6%) disagreed.

***IDENTIFY CURRICULAR WEAKNESSES*** *(Proficiency testing has helped us identify curricular weaknesses)*

While most teachers (61.9%) agreed that proficiency testing has helped educators identify curricular weaknesses, less than one of six did so strongly (14.7%). A significant difference between gender was found in relation to the survey item. An overwhelming 70.4% of females, compared with only 36.9% of males, indicated that proficiency testing has helped educators identify curricular weaknesses.

***HELD ACCOUNTABLE*** *(Proficiency testing has resulted in teachers being held accountable for results)*

Three of four teachers (75.4%) agreed that proficiency testing has resulted in teachers being held accountable for results, with close to one in three (30.9%) doing so strongly.

***TEST TAKING SKILLS*** *(Proficiency testing has helped students test taking skills)*

Only 44.9% of teachers agreed that proficiency testing has helped students' test taking skills.

***LEARNING DIFFICULTIES*** *(Proficiency testing is overwhelming for students with learning difficulties)*

The majority of teachers (86.7%) agreed that proficiency testing is overwhelming for students with learning difficulties.

***PARENTAL INVOLVEMENT*** *(Proficiency testing has encouraged parents to become more involved in our schools)*

Only 36.7% of teachers agreed that proficiency testing has encouraged parents to become more involved in Perrysburg schools. No significant differences were found according to gender, building, years employed, or subject taught.

***MORALE*** *(Proficiency testing has adversely impacted morale among faculty and staff)*

More than two of three teachers (68%) agreed that proficiency testing has adversely impacted morale among faculty and staff, with 37.6% doing so strongly. There was a difference among teachers by building, due to the strength of agreement of elementary teachers (59.1% at Fort Meigs, 65% at Woodland) compared with secondary teachers (only 20% at the junior high and 25% at the high school). Thus, elementary teachers are experiencing more adverse impacts on morale as a result of proficiency testing than are secondary teachers.

***COMFORT*** *(Proficiency testing has become more comfortable for me as I have gained experience)*

Only a slight majority of teachers (54.5%) agreed that proficiency testing has become more comfortable for them as they have gained experience.

***PRESSURE*** *(Proficiency testing has put too much pressure on students)*

The vast majority of teachers (72.4%) reported that proficiency testing has placed too much pressure on students. There was significant difference by grade level, subject taught, and building. By grade level, there was a high level of agreement with the statement. At the elementary level, 97.2% of K-3 agreed (82.4% strongly), 100% of fourth grade teachers (79.9% strongly), 100% of fifth grade teachers (all strongly), but then only 64.7% of sixth grade teachers (29.4% strongly). At the secondary level, the level of agreement also waned by increasing grade level, with 68.8% of seventh grade teachers (18.8% strongly), 42.1% of eighth grade teachers (26.3%) strongly and 51.7% of senior high teachers (27.6% strongly) agreeing.

With regard to subject area, 71.5% of citizenship, 62.6% of science, and 60% of math teachers agreed that proficiency testing has placed too much pressure on students, while only 40% of writing teachers agreed. By building, a greater number of high school teachers disagreed (47.6%) than junior high teachers (37.1%). However, the real major difference was in the elementary buildings where only 9.1% at Fort Meigs, 6.3% at Frank, 13.6% at Toth, and 9.7% at Woodland disagreed with the survey statement.

***APPLY KNOWLEDGE*** *(Proficiency testing has increased students' ability to apply the knowledge they have gained)*

Only 33.2% of teachers believed that proficiency testing has increased students' ability to apply knowledge. There was heavy disagreement with the survey statement in all subjects, with a higher proportion of science (88.2%) and math (80%) teachers disagreeing with the item than citizenship (71.2%) and writing (70%) teachers.

***RESULTS ARRIVE LATE*** *(Proficiency testing results arrive too late for successful intervention response)*

More than seven of ten teachers (70.9%) agreed that proficiency test results arrive too late for successful intervention response. One difference was noted according to subject taught, in that 80% of gifted and talented teachers disagreed with the survey statement, while only 13.4% of math teachers did.

***FOSTERED COLLABORATION*** *(Proficiency testing has fostered more collaboration among teachers)*

Teachers (50.3%) were divided in relation to whether proficiency testing has fostered more collaboration among teachers. Female teachers (56%), as opposed to male teachers

(33.3%), were also more inclined to agree that proficiency testing has fostered more collaboration. There was also a significant difference in the level of agreement according to building, with only 34.9% of high school teachers agreeing with the statement, while 75% of those at Frank and 81.8% at Toth agreed.

### INCREASED COMPETITION *(Proficiency testing has increased competition among school districts)*

More than nine of ten teachers (92.9%) agreed, with two of three doing so strongly (64.3%), that proficiency testing has increased competition among school districts.

### ALIGN CURRICULUM BETWEEN GRADES *(Proficiency testing has helped the school district align curriculum between grade levels)*

A total of 63.5% of Perrysburg teachers agreed that proficiency testing has helped the school system align curriculum between grade levels. Thus, two of three teachers agreed with the survey statement, although only 13% did so strongly. A major gender difference was also found, for 67.8% of females, compared with only 50.1% of males, reported that proficiency testing has helped the school system align curriculum between grade levels.

### IMPOSED UPON DISTRICT *(Proficiency testing has been imposed upon rather than sought input from the school district)*

This survey statement received the most agreement by teachers. An overwhelming 96.2% of teachers responded that proficiency testing has been imposed upon the school district rather than policy makers seeking input from the district. Two of three teachers (67%) agreed strongly. Importantly, there is a difference by years of experience, as new teachers agree far less strongly (33.4%) than more experienced teachers do (77.1% for teachers with four to ten years of experience, 77.4% for those with 11-20 years, and 73.2% for those with more than 20 years).

### EMPHASIS ON MATH AND SCIENCE *(Proficiency testing has placed greater emphasis on math and science curricula)*

Regarding whether proficiency testing has indeed placed greater emphasis on math and science curricula, 63.1% of the teachers agreed. There was a significant difference according to gender, with more females (65.7%) than males (56.8%) agreeing. Interestingly, there were no differences according to building, years employed, grade level taught, or subject taught.

### ADD-ON *(Proficiency testing has been treated as an add-on rather than a regular part of the school year)*

Less than half of the teachers (48.7%) agreed that proficiency testing has been treated as an add-on rather than a regular part of the school year. In other words, 51.3% of teachers disagreed with this statement and close to one in five (18.2%) did so strongly. There was a difference between grade level taught, for only 20% of sixth grade teachers and 31.6% of fourth grade teachers agreed with the survey statement, whereas 63.1% of the high school teachers agreed. The difference was also apparent in the by building analysis, for more high school teachers agreed (62.9%) than elementary school teachers (25% at Toth, 36.9% at Fort Meigs, and 34.5% at Woodland).

*EDUCATIONAL OUTCOMES (Proficiency testing has made us more conscious of educational outcomes)*

More than seven of ten teachers agreed (70.4%) that proficiency testing has made educators more conscious of educational outcomes, while more than one of five (22.4%) did so strongly.

*RAISING THE BAR (Proficiency testing has resulted in a constant "raising of the bar" by state officials)*

The majority of teachers (82.2%) concurred (and 45% did so strongly) that proficiency testing has resulted in a constant "raising of the bar" by state officials. A significant difference was found for gender in that an overwhelming 89.6% of women, compared with 60.9% of men, agreed that proficiency testing has resulted in a constant "raising of the bar." There were also significant differences by grade level taught, as only one K-3 teacher and no fourth, fifth and sixth grade teachers disagreed, while 41.2% of eighth grade and 39.2% of high school teachers disagreed with the statement. By building, the difference was evidenced by 40% of high school teachers and 21.9% of junior high teachers disagreeing with the statement, while only one teacher at one of the elementary schools disagreed. There was also a significant difference by years of experience. Those with 4-10 years agreed less strongly (8.3%) with the survey statement than those with 20 or more years of experience (30.2%).

*THINK CRITICALLY (Proficiency testing has helped students to think critically)*

Only 38.9% of the teachers agreed that proficiency testing has helped students' ability to think critically. There was significant difference by grade level taught, in that the higher percentages of agreement with the statement are found among fourth grade teachers (57.9%) and fifth grade teachers (64.3%), than with K-3 teachers (48.6%) or sixth grade teachers (46.7%). A difference in agreement was also found between seventh grade teachers (56.3%) and eighth grade teachers (15.8%). Only 22.4% of high school teachers agreed.

Likewise, differences were also revealed per building. Elementary school teachers were more in agreement with the statement than high school teachers were. To illustrate, only 25% of high school teachers agreed, while 36% of junior high school teachers agreed. At the elementary schools, the majority of teachers at Woodland (62%) agreed that proficiency testing has helped students think critically, whereas teachers at Toth (51%) and Frank (50%) were split in agreement. Much fewer teachers at Fort Meigs (38.1%) agreed with the survey statement.

**SINGLE TEST** *(Proficiency testing places too much emphasis on a single test)*

Almost nine of ten teachers (89.9%) agreed that proficiency testing places too much emphasis on a single test. A significant difference by gender was apparent, in that an overwhelming 92.3% of females, as opposed to 80.5% of males, agreed with the survey statement. There were also some differences by subject taught, as evidenced by 100% of citizenship, 88.2% of science, 80% of writing, and 66.7% of math teachers agreeing with the statement.

There was also a significant difference by subject taught. While the majority of citizenship teachers (57.1%) agreed, writing (42.1%), math (20%), and science (17.6%) teachers expressed much lower levels of agreement. A significant difference also existed by building with higher percentages of teacher agreement at the elementary schools (100% at Fort Meigs, Frank, and Toth; and 90.3% at Woodland), compared with 85.3% at the junior and 81.6% at the senior high school.

**PUBLIC SUPPORT** *(Proficiency testing results have increased public support for our district)*

Teachers were almost equally divided (50.3%) over whether proficiency testing results have increased public support for the Perrysburg school district.

**APPEASE PUBLIC** *(Proficiency testing is used more to appease public concern about education rather than to improve it)*

Most teachers (87%) agreed that proficiency testing is used more to appease public concern about education rather than to improve it.

**LEARNING OUTCOMES** *(Proficiency testing has helped us focus on learning outcomes rather than just curricular inputs)*

Regarding whether proficiency testing has helped the education system focus on learning outcomes rather than just curricular inputs, 58.4% of the teachers agreed. Although there is not a statistically significant difference by gender, it should be noted that only 43.2% of men agreed compared with 64.4% of women.

**READING COMPREHENSION** *(Proficiency testing tests a student's reading comprehension more than knowledge in a particular subject area)*

Nine of ten teachers (90.1%) agreed (with 54.5% doing so strongly) that proficiency testing tests a student's reading comprehension more than knowledge in a particular subject area. There was a significant difference in strength of agreement among elementary teachers, where 92.9% of fifth grade teachers strongly agreed compared with only 26.3% of the high school teachers.

**APPLY INFORMATION** *(Proficiency testing helps students apply rather than just recall information)*

A majority of teachers (62.1%) agreed (although only 12.8% did so strongly) that proficiency testing helps students apply rather than just recall information. A significant gender difference was evidenced in that 70.2% of females, as opposed to only 39.2% of males, reported that proficiency testing helps students apply information. A difference was also found between buildings, with far more agreement among teachers at Woodland (83.3%) and Frank (75.1%) elementary schools compared with 43.7% agreement among high school teachers.

**CURRICULUM CONSTRICTED** *(Proficiency testing has resulted in having to teach nine months of curriculum in six months)*

Almost three of four teachers (73.5%) agreed, with 46.5% of the teachers agreeing strongly, that proficiency testing has resulted in having to teach nine months of curriculum in six months. There was a significant difference by grade level, as no fourth or fifth grade teachers disagreed; however, 56.9% of high school teachers disagreed.

**MEASURE LEARNING** *(Proficiency testing is a valid way to measure students' learning)*

A mere 16.8% of teachers agreed that proficiency testing is a valid way to measure students' learning. Of the 83.2% of teachers in disagreement with the survey statement, four of ten teachers (40.3%) did so strongly. The difference at the building level was that more high school teachers (24.6%) agreed that proficiency testing is a valid measure of student learning than elementary teachers (i.e., 9.5% at Fort Meigs and 9.1% at Toth) did.

**CREATIVE TEACHING** *(Proficiency testing does not allow for creative teaching activities)*

A total of 64% of teachers agreed that proficiency testing does not allow for creative teaching activities. Thus, two of three teachers agreed with this statement, and one of three (32%) did so strongly. There was a significant difference, however, by grade level because elementary teachers strongly agreed (85.7% for fifth grade teachers and 83.3% for K-3), while only 21.1% of eighth grade teachers agreed. Interestingly, there was a difference by subject taught, with 20% of writing teachers disagreeing with the survey statement compared to no disagreement among math, science, and citizenship teachers. A major difference was evidenced at the building level, where 40.2% of high school and 61.8% of junior high school teachers disagreed with the survey statement, whereas only 6.3% at Frank, 27.2% at Fort Meigs and Toth, and 29% at Woodland disagreed.

**DEVELOPMENTALLY APPROPRIATE** *(Proficiency testing is developmentally-appropriate for the ages of students who take them)*

Relatively few teachers (32.6%) indicated that proficiency testing is developmentally-appropriate for the ages of students who take them. That is, more than two of three teachers (67.4%) disagreed with this statement, and close to four of ten did so strongly (39.6%). A significant difference was found by years of experience for teachers. Those with four to ten years of experience disagreed far more (89.6%) than other teachers, especially those with over 20 years of experience (of whom 59.5% disagreed with the survey statement). At the building level, 47.5% of high school and 51.6% of junior high teachers agreed, while only 10.3% at Woodland, 9.5% at Fort Meigs, and 6.3% at Frank agreed.

*UNRELIABLE FOR TEACHER EVALUATION (Proficiency testing results are not a reliable way to evaluate teacher performance)*

An overwhelming 94.4% of teachers agree that proficiency test results are not a reliable way to evaluate teacher performance, indicating that teachers are not in favor of proficiency test results being attributed to teacher performance or used to judge teacher effectiveness.

*SELF-ESTEEM (Proficiency testing has increased students' self-esteem)*

The statement of whether proficiency testing has increased students' self-esteem received very minimal support from teachers, with only 9.5% agreeing. Significant differences were found by grade level taught and building. At the elementary grade level, only one K-3 teacher and one sixth grade teacher agreed with the survey statement; at the high school level, however, 12 teachers agreed. At the building level, 13 high school teachers, compared with only one elementary teacher, agreed with the survey statement.

*STUDENT CREATIVITY (Proficiency testing has tended to stifle student creativity in the classroom)*

A majority of teachers (60.6%) agreed, with three of ten (29.8%) doing so strongly, that proficiency testing has tended to stifle student creativity in the classroom. The difference at the grade level is that only 20% of K-3 teachers disagreed compared to 66.7% of seventh grade teachers. At the building level, a significant difference was evidenced in that 67.7% of junior high and 43.4% of high school teachers disagreed, while only 18.8% at Frank and 27.3% at both Toth and Woodland disagreed.

## THEMATIC RESPONSES

### Support and Administrative Staff

*Impact on Student Learning Behavior*
    Motivation
    Increased Anxiety
    Test Taking Skills
    Pressure
    Apply Knowledge              = Eight Items
    Think Critically
    Reading Comprehension
    Apply Information

*Impact on Professional Job Environment*
    Stress
    School Climate
    Workload
    Held Accountable
    Morale
    Comfort
    Fostered Collaboration           = Thirteen Items
    Imposed On District
    Raising The Bar
    Increased Accountability
    Professional Duties
    Greater Responsibility
    District Budget

*Impact on Curriculum*
    Alignment of Curriculum with Proficiencies
    Teaching To Test
    Identify Curricular Weaknesses
    Align Curriculum Between Grades      = Seven Items
    Emphasis On Math And Science
    Add-On
    Educational Outcomes
    Learning Outcomes

*Impact on Response to Student Learning Needs*
    Helped With Academic Problems
    Learning Difficulties
    Results Arrive Late            = Six Items
    Single Test
    Developmentally Appropriate
    Self-Esteem

*Community Relations*
    Parental Involvement
    Increased Competition
    Public Support              = Five Items
    Appease Public
    Measure Learning

## SUPPORT AND ADMINISTRATIVE STAFF

## General Comments:

*Impact on Students' Learning Behavior*

The support and administrative staff members are concerned about the impact proficiency testing is having on the students' learning environment and are less than convinced that it is resulting in better student learning skills, although they do feel it has helped motivate students. They do believe it is resulting in students taking their studies more seriously, but are concerned that it has increased student anxiety toward school and that it has placed too much pressure on students. The support and administrative staff are split as to whether or not it has improved test taking skills or to think critically, but do agree that it has helped students to apply the knowledge they have gained.

*Impact on Professional Job Environment*

There is no question the proficiency testing has impacted the job environment for support and administrative staff. They do believe it has created excess stress and increased their workload. They feel it has placed greater responsibility on them as well as resulted in teachers being held more accountable. Most feel that it has fundamentally changed their professional duties, particularly guidance counselors. Administrative staff definitely do not believe that it has improved school climate and has, in fact, adversely impacted school morale among faculty and staff. Part of the reason for this would seem to be the feeling that proficiency testing has been imposed upon the system without adequate input from educators within the district and that state officials are constantly raising standards that denote proficiency.

On the positive side, a majority of staff think that proficiency testing has fostered collaboration among teachers and that they are becoming more comfortable with it as they gain more experience.

*Impact on Curriculum*

Administrative and support staff are more positive about this aspect of proficiency testing. They do believe that teachers have been forced to teach to the test and that they have had to work with teachers to align curriculum to fit proficiencies. They also feel that the district has aligned its curriculum between grades by identifying curricular weaknesses. Administrative staff do not feel that it has been merely treated as an add-on to the curriculum, and they have worked with teachers to both become more conscious of educational outcomes and to focus attention on learning outcomes.

*Impact on Student Learning Needs*

While they are convinced that proficiency testing has not increased students' self-esteem, staff does believe that it has helped identify academic problems of individual students. However, administrative staff is concerned that the tests are overwhelming for students with learning difficulties. The majority feels that they are not developmentally appropriate for the students who take them. They firmly believe that proficiency testing places too much emphasis on a single test and that the results arrive too late for timely intervention to help those who fail.

*Community Relations*

Insofar as increasing parental involvement in the schools is one of the goals of proficiency testing, administrative/support staff do not believe that this has been one of the results. However, they do believe that the generally fine performance of Perrysburg students on the tests has increased public support for the district; they also believe the results have been more to appease the public than to improve education. This could be tied to the feeling of a majority of administrative/support staff that proficiency test results are not a valid way to measure student learning.

## Support and Administrative Staff Findings Listed in Descending Order of Agreement

| Wording of Statement | Heart of Statement | Percentage of Agreement |
|---|---|---|
| (+) | curriculum aligned | 96.9 |
| (-) | increased competition among schools | 93.9 |
| (-) | imposed upon district | 93.8 |
| (-) | raising the bar | 90.9 |
| (-) | emphasis on a single test | 87.9 |
| (+) | identify academic problems | 87.1 |
| (+) | conscious of outcomes | 84.8 |
| (-) | greater responsibility on school administrators | 84.4 |
| (+) | focus on learning outcomes | 81.8 |
| (-) | increased anxiety | 81.3 |
| (-) | increased workload | 81.3 |
| (-) | teach to test | 78.8 |
| (-) | reading comprehension than knowledge | 77.4 |
| (-) | overwhelming for students with learning difficulties | 75.8 |
| (-) | results arrive too late | 75.8 |
| (-) | too much pressure on students | 75 |
| (+) | identify curricular weaknesses | 72.7 |
| (-) | excess stress | 72.7 |
| (-) | appease public | 71.9 |
| (+) | aligned curriculum between grades | 71.9 |

| | | |
|---|---|---|
| (+) | increased public support | 71.9 |
| (-) | teachers held accountable | 69.7 |
| (-) | adversely impacted morale | 68.8 |
| (+) | emphasis on math and science | 68.8 |
| (-) | fundamentally changed my professional duties | 68.8 |
| (+) | apply rather than recall information | 65.6 |
| (-) | adversely impacted district budget | 64.3 |
| (+) | motivate students | 63.7 |
| (+) | comfortable with experience | 61.3 |
| (+) | more collaboration | 60.6 |
| (+) | developmentally-appropriate | 56.2 |
| (+) | test-taking skills | 51.6 |
| (+) | think critically | 50.1 |
| (-) | treated as add-on | 48.5 |
| (+) | encourage parental involvement | 48.5 |
| (+) | apply knowledge | 45.5 |
| (-) | not increased my sense of accountability | 42.9 |
| (+) | measures student learning | 38.7 |
| (+) | improved climate | 9.1 |
| (+) | increased students' self-esteem | 3.3 |

## ITEM ANALYSIS OF SUPPORT AND ADMINISTRATIVE STAFF

### Responses to Survey Statements

***MOTIVATION*** *(Proficiency testing has helped motivate students to take their studies more seriously)*

Close to two of three (63.7%) support and administrative staff (henceforth called administrative staff members) believe that proficiency testing has helped motivate students to take their studies more seriously, although less than one in five (18.2%) chose "strongly agree" and none chose "very strongly agree." Though not statistically significant because of the very low numbers involved, only 28.6% of high school staff members agreed with the statement while 78.9% of elementary school staff members did so.

***STRESS*** *(Proficiency testing has created excess stress in my job)*

Close to three of four (72.7%) administrative staff members agreed with this statement, and four of ten (39.4%) strongly agreed. On this item, there was significant difference according to the professional capacity of the staff with all guidance counselors agreeing (83.3% strongly) while only 66.7% of the remaining staff agreed (with only one in four doing so strongly).

***ALIGNMENT OF CURRICULUM*** *(Proficiency testing has resulted in school curriculum being aligned to fit proficiencies)*

Administrative staff members firmly agreed with this statement (96.9%) with more than seven of 10 doing so strongly. There were no significant differences among staff.

***TEACHING TO THE TEACH*** *(Proficiency testing has forced teachers to teach to the test)*

While close to eight of 10 administrative staff members agreed (78.8%) with this statement, less than one of two (45.5%) did so strongly. There were no significant differences among staff.

***SCHOOL CLIMATE*** *(Proficiency testing has improved school climate)*

More than nine of 10 (90.9%) administrative staff members disagreed with this statement, although only one of five did so strongly (21.2%). There were no differences among staff.

***WORKLOAD*** *(Proficiency testing has increased my workload)*

More than eight of 10 (81.3%) administrative staff agreed with this statement and half (50%) did so strongly. While there were no significant differences among staff, it should be noted that all of the guidance counselors very strongly agreed while only one of five (22.2%) administrators did so.

***HELPED WITH ACADEMIC PROBLEMS*** *(Proficiency testing has helped us identify academic problems of individual students)*

Close to four of five administrative staff members agreed (87.1%) and one of five (21.2%) did so strongly. There were no significant differences among staff.

***INCREASED ANXIETY*** *(Proficiency testing has increased the anxiety students feel toward school)*

More than eight of 10 (81.3%) administrative staff members agreed with this statement and half (50%) did so strongly. While not statistically significant, all guidance counselors, school psychologists and other instructional support staff agreed.

***IDENTIFY CURRICULAR WEAKNESSES*** *(Proficiency testing has helped us identify curricular weaknesses)*

More than seven of 10 (72.7%) administrative staff members agreed with this statement and one in five (21.25) did so strongly. There were no differences among staff.

***HELD ACCOUNTABLE*** *(Proficiency testing has resulted in teachers being held accountable for results)*

Close to seven of 10 administrative staff agreed (69.7%) while 27.3% did so strongly. There were no differences among staff.

**TEST TAKING SKILLS** *(Proficiency testing has helped students' test taking skills)*

Administrative staff members were split on this item with only 51.6% agreeing and less than one of 10 doing so strongly. While three of four administrators agreed with the statement, only one of three guidance counselors did so.

**LEARNING DIFFICULTIES** *(Proficiency testing is overwhelming for students with learning difficulties)*

Three of four (75.8%) administrative staff members agreed with this statement and close to seven of 10 (69.7%) did so strongly. There were no differences among staff on this item.

**PARENTAL INVOLVEMENT** *(Proficiency testing has encouraged parents to become more involved in our schools)*

Less than half the administrative staff members (48.5%) agreed with this statement and less than one of five did so strongly. Female administrative staff members were far more in agreement with this statement (66.7%) while only 10% of male administrative staff members agreed. There were no other significant differences for staff.

**MORALE** *(Proficiency testing has adversely impacted morale among faculty and staff)*

More than two of three (68.8%) administrative staff members agreed with one of five (21.9%) doing so strongly. There were no significant differences among staff, although it should be noted that all secretarial support staff members agreed with this statement.

**COMFORT** *(Proficiency testing has become more comfortable for me as I have gained experience)*

More than six of 10 (61.3%) administrative staff members agreed with this statement, although only 16.1% did so strongly. There were no significant differences among staff, but 71.4% of secretarial staff disagreed with this item.

**PRESSURE** *(Proficiency testing has put too much pressure on students)*

Three of four (75%) staff agreed with this statement, and one of two (50%) did so strongly. The main point of difference among administrative staff was that only 33% of administrators agreed with the statement, while all of the guidance counselors and the school psychologists did so.

**APPLY KNOWLEDGE** *(Proficiency testing has increased students' ability to apply the knowledge they have gained)*

Less than half (45.5%) of the administrative staff members agreed with this statement. There were no differences among staff.

**RESULTS ARRIVE LATE** *(Proficiency testing results arrive too late for successful intervention response)*

More than three of four (75.8%) administrative staff members agreed with this statement and over one of three (36.4%) did so strongly. There were no significant differences among the group.

**FOSTERED COLLABORATION** *(Proficiency testing has fostered more collaboration among teachers)*

A majority (60.6%) of administrative staff members agreed with this statement although less than one of five (18.2%) did so strongly. There were significant differences by gender since more than eight of ten (81%) women agreed while only 20% of the men did so.

**INCREASED COMPETITION** *(Proficiency testing has increased competition among school districts)*

More than nine of 10 (93.9%) administrative staff members agreed with this statement and close to two of three (63.6%) did so strongly. There were no differences among the group.

**ALIGN CURRICULUM BETWEEN GRADES** *(Proficiency testing has helped the school district align curriculum between grade levels)*

More then seven of 10 (71.9%) administrative staff members agreed with this statement and over one of five (21.9%) did so strongly. There were no group differences.

**IMPOSED UPON DISTRICT** *(Proficiency testing has been imposed upon rather than sought input from the school district)*

There was overwhelming (93.8%) agreement among administrative staff members on this statement, although less than half (43.8%) did so strongly. There were no differences among the group.

**EMPHASIS ON MATH AND SCIENCE** *(Proficiency testing has placed greater emphasis on math and science curricula)*

Almost seven of 10 (68.8%) administrative staff members agreed with this statement, although less than one of ten (9.4%) did so strongly. While not statistically significant, it should be noted that 90.9% of guidance counselors and other instructional staff agreed while only 55.6% of administrators did so.

**ADD-ON** *(Proficiency testing has been treated as an add-on rather than a regular part of the school year)*

Administrative staff members were fairly well split on this item with just over half (51.5%) disagreeing with the statement. There were no differences among the group.

**EDUCATIONAL OUTCOMES** *(Proficiency testing has made us more conscious of educational outcomes)*

More than eight of 10 (84.8%) administrators agreed with this statement, although only one in five (21.4%) did so strongly. There were no group differences on this item.

**RAISING THE BAR** *(Proficiency testing has resulted in a constant "raising of the bar" by state officials)*

More than nine of 10 administrative staff members (90.9%) agreed with this statement and more than one of two (56.6%) did so strongly. There were differences among the group.

**THINK CRITICALLY** *(Proficiency testing has helped students to think critically)*

Administrative staff members were split on this item, and only 50.1% agreeing with 15.7% doing so strongly. There were no group differences.

**SINGLE TEST** *(Proficiency testing places too much emphasis on a single test)*

Close to nine of 10 (87.9%) agreed with this statement and 57.6% did so strongly. There were no differences among the group.

**PUBLIC SUPPORT** *(Proficiency testing results have increased public support for our district)*

More than seven of ten administrative staff members (71.9%) agreed with this item and close to half (46.9%) did so strongly. Though not statistically significant, more administrators (75%) than any other category agreed with this statement.

**APPEASE PUBLIC** *(Proficiency testing is used more to appease public concern about education rather than it improve it)*

Seven of 10 (71.9%) administrative staff members agreed with this statement and close to half (46.9%) did so strongly. There were no differences by group.

**LEARNING OUTCOMES** *(Proficiency testing has helped us focus on learning outcomes rather than just curricular inputs)*

More than eight of 10 administrative staff members (81.8%) agreed with this statement, although less than one in five (18.2%) did so strongly. There were no differences by group.

**READING COMPREHENSION** *(Proficiency testing tests a student's reading comprehension more than knowledge in a particular subject area)*

More than three of four (77.4%) administrative staff agreed with this statement and close to half (45.2%) did so strongly. There were no differences within the group.

**APPLY INFORMATION** *(Proficiency testing helps students apply rather than just recall information)*

Two of the three administrative staff members (65.6%) agreed with this statement and close to one of five (18.8%) did so strongly. There were no differences within the group.

**INCREASED ACCOUNTABILITY** *(Proficiency testing has not increased my sense of accountability)*

A majority (57. 1%) of administrative members disagreed with this statement, although only 14.3% did so strongly. There were no differences within the group.

**MEASURE LEARNING** *(Proficiency testing is a valid way to measure students' learning)*

More than six of 10 administrative staff members (61.3%) disagreed with this statement, but only 16.1% did so strongly. While 66.7% of administrators agreed with this statement, 75% of the rest of the administrative staff, including 100% of guidance counselors, did not.

**PROFESSIONAL DUTIES** *(Proficiency testing has fundamentally changed my professional duties)*

Close to seven of ten (68.8%) of the administrative staff members agreed with this statement while 28.1% did so strongly. The significant difference was found between guidance counselors, who not only had 100% agreement, but also 100% strongly agreed, while 44.4% of administrators disagreed (and only 11.1% strongly agreed). There were also significant differences by building, as 90.9% of high school and junior high administrative staff members agreed, but only 50% of elementary administrative staff members agreed.

**DEVELOPMENTALLY APPRORPIATE** *(Proficiency testing is developmentally-appropriate for the ages of students who take them)*

A majority (56.2%) of administrative staff members agreed with this statement, and one of four (25%) did so strongly. There were no differences by group.

**GREATER RESPONSIBIITY** *(Proficiency testing has placed greater responsibility on school administrators)*

More than eight of 10 (84.4%) administrative staff members agreed with this statement and more than four of 10 (43.8%) did so strongly. Close to two of three women agreed (64.4%) while only 43.2% of men did so.

**SELF-ESTEEM** *(Proficiency testing has increased students' self-esteem)*

An overwhelming number (96.7%) of administrative staff members disagreed with this statement and more than four of 10 (43.3%) did so strongly. There were no differences by group.

**DISTRICT BUDGET** *(Proficiency testing has adversely impacted the district's budget)*

About two of three (64.3%) administrative staff members agreed with this statement, although less than one of five (17.9%) did so strongly. Seven of 10 (70.2%) women agreed while less than four of 10 men did (39.2%). While 80% of the guidance counselors agreed, only 44.4% of administrators did so.

## THEMATIC RESPONSES

### Elementary & Secondary Students

*Impact on Students' Learning Behavior*
    Motivation
    Stress
    Too Nervous
    Pressure
    Think Critically                    =Nine Items
    Apply Not Recall
    Get Them Over
    Pay More Attention
    Apply Knowledge
*Impact on Learning Needs*
    Help Weaknesses
    Self-Esteem
    Learning Problems
    What Is Important
    Better Prepared
    Unfair To Students                   =Fifteen Items
    Know Learning
    Bad Day
    Single Test
    Gifted And Talented
    Measure Knowledge
    Extra Help
    How Well Teachers Teach
    Buckle Down Books
    Comfort

*Impact on Teaching and Learning Environment*
    Teaching to the Test
    Workload
    School Activities
    Teach Better
    Emphasis On Math And Science
    Rating Teachers
    Material Covered                     =Thirteen Items
    Preparation
    Cramming Of Material
    Limited Creativity

Pace Of Learning
Stressed Teachers
Increased Competition

*Parent/Community Relations*
   Parent Involvement
   Meaning To Parents             =Three Items
   Pride In Perrysburg

# ELEMENTARY STUDENTS

## General Comments:

*Impact on Students' Learning Behavior*

It is obvious that elementary students are far more positive about proficiency testing than their secondary school counterparts. The fact that fourth graders are more positive than sixth graders might suggest that some naivete is involved in some of their responses, but there seems to be a clear trend toward a diminishment of positivism as the grade levels get higher. The elementary students firmly agreed that proficiency testing has caused them to take their studies more seriously. However, more fourth graders were more in agreement than sixth graders.

The elementary students did agree that proficiency testing has placed more stress in their school day, but significantly more fifth graders reported this than fourth graders. An even greater number agreed that proficiency testing puts too much pressure on students. It is telling that close to eight of 10 fifth graders, who have taken the tests, agreed while only two of three fourth graders, who have not, agreed. Still, the elementary students did not seem to let this pressure impact their attitude toward the tests. A majority disagreed with the statement that proficiency tests make them too nervous to do their best, and more than two-thirds rejected the thought that they just wanted to get them over with rather than to do their best.

As far as developing the skills to handle the test is concerned, more than three of four agreed that proficiency testing has helped them to think critically. This is quite different from the responses of secondary students. Additionally, more than eight of 10 agreed that proficiency testing has increased their ability to apply the knowledge they have gained and an equal number believe that the tests have allowed them to apply rather than just recall information. Furthermore, elementary students were much more affirmative than secondary students about the impact that proficiency testing has had on their need to pay attention to their teachers. As with most of the items, fourth grade students were significantly more positive in their responses to these statements than sixth grade students.

## Impact on Learning Needs

An overwhelming number of elementary students believe that proficiency testing has helped their teachers find out what their weaknesses are so that they can correct them. Furthermore, close to three of four feel that proficiency testing causes teachers to help students who need extra help. More than eight of 10 believe that proficiency testing does make them more aware of what is important in school, and a similar number agree that the tests allow them to know how well they are learning as well as how much they know about a particular subject. As with most of the items, it should be noted that the inexperienced fourth graders are far more convinced about this than the more experienced sixth graders. Finally, more than eight of 10 elementary students believe that proficiency testing will prepare them better for learning in the future.

As to whether the tests are serving their psychological needs for learning, there was again more positivism among elementary students than among their secondary counterparts. A majority actually indicated that they believed that proficiency testing has helped their self-esteem although the fourth graders who have not taken the test were significantly in more agreement than the sixth graders who have. As with the secondary students, there was the interesting finding that the students with the least experience with the tests indicated that they have become more comfortable with them as they have gained experience.

The elementary students did maintain that the tests are too hard for students with learning problems, and they were split in their opinion that proficiency testing is unfair to students who do not test well. However, a majority of elementary students did not accept the premise that proficiency testing is unfair to students who are just having a bad day. However, they did agree that proficiency testing places too much emphasis on one test.

## Impact on Teaching and Learning Environment

While there was agreement that proficiency testing has forced teachers to teach to the test, more sixth graders believed this than fourth graders. A majority disagreed that their teachers acted stressed out in class because of the tests and a majority also does not believe that testing has increased competition among students or schools. Unlike secondary students, a majority does not think that proficiency testing has resulted in an increase in homework, although two of three agree that proficiency testing requires too much preparation just for the tests. They firmly believe that their participation in school activities has not been adversely affected. Furthermore, they were split about whether proficiency testing has speeded the pace of learning or has required too much cramming in of material. However, there were a significantly higher number of fourth graders who disagreed with the adverse impact than sixth graders.

Aside from agreeing that proficiency tests have forced their teachers to teach to the test, the elementary students do not affirm or refute that proficiency testing get teachers to teach better. However, they do agree that the tests reduce the number of creative activities that can be done in class. A slight majority does believe that the test results reveal how well teachers have been teaching, but also a majority agree that proficiency test results do not tell how good their teachers are.

*Parent/Community Relations*

Unlike their secondary student counterparts, elementary students indicated that they do take more pride in living in Perrysburg because of the test results. Furthermore, more than seven of ten believed that their parents had been encouraged to become more involved in their studies. They did not agree that the test scores mean more to their parents than to themselves.

**Elementary Students Findings Listed in Descending Order of Agreement**

| Wording of Statement | Heart of Statement | Percentage of Agreement |
|---|---|---|
| (+) | helped teachers find my weaknesses to correct them | 88.6 |
| (+) | measures what I know about subjects | 84.2 |
| (+) | prepares me for future learning | 83.8 |
| (+) | participation in school activities | 83.4 |
| (+) | motivate students | 83.2 |
| (+) | allows me to know how well I am learning | 82.3 |
| (+) | more aware of what is important in school | 81.5 |
| (+) | apply knowledge | 81 |
| (+) | apply rather than recall information | 80.8 |
| (+) | comfortable with experience | 80.4 |
| (+) | think critically | 75.7 |
| (+) | Buckle Down books are helpful test preparation | 74.3 |
| (+) | causes teachers to help students who need it | 73.1 |
| (-) | too much pressure on students | 72.5 |
| (-) | too hard for students with learning problems | 71.5 |
| (+) | encourage parental involvement | 70.1 |
| (-) | teach to test | 70 |
| (-) | emphasis on a single test | 68.7 |
| (+) | emphasis on math and science | 66.7 |
| (-) | requires too much preparation just for tests | 65.2 |
| (-) | excess stress | 65.2 |
| (+) | pay more attention to my teacher | 64.3 |
| (+) | more pride in living in Perrysburg | 62.5 |
| (+ or -) | selection into gifted and talented programs | 62 |
| (-) | do not tell how good my teachers are | 61.5 |
| (+) | increased students' self-esteem | 61 |
| (-) | do not show how well teachers teach | 54.8 |
| (-) | requires cramming of material | 53.3 |
| (-) | covers material never had in class | 52.3 |
| (-) | speeds up pace of learning | 51 |
| (-) | limits creative classroom projects | 49.8 |

| (+) | gets my teachers to teach better | 47.3 |
| (-) | unfair to students who do not test well | 46.8 |
| (-) | unfair because might be having a bad day | 45.8 |
| (-) | increased competition among schools | 45.1 |
| (-) | too nervous to do my best | 43.9 |
| (-) | increased workload | 43.6 |
| (-) | scores mean more to parents than students | 40.9 |
| | | |
| (-) | teachers more stressed out in class | 31.5 |
| (-) | get them over with rather than do my best | 30.5 |

## ITEM ANALYSIS FOR ELEMENTARY STUDENTS

### Responses to Survey Statements

*MOTIVATION (Proficiency testing has helped motivate students to take their studies more seriously.)*
    More than four of five (83.2%) elementary students agreed with this statement, and more than four of 10 (42.7%) did so strongly. Interestingly, more than nine of 10 fourth graders agreed with a majority (55.2%) doing so strongly, compared to 79.2% for sixth graders with only one of three (32.4%) doing so strongly.

*STRESS (Proficiency testing has created excess stress in my school day)*
    Two of three students (65.2%) agreed with this statement. While over seven of ten fifth graders (71%) agreed, only 58.3% of fourth graders did so. This, of course, might be tied to the fact that fourth graders had not yet been tested when they took this survey.

*HELPED WEAKNESSES (Proficiency testing has helped teachers find out my weaknesses so they can correct them)*
    Elementary students were in very firm agreement (88.6%) with this statement with six of 10 (60%) doing so strongly. When it came to responding to the "very strongly agree" option, more than half the fourth graders (55.6%) did so while only one quarter (25.7%) of the sixth graders did so.

*TEACHING TO THE TEST (Proficiency testing has forced teachers to teach to the test)*
    Seven of 10 (70%) of the students agreed with this statement and over four of ten (40.8%) did so strongly. Once again, the higher the grade level, the more negative the students were toward the impact of proficiency testing on their lives. While only 57.3% of fourth graders agreed with one in three (35.6%) doing so strongly, more than three of four (75.7%) sixth graders agreed (with 52.4% of fifth and 40.9% of sixth graders doing so strongly).

**SELF-ESTEEM** *(Proficiency testing has increased students' self-esteem)*
Elementary students were far more in agreement (61%) than their secondary student counterparts (31.8%). It is interesting that the most positive were the fourth graders where close to two of three (65%) agreed. While two of three fourth graders agreed (65%) and more than a third did so strongly (35.4%), just over half (52.9%) of sixth graders agreed and 22.7% did so strongly.

**WORKLOAD** *(Proficiency testing has increased my amount of homework)*
Less than half (43.6%) of elementary students agreed with this statement.
The fourth graders were more in disagreement with the statement (61.9%) than the sixth graders (54%).

**PARENT INVOLVEMENT** *(Proficiency testing has encouraged my parents to become more involved in my studies)*
More than seven of 10 students (70.1%) agreed with this statement which was opposite from what was found with secondary students. Elementary students were four times as likely to agree strongly than their secondary student counterparts. Once again, fourth graders were in more agreement (77%), with more than half strongly agreeing, than sixth graders (62.2%) with only one in three (33.7%) strongly agreeing.

**MEANING TO PARENTS** *(Proficiency test scores mean more to my parents than they do to me)*
The majority of students (59.2%) disagreed with this statement with twice as many of them strongly disagreeing with the statement (35%) than their secondary student counterparts. There were no differences within the group.

**SCHOOL ACTIVITIES** *(Proficiency testing has not had a negative impact on my participation in school activities)*
More than eight of ten (83.4%) students agreed that the level of their participation had not been affected. Close to six of 10 (59%) strongly agreed with the statement. There were no differences within the group in this item.

**TOO NERVOUS** *(Proficiency testing causes me to be too nervous to do my best)*
A majority of elementary students disagreed with this statement (43.9%), and fourth graders disagreed more often than sixth graders.

**COMFORT** *(Proficiency testing has become more comfortable for me as I have gained experience)*
As pointed out in the upcoming analysis of secondary students, there is a curious finding on this item because the lower the grade level, the more the agreement which is opposite from what one would expect for a statement that affirms the worth of experience in creating comfort. More than eight of ten (80.4%) elementary students were in agreement. The main difference in grade level related to the strength of the agreement

where more than half the fourth graders (54.3%) strongly agreed while only 39% of sixth graders did so. It was also statistically significant that more males agreed (82.5%) than females (78%) and that their level of agreement (52.5% strongly) was higher than females (41.8%).

**STRESSED TEACHERS** *(Proficiency testing has resulted in my teachers acting more stressed out in class).*

The majority of elementary students disagreed with this statement (68.5%). Six of ten fourth graders disagreed, while only half of sixth graders did so.

**APPLY KNOWLEDGE** *(Proficiency testing has increased students' ability to apply the knowledge they have gained)*

Elementary students firmly agreed with this statement (81%) and close to half (45.9%) did so strongly. The only difference within the group was that fourth graders strongly agreed over half the time (55%) while sixth graders did so only 37.4% of the time.

**INCREASED COMPETITION** *(Proficiency testing has increased competition among students and schools).*

A majority of elementary students (54.9%) disagreed with this statement with one in three (33.4%) doing so strongly. Fourth graders had a higher percentage of disagreement (63.1%) than sixth graders (49.3%).

**PRIDE IN PERRYSBURG** *(Proficiency tests results have given me more pride in living in Perrysburg)*

The majority (62.5%) of students agreed with this statement which was quite different from their secondary counterparts. Furthermore, one of three (35.9%) did so strongly. Close to half the fourth graders (49.6%) strongly agreed while just over one in five (21.7%) of the sixth graders did so.

**LEARNING PROBLEMS** *(Proficiency testing is too hard for students with learning problems)*

More than seven of 10 students (71.5%) were in agreement with this item and four of 10 (40%) did so strongly. Once again, more fourth graders (56.2%) strongly agreed than fifth graders (41.6%).

**EMPHASIS ON MATH AND SCIENCE** *(Proficiency testing has placed greater emphasis on math and science curricula)*

Two out of three elementary students (66.7%) agreed with this statement with more than one third (35.8%) doing so strongly. On this particular item, the sixth graders actually felt more strongly in agreement (42.8%) than their younger counterparts in fifth grade (34.5%).

**PRESSURE ON STUDENTS** *(Proficiency testing has placed too much pressure on students)*

Close to three of four students (72.5%) agreed with this item. The main difference was at the grade level where 78.3% of fifth graders agreed, with more than half (51.5%) doing so strongly, while only 63.8% of fourth graders agreed and four of ten (41.2%) did so strongly.

**WHAT IS IMPORTANT** *(Proficiency testing has made me more aware of what is important in school)*

More than eight of 10 students (81.5%) agreed with this statement and close to one out of two (49.8%) did so strongly. Fourth graders agreed more often (85.8%) than sixth graders (76.3%).

**RATING TEACHERS** *(Proficiency testing results do not tell how good my teachers are)*

This is one item where elementary students are less in agreement than their secondary counterparts. Just over six of 10 (61.5%) agree, although more than four of 10 strongly agreed (42.4%). More fourth graders disagreed (47.3%) than sixth graders (34.8%).

**THINK CRITICALLY** *(Proficiency testing has helped students to think critically)*

More than three of four elementary students agreed (75.7%) with this statement with close to four in 10 (39.7%) doing so strongly. While more than half (52.2%) of the fourth graders strongly agreed, less than one of three sixth graders (31.4%) did so.

**MATERIAL COVERED** *(Proficiency testing covers a lot of material I never had in class)*

Just over half of the elementary students (52.3%) agreed with this statement. There were no differences within the group. To the credit of the fourth graders, they were split on this item which is reasonable since they have not yet taken the tests and had no basis for judgment.

**BETTER PREPARED** *(Proficiency testing will prepare me better for learning in the future)*

More than eight of 10 (83.8%) elementary students agreed with this statement while more than half did so strongly (51.1%). This shows their positivism about the test compared with their secondary student counterparts. Again, more than twice as many fourth graders strongly agreed (54.3%) then sixth graders (36.7%).

**UNFAIR TO STUDENTS** *(Proficiency testing is unfair to students who do not test well)*

Elementary students were split on this item with more disagreeing (53.2%) than agreeing. Interestingly, more fourth graders strongly agreed (33.5%) than sixth graders (23.4%).

***TEACH BETTER*** *(Proficiency testing gets my teachers to teach better).*

The students were fairly split on this item, but a majority of them (52.7%) disagreed with the statement. The only difference among the group was that fourth graders more often strongly agreed (28.9%) than sixth graders (16.1%).

***PREPARATION*** *(Proficiency testing requires too much preparation just for the tests)*

Two of three elementary students (65.2%) agreed with this item, but the only difference within the group was that more fourth graders strongly disagreed (19.9%) than sixth graders (12.2%).

***PAY MORE ATTENTION*** *(Proficiency testing makes me pay more attention to my teacher)*

This was an interesting item more for the comparison between elementary and secondary students than for either group individually. Whereas two of three (64.3%) elementary students agreed with the statement, a like number of secondary students disagreed with it. As far as difference within the group, fourth graders more strongly agreed (47.3%) than sixth graders (29.5%).

***CRAMMING OF MATERIAL*** *(Proficiency testing requires too much cramming in of material during class)*

The elementary students were fairly split on this item with just over half (53.3%) agreeing, but fourth graders disagreed much more (57.4%) than sixth graders (29.9%).

***KNOW LEARNING*** *(Proficiency testing has allowed me to know how well I am learning)*

More than eight of 10 elementary students (82.3%) agreed with this statement with close to half strongly agreeing (49%). There were no differences within the group.

***BAD DAY*** *(Proficiency testing is unfair because you might be just having a bad day)*

It was interesting that a majority of elementary students (54.2%) disagreed with this statement while a majority of secondary students (59.4%) agreed with it. As is the trend, fourth graders more strongly disagreed (40.6%) than sixth graders (27.8%).

***APPLY NOT RECALL*** *(Proficiency testing gets me to apply rather than just recall information)*

More than eight of 10 elementary students (80.8%) agreed with this statement with four of 10 (40.2%) doing so strongly. Once again, more fourth graders strongly agreed (48.6%) than sixth graders (33.5%).

***SINGLE TEST*** *(Proficiency testing places too much emphasis on a single test)*

More than two of three (68.7%) students agreed with this statement. Once again, the negative reaction to the test tied to grade level was displayed by the fact that less than half of the fourth graders agreed (46.2%) while three of four (75%) sixth graders did so.

**GIFTED AND TALENTED** *(Proficiency testing is a way to select students into gifted and talented programs)*

A majority of elementary students (62%) agreed with this statement, but more than twice as many strongly agreed (38.1%) than their secondary student counterparts (17.4%). There were no group differences for this item.

**GET THEM OVER** *(Proficiency testing just makes me want to get them over with rather than to do my best)*

More than two-thirds (69.5%) of elementary students disagreed with this statement with close to one of two (49.5%) doing so strongly. More fourth graders disagreed (84.3%) and more strongly (68.6%) than sixth graders (60.2%) with only 35% doing so strongly.

**MEASURE KNOWLEDGE** *(Proficiency testing is a good way to measure how much I know about particular subjects)*

More than eight of 10 elementary students (84.2%) agreed with this statement with close to half (47.6%) doing so strongly. When it came to very strongly agreeing, more than twice as many fourth graders did so (38.9%) than sixth graders (18.6%).

**LIMITED CREATIVITY** *(Proficiency testing has limited the number of creative classroom projects that we do)*

Elementary students were split on this item (50.2% disagreeing), but more fourth graders (61.9%) than sixth graders (50%) disagreed.

**EXTRA HELP** *(Proficiency testing causes teachers to help students who need extra help)*

Close to three of four elementary students (73.1%) agreed with this statement with more than four of 10 (42.5%) doing so strongly. Fourth graders more strongly agreed (47.9%) than sixth graders (34.7%).

**HOW WELL TEACHERS TEACH** *(Proficiency testing does not show how well teachers have been teaching you)*

A majority (54.8%) of elementary students agreed with this statement with 35% doing so strongly. Fourth graders more strongly disagreed (33.1%) than sixth graders (20.1%).

**BUCKLE DOWN BOOKS** *(Proficiency testing Buckle Down books are helpful in preparing for tests)*

Close to three of four elementary students (74.3%) agreed with this statement with more than four of 10 (43.7%) doing so strongly. More fourth graders strongly agreed (53.5%) than sixth graders (38.6%), although it is questionable as to how much exposure fourth graders have had to these books.

**PACE OF LEARNING** *(Proficiency testing has resulted in speeding up the pace of how fast I have to learn)*

Elementary students were split on this item with only 51% agreeing. Close to two of three fourth graders (64.2%) disagreed while the majority of sixth graders (57.7%) agreed with the statement.

## SECONDARY STUDENTS

## General Comments:

*Impact on Students' Learning Behavior*

According to how they responded to this survey, secondary students do not perceive that proficiency testing has positively impacted them. Less than half felt that they have been motivated to take their studies more seriously. Of course, it should be kept in mind that many of them might have felt that they already take their studies seriously. A trend that played itself out throughout the survey responses was that the higher the grade level responding, the lower the level of positive response toward proficiency testing. It should be realized that, for comparison purposes, seniors were excluded from consideration because it was decided by school officials that it was most appropriate to use social studies classes to administer the survey instrument. Unfortunately, this only captured 29 seniors. Thus, comparisons herein are made using seventh through eleventh graders.

As far as stress and pressure are concerned, close to three of four students agreed that proficiency testing has caused these behavioral factors to be excessive. A majority of students also believe that they become too nervous to do their best work on the tests and that the tests do not take into consideration that they might just be having a bad day. Over two-thirds of the students indicated that they just want to get the tests done, and close to three out of four eleventh graders felt this way. This seems to be an internal conflict because a majority of them disagreed that they feel too much competition with other students.

As far as the developing of skills to handle the tests is concerned, less than half of the students felt that proficiency testing has helped their ability to think critically and only one of three eleventh graders thought so. A similar number of eleventh graders felt that proficiency testing has increased their ability to apply the knowledge they have gained, even though a majority of secondary students agreed that it did. While a slight majority of students agreed that proficiency testing makes them apply rather than just recall information, once again, only about a third of eleventh graders agreed. In addition two-thirds of the students disagreed that proficiency testing makes them pay more attention in class, and a similar number felt that too much preparation is required to take the tests.

*Impact on Learning Needs*

A majority of students do believe that proficiency testing has helped teachers find out their weaknesses so that they can correct them, and close to two of three believe that proficiency testing is a good way to measure how much they know about a particular subject. This is also aligned with the finding that a majority believe that proficiency testing has allowed them to know how well they are learning, although only one-third of eleventh graders believe this to be so. However, secondary students were split on their opinion as to whether proficiency testing has made them more aware of what is important in school and less than one-third of eleventh graders think so. They were also split as to whether proficiency testing will prepare them better for learning in the future and, once again, less than one-third of eleventh graders believed it will.

As to whether proficiency testing is serving their psychological needs for learning, there was significant negativity. Close to seven of ten students disagreed that proficiency testing has helped their self-esteem. They felt that such testing is unfair to students with learning difficulties and who do not test well, thereby putting too much emphasis on a single test. While a majority of all secondary students agreed that they have become more comfortable as they have gained experience, a majority of those with the most experience in the upper grades actually disagreed. This might be attributed to the general negativity of upper grade students to the tests.

*Impact on Teaching and Learning Environment*

Even though there was some negativity regarding the impact that proficiency testing has had on the school environment of secondary students, the survey findings tend to affirm the sense of professionalism and competence students perceive about their teachers in Perrysburg. A majority of students disagreed with the statement that proficiency testing resulted in their teachers acting more stressed out in class, but they do agree that it has caused teachers to help students who need extra help. They disagreed that proficiency testing results tell how good their teachers are. They also disagreed that proficiency has made their teachers teach better, although a majority believes that their teachers have been forced to teach to the test.

As for their own school life, more then seven of ten agreed that proficiency testing has not impacted their participation in school activities, but a majority did feel that it has increased the amount of their homework. They were fairly split as to whether proficiency testing has speeded up the pace of learning, but they do believe that it requires too much cramming in of material during class. Furthermore, a majority of students feels that the tests cover a lot of material they never had in class, although they do agree that the Buckle Down books have helped them prepare for the tests. A similar majority does believe that proficiency testing has limited the number of creative classroom projects that they do.

*Parent/Community Relations*

Even though the high performance of Perrysburg students would seem like a source of pride to the students, their response to this statement was firmly negative. They also disagreed that proficiency testing has encouraged their parents to become more involved in their studies. Even though six of 10 eleventh graders felt that their test scores were more important to their parents than to them, a majority of secondary students disagreed.

## Secondary Students Findings Listed in Descending Order of Agreement

| Wording of Statement | Heart of Statement | Percentage of Agreement |
|---|---|---|
| (-) | emphasis on a single test | 77.5 |
| (-) | excess stress | 75.4 |
| (-) | too much pressure on students | 74.7 |
| (-) | do not tell how good my teachers are | 72.2 |
| (+) | participation in school activities | 70.1 |
| (-) | requires too much preparation just for tests | 68.5 |
| (+) | emphasis on math and science | 66.7 |
| (-) | requires cramming of material | 65.6 |
| (-) | do not show how well teachers teach | 64.5 |
| (+) | Buckle Down books are helpful test preparation | 63.1 |
| (+) | measures what I know about subjects | 62.6 |
| (+) | comfortable with experience | 62.1 |
| (-) | teach to test | 62.1 |
| (-) | unfair to students who do not test well | 60.6 |
| (+) | helped teachers find my weaknesses to correct them | 60.3 |
| (-) | limits creative classroom projects | 60.3 |
| (-) | too hard for students with learning problems | 60.2 |
| (-) | covers material never had in class | 59.9 |
| (-) | unfair because might be having a bad day | 59.4 |
| (-) | too nervous to do my best | 59.2 |
| (+) | allows me to know how well I am learning | 56.3 |
| (+) | apply knowledge | 54.9 |
| (+) | apply rather than recall information | 54.8 |
| (-) | increased workload | 53 |
| (-) | get them over with rather than do my best | 52.6 |
| (+) | causes teachers to help students who need it | 52 |
| (+) | more aware of what is important in school | 51.9 |
| (+) | prepares me for future learning | 51.1 |
| (-) | speeds up pace of learning | 51 |
| (+ or -) | selection into gifted and talented programs | 50.3 |
| (+) | think critically | 50 |
| (-) | scores mean more to parents than students | 48.7 |
| (-) | increased competition among schools | 46 |
| (+) | motivate students | 45.2 |
| (-) | teachers more stressed out in class | 43.9 |
| (+) | pay more attention to my teacher | 37.7 |
| (+) | more pride in living in Perrysburg | 36.4 |
| (+) | encourage parental involvement | 36 |
| (+) | gets my teachers to teach better | 32 |
| (+) | increased students' self-esteem | 31.9 |

# ITEM ANALYSIS OF SECONDARY STUDENTS

## Responses to Survey Statements

**MOTIVATION** *(Proficiency testing has helped motivate students to take their studies more seriously)*

There was more disagreement (54.8%) than agreement among secondary students and only one of 10 strongly agreed with this statement. There was significant difference according to grade level, which is a trend that runs throughout the survey results. The higher the grade levels the more negative the response concerning proficiency testing. In this instance, close to two of three (65.2%) seventh graders agreed with the statement while only 29.6% of eleventh graders did so. Keep in mind that twelfth graders are not included in the comparisons because the number surveyed was too low for representative results.

**STRESS** *(Proficiency testing has created excess stress in my school day)*

More than three of four (75.4%) students agreed with this statement, and close to half (45.7%) did so strongly. There was significant difference by grade, but this time it was because the seventh graders were more stressed (79.3%) than eleventh graders (66.1%).

**HELPED WEAKNESSES** *(Proficiency testing has helped teachers find out my weaknesses so they can correct them)*

More than six of 10 (60.3%) students agreed with this statement and more than one of five (21.4%) did so strongly. More than twice as many seventh graders were in agreement (75.7%) than were eleventh graders (35.3%).

**TEACHING TO THE TEST** *(Proficiency testing has forced teachers to teach to the test)*

A majority of secondary students agreed with this statement (62.1%) while just over one of five (22.1%) did so strongly. There were differences by grade level with close to three of four (72.7%) seventh graders agreeing while only half (50.7%) of the eleventh graders did so.

**SELF-ESTEEM** *(Proficiency testing has increased students' self-esteem)*

Close to seven of 10 (68.2%) students disagreed with this statement and less than one of 10 agreed strongly. The higher the grade level, the more disagreement there was. Among seventh graders, close to four of 10 (39.8%) agreed with 10.7% doing so strongly while less than one of five (19.3%) of eleventh graders did so (and only 3% did so strongly).

**WORKLOAD** *(Proficiency testing has increased my amount of homework)*

More than half (53%) of the secondary students agreed with this statement, although a larger percentage (16.6%) of males than females (9.9%) disagreed strongly on this item. There was also significant difference at the grade level, where 65.8% of eighth graders agreed (35.1% strongly) while only 34.4% of tenth, eleventh, and twelfth graders did so (only 13.7% strongly).

**PARENT INVOLVEMENT** *(Proficiency testing has encouraged my parents to become more involved in my studies)*

Close to two-thirds (64%) of secondary students disagreed with this statement and close to one of four (23.9%) did so strongly. Close to eight of 10 eleventh graders disagreed while less than half (49.9%) of seventh graders did so.

**MEANING TO PARENTS** *(Proficiency test scores mean more to my parents than they do to me)*

Less than half (48.7%) of the secondary students agreed with this statement. Once again, the higher the grade level, the more negative the response, with only 47.3% of seventh graders agreeing while 61.9% of eleventh graders did so.

**SCHOOL ACTIVITIES** *(Proficiency testing has not had a negative impact on my participation in school activities)*

More than seven of ten (70.1%) secondary students agreed with this statement and close to one of four (23.6%) did so strongly. Males were somewhat more positive about this with 26% agreeing strongly than females (where 20% agreed strongly).

**TOO NERVOUS** *(Proficiency testing causes me to be too nervous to do my best)*

It is interesting that a majority (59.2%) of secondary students agreed with this statement while a majority (52.4%), of elementary students disagreed with it since one would think that the older students would be less nervous. This might be explained by the general tendency of elementary students to be positive about proficiency testing while secondary students are generally negative.

**COMFORT** *(Proficiency testing has become more comfortable for me as I have gained experience)*

Less than two of three secondary students agreed with this statement (62.1%), and less than one of five (18.7%) did so strongly. At the grade level, there was a finding that would not seem logical in that more than one of four (26.8%) seventh graders strongly agreed with the statement while only 7.3% of eleventh graders did so. While one would think that the higher grades would have far more experience with the testing, the overall negativity toward the testing seems to prevail in the responses.

**STRESSED TEACHERS** *(Proficiency testing has resulted in my teachers acting more stressed out in class)*

A majority (56.1%) of secondary students disagreed with this statement. More seventh graders disagreed (62.5%) than eleventh graders (55.8%). This would appear to be to the credit of Perrysburg teachers who generally are negative about the testing, but by and large do not show this in the classroom so as to affect the attitudes of students.

*APPLY KNOWLEDGE (Proficiency testing has increased students' ability to apply the knowledge they have gained)*

Just over half (54.9%) of the secondary students agreed with this statement with only 13.5% doing so strongly. A higher percentage of males (18.9%) than females (12.5%) strongly disagreed with this statement. Again, the agreement at the lower grades was significantly higher than at the upper grades. Among seventh graders, 83.1% agreed (with 15.8% doing so strongly) while in the eleventh grade only 36% agreed (and 5% agreed strongly).

*INCREASED COMPETITION (Proficiency testing has increased competition among students and schools)*

A majority (54%) of secondary students disagreed with this statement with one of five (20.5%) doing so strongly. There were no differences within the group.

*PRIDE IN PERRYSBURG (Proficiency tests results have given me more pride in living in Perrysburg)*

Close to two of three (63.6%) secondary students disagreed with this statement, and close to one of three (31.6%) did so strongly. Whereas more than four of ten (43%) seventh graders agreed with this statement, only one of four (26.9%) of the eleventh graders did so.

*LEARNING PROBLEMS (Proficiency testing is too hard for students with learning problems)*

A majority (60.2%) of students agreed with this statement while approximately one in four (26.6%) did so strongly. A greater number of males (28.6%) than females (23%) strongly agreed with this statement.

*EMPHASIS ON MATH AND SCIENCE (Proficiency testing has placed greater emphasis on math and science curricula)*

Two of three students (66.7%) agreed with this statement, although only one of five (21.4%) did so strongly. Male students were stronger in their agreement (29.6% strongly) than females students (23% strongly). Seventh graders agreed more than seven of 10 times (71%) with more than one of four (26.3%) doing so strongly, while eleventh graders agreed less than six of 10 times (59.6%) and less than one of five did so strongly (18.7%).

*PRESSURE ON STUDENTS (Proficiency testing has placed too much pressure on students)*

Three of four (74.7%) students agreed with this statement and over four of 10 (43.7%) did so strongly. Once again, as with the question on stress, a greater number of lower grade students agreed than upper level students. Among seventh graders, more than three of four agreed (75.7%) while less than six of 10 eleventh graders (59.7%) did so.

**WHAT IS IMPORTANT** (*Proficiency testing has made me more aware of what is important in school*)

Unlike elementary students who were positive toward this item, secondary students were largely split with only 51.9% in agreement and only 13.6% strongly. More than twice as many seventh graders agreed with this (67.7%) than eleventh graders (32%).

**RATING TEACHERS** (*Proficiency testing results do not tell how good my teachers are*)

On this item, close to three of four secondary students agreed with the statement (72.2%) and one in three (32.2%) did so strongly. There were no group differences.

**THINK CRITICALLY** (*Proficiency testing has helped students to think critically*)

Only half of the secondary students agreed with this statement (50%), and only about one in 10 (11.6%) agreed strongly. As with the statement on applying knowledge, males tended to disagree more strongly (23.7%) than females (15.2%). As is the trend, seventh graders agreed much more often (65.4%) and more strongly (15.6%) than eleventh graders (34%) with only 3.9% doing so strongly.

**MATERIAL COVERED** (*Proficiency testing covers a lot of material I never had in class*)

Close to six of 10 secondary students (59.9%) agreed with this statement. More seventh graders agreed (68%) than eleventh graders (51%), which is significant because this is one of the only items in which seventh graders were more negative than eleventh graders.

**BETTER PREPARED** (*Proficiency testing will prepare me better for learning in the future*)

Secondary students were fairly split on this item (51.1% in agreement) which was much less than elementary students. Two of three (66.3%) seventh graders agreed while less than a third (30.6%) of eleventh graders did so.

**UNFAIR TO STUDENTS** (*Proficiency testing is unfair to students who do not test well*)

Six of 10 (60.6%) secondary students agreed with this statement. There were no group differences on this item.

**TEACH BETTER** (*Proficiency testing gets my teachers to teach better*)

More than two of three (68%) secondary students disagreed with this statement. More females disagreed (70.8%) than males (64.5%). Close to eight of 10 (79.6%) eleventh graders disagreed whereas less than six of 10 seventh graders (59.2%) disagreed.

**PREPARATION** (*Proficiency testing requires too much preparation just for the tests*)

More than two of three (68.5%) secondary students agreed with this statement and more than one-third (34.4%) did so strongly. There were no group differences on this item.

***PAY MORE ATTENTION*** *(Proficiency testing makes me pay more attention to my teacher)*

Close to two-thirds of the secondary students (62.3%) disagreed with this statement, whereas two-thirds of elementary students agreed with the statement. While a majority (55.7%) of seventh graders disagreed with the statement, more than eight of 10 (81.1%) eleventh graders did so.

***CRAMMING OF MATERIAL*** *(Proficiency testing requires too much cramming in of material during class)*

Close to two of three (65.6%) secondary students agreed with this statement and there were no group differences.

***KNOW LEARNING*** *(Proficiency testing has allowed me to know how well I am learning)*

Although over fifty-six percent of secondary students agreed with this statement, less than one of five (18.2%) did so strongly. While close to three of four seventh graders agreed (72.7%), only one of three eleventh graders (33.9%) did so.

***BAD DAY*** *(Proficiency testing is unfair because you might be just having a bad day)*

A majority (59.4%) of secondary students agreed with this statement, but there were no group differences for this item.

***APPLY NOT RECALL*** *(Proficiency testing gets me to apply rather than just recall information)*

As with several of the items, while a majority (54.8%) of secondary students agreed with this statement, this was far less than the level of agreement found among elementary school children. Furthermore, only 14.5% strongly agreed. More than twice as many seventh graders (70%) agreed than eleventh graders (34.4%)

***SINGLE TEST*** *(Proficiency testing places too much emphasis on a single test)*

More than three of four (77.5%) students agreed with this statement and, in this instance, there were no differences by gender or grade level.

***GIFTED AND TALENTED*** *(Proficiency testing is a way to select students into gifted and talented programs)*

Secondary students were split on this item with 50.3% in agreement and less than half as many strongly agreeing (17.4%) than their elementary counterparts. Once again, seventh graders agreed (62%) much more often than eleventh graders (34.9%).

***GET THEM OVER*** *(Proficiency testing just makes me want to get them over with rather than to do my best)*

A slim majority of students (52.6%) agreed with this statement which is diametrically different from their elementary counterparts. One third of the students (33.4%) strongly agreed with the statement. Close to three of four eleventh graders agreed with the statement while only half (53.7%) of the seventh graders did so.

**MEASURE KNOWLEDGE** *(Proficiency testing is a good way to measure how much I know about particular subjects)*

While a majority (62.6%) of secondary students agreed with this statement, less than one in five (19%) did so strongly. While three of four (74.1%) of seventh graders agreed with the statement, just over four of ten (41.4%) of eleventh graders did so.

**LIMITED CREATIVITY** *(Proficiency testing has limited the number of creative classroom projects that we do)*

A majority (60.3%) of secondary students agreed with this statement and there were no group differences.

**EXTRA HELP** *(Proficiency testing causes teachers to help students who need extra help)*

A slight majority (52%) of secondary students agreed with this statement, but only 15.5% did so strongly. While two of three (65.4%) seventh graders agreed, only one of three (33.1%) eleventh graders agreed.

**HOW WELL TEACHERS TEACH** *(Proficiency testing does not show how well teachers have been teaching you)*

Close to two of three (64.5%) secondary students agreed with more than one-third (35%) doing so strongly. There were no group differences on this item.

**BUCKLE DOWN BOOKS** *(Proficiency testing Buckle Down books are helpful in preparing for tests)*

Over sixty-three percent of secondary students agreed with this statement, and one of four (24.1%) did so strongly. There were more females who agreed (69.7%) than males (57.7%)

**PACE OF LEARNING** *(Proficiency testing has resulted in speeding up the pace of how fast I have to learn)*

Secondary students were fairly split on this item (51% in agreement), and there were no significant differences by group.

## COMMUNITY MEMBERS/PARENTS

Because these respondents were not asked demographic background questions as the other constituencies were, no item by item analysis is necessary. Instead, simply the main themes of the survey will be considered with regard to community member/parent response. It should be kept in mind in reviewing these findings that they represent only the 129 community members/parents who responded to the survey that was included as an insert in <u>Perryscope</u>. For the sake of brevity, the term 'parents' will be used to include both community members and parents when referring to these respondents.

## General Comments:

*Impact on Students' Learning Behavior*

Parents disagreed (69%) that proficiency testing has helped motivate students, but they definitely agreed (83.3%) that it has increased the anxiety students feel toward school. Furthermore, close to eight of 10 disagreed (79.4%) that proficiency testing has helped their child keep focused on school performance. They also felt that proficiency testing has created more stress on them as parents (75.7% and one of two strongly), but a majority (55.6%) think that it has not affected their concern about their child's academic performance. They do feel (79.3% and 57.8% strongly) that proficiency testing does put more pressure on their child, although they do perceive that proficiency testing is helping their child's test taking skills (76.3%). However, more than three of four (75.8%) did not agree that proficiency testing helps student apply rather than just recall information.

*Impact on Professional Job Performance of Teachers and Administrators*

Even though it might be supposed that one of the main goals of proficiency testing would be to increase the public's sense of accountability among faculty and staff, parents responding to this survey were split (50%) on this item. However, a majority (60%) of the parents did agree that teachers are being held more accountable for the results. However, close to nine of 10 (87.8%) respondents agreed that these test results are not a reliable source to evaluate teacher performance. Also, three of four disagreed with the statement that proficiency testing scores reveal how well teachers have been teaching their child. Furthermore, more than nine of 10 (90.4%) agreed that proficiency testing does not demonstrate who are the most outstanding teachers.

With regard to administrators, three of four (75.2%) agreed that proficiency testing has placed greater responsibility on administrators. However, more than four of five parents (81.7%) disagreed with the statement that proficiency testing has pleased them because it has improved accountability. Finally, close to eight of 10 parents perceived that proficiency testing has adversely impacted morale among faculty and staff.

*Impact on Curriculum*

One of the positive responses (79.3%) from parents was that proficiency testing has helped identify weak areas in the school's curriculum. Unfortunately, this perception did not translate into agreement that proficiency testing has improved the quality of education in Perrysburg schools because more than eight of 10 (84.3%) disagreed with this statement. Two of three parents (66.7%) also disagreed with the statement that proficiency testing has helped students realize what they need to know. Further evidence of the basically negative response from these parents toward proficiency testing reveals that more than nine of 10 (94.1%) agreed that proficiency testing has forced teachers to teach to the test, but close to six of 10 (59.6%) disagreed that this has helped the school district align its curriculum.

*Impact on Response to Student Learning Needs*

One of the primary areas surveyed with parents was their perception as to whether proficiency testing was resulting in a better atmosphere for and service to their children. There was a split (with 51.8% disagreeing) on the statement that proficiency testing helps identify the academic problems of individual students, and one half (50%) of the respondents disagreed that it causes teachers to help students who need extra help.

There was concern displayed through parents' response to items related to the impact proficiency testing is having on their children's feelings about school. Close to nine of 10 (89.6%) agreed that proficiency testing has not increased their child's self-esteem and just over half (50.9%) agreed that proficiency testing has adversely affected their child's confidence to do well in regular school subjects.

There are definite perceptions among the respondents that proficiency testing is not an appropriate way to measure student learning with more than three of four (87.8%) parents (75.8%) disagreeing. Furthermore, more than eight of 10 felt that proficiency testing was not an appropriate way to select students into gifted and talented programs.

As might be expected, there was firm agreement (85.6%) that proficiency testing places too much emphasis on a single test, and an equal number of parents (85.6%) felt that too much emphasis was being placed on test scores.

*Community Relations*

Several of the items surveyed parent attitudes toward how the proficiency testing has impacted community relations and their own relationship to the schools. Close to nine of 10 (88.9%) disagreed that proficiency testing has encouraged them to become more involved in the schools, and seven of 10 (70.8%) disagreed that it has fostered more communication between teachers and parents. Seven of 10 (69.2%) disagreed that proficiency testing results have not been well explained to them. Close to nine of 10 (87.2%) felt that proficiency testing was used more to appease the public than improve education.

Despite the fact that close to nine of 10 (87.2%) agree that proficiency testing has increased competition among school districts, close to two of three (62.3%) disagreed that proficiency testing results have increased community pride about the school district. An equal number (62.3%) disagreed that proficiency testing has increased public support of the schools. Just over half (51.9%) agreed that the test results have helped real estate values in Perrysburg, but close to three in four (73.5%) disagreed that proficiency testing results reflect how good the school district is.

## COMPARATIVE ANALYSIS

### Comparing Teachers and Support/Administrative Staff

Only four statistically significant differences were found between teachers and support staff in relation to proficiency testing. Specifically, differences were found regarding whether proficiency testing has: (1) forced teachers to teach to the test; (2) put too much pressure on students; (3) helped students' ability to think critically; and, (4) been seen as a valid way to measure students' learning. An overwhelming majority of teachers (89.9%), compared with 78.8% of support staff, agreed that proficiency testing has forced teachers to teach to the test. Although there are similar levels of agreement between teachers (72.4%) and support staff (75%) that proficiency testing has put too much pressure on students, there was significant difference in the strength of disagreement on the part of teachers. Forty-six of the 198 teachers responding to this survey item disagreed (23.2%), with 10 teachers (5%) strongly or very strongly disagreeing that proficiency testing has placed too much pressure on students. In contrast, only six of 32 support staff (18.8%) disagreed, with no one strongly or very strongly disagreeing with the survey item.

A major difference is apparent between teachers and support staff regarding the impact of proficiency testing on students' critical thinking. Only 38.9% of the teachers, compared with 50.1% of support staff, reported that proficiency testing has helped students' ability to think critically. Great levels of disagreement were found among the teachers, with 42% disagreeing, 11.4% strongly disagreeing, and 7.8% very strongly disagreeing that proficiency testing has positively impacted students' ability to think critically. Similarly, teachers (83.2%) are much more negative than support staff (61.1%) about proficiency tests as a valid measure of students' learning.

Much agreement of opinion exists between the two groups. Both support staff (96.9%) and teachers (94%) agree that proficiency testing has resulted in school curriculum being aligned to fit the proficiencies. Similar levels of disagreement exist among teachers (91.4%) and support staff (90.9%) indicating that both do not believe that proficiency testing has improved school climate. Rather, teachers (86%) and support staff (81.3%) reported that proficiency testing has increased the anxiety students feel toward school. Similarly, both support staff (68.8%) and teachers (68%) indicated that proficiency testing has adversely impacted morale among faculty and staff, with more teachers (17.8%) than administrators (3.1%) very strongly agreeing that proficiency has had a negative impact on morale. Moreover, both support staff (75.8%) and teachers (70.9%) agreed that proficiency testing results arrive too late for successful intervention. Both support staff (93.9%) and teachers (92.9%) perceive that proficiency has increased competition among school districts. Both teachers (96.2%) and support staff (93.8%) overwhelmingly agree that proficiency testing has been imposed upon the school district as opposed to seeking input from the district.

Regarding whether proficiency testing has been treated as an add-on rather than a regular part of the school year, a slight majority of teachers (51.3%) disagreed with this statement and close to one in five (18.2%) did so strongly. Likewise, a slight majority of support staff disagreed (51.5%), but none did so strongly. Teachers (90.1%) overwhelmingly agreed that proficiency testing tests a student's reading comprehension more than knowledge in a particular subject area, with more than half doing so strongly (54.5%). Support staff also firmly agreed (77.4%), with 45.2% doing so strongly. A majority of teachers agreed (62.1%) that proficiency testing helps students apply rather than just recall information, although only 12.8% did so strongly. Two of three support staff agreed (65.6%), with close to one in five doing so strongly (18.8%). More than two of three teachers (67.4%) disagreed that proficiency testing is developmentally-appropriate for the ages of students who take them, and close to four of ten teachers disagreed strongly (39.6%). A slight majority of support staff (53.8%) disagreed, with one of four (25%) disagreeing strongly. Finally, both support staff (96.7%) and teachers (90.5%) overwhelming disagreed that proficiency testing has increased students' self-esteem.

## Comparing Elementary and Secondary Students

In relation to the positively-worded survey statements, 83.2% of elementary students overwhelmingly agreed that proficiency testing has helped motivate them to take their studies more seriously, whereas less than half of the secondary students (45.2%) agreed. The majority of both elementary (88.6%) and secondary (60.3%) students reported that proficiency testing has helped teachers find out their weaknesses so that teachers can correct them. Exactly the same percentage of elementary and secondary students (66.7%) responded that proficiency testing has placed greater emphasis on math and science ability.

However, major differences in perceptions exist between elementary and secondary students regarding proficiency testing. First, almost twice as many elementary students (61%) as secondary students (31.9%) reported that proficiency testing has helped their self-esteem. Second, regarding whether proficiency testing has encouraged parents to become more involved in their child's studies, 586 of 835 elementary students (70.1%) compared with only 408 of 1134 secondary students (36%) responded that proficiency testing has encouraged such parental involvement. Third, in relation to the impact of proficiency testing on students' participation in school activities, an overwhelming 83.4% of elementary students and 70% of secondary students reported that proficiency testing has not had a negative impact on their participation. Fourth, an overwhelming 81% of elementary students, compared with only 54.9% of secondary students, reported that proficiency testing has increased their ability to apply the knowledge they have gained. Likewise, elementary students (81.5%) are much more convinced that proficiency testing has made them more aware of what is important in school than are secondary students (51.9%). Elementary students (75.7%) are also much more convinced than their secondary counterparts (50%) that proficiency testing has helped their ability to think critically.

Although both groups reveal agreement that they have become more comfortable with proficiency testing as they have gained experience, elementary students (80.4%) are more positive about it than secondary students (62.1%). A major difference is apparent between the groups as to whether proficiency test results have given students more pride in living in Perrysburg. For elementary students, 62.5% agreed that proficiency test results have increased their pride in Perrysburg, while only 36.4% of secondary students agreed. Elementary students (83.8%) are also much more convinced than secondary students (51.1%) that proficiency testing will prepare them better for learning in the future. However, neither elementary (47.3%) nor secondary (32%) students were convinced that proficiency testing gets their teachers to teach better.

Overwhelming, more elementary students (80.8%) than secondary students (54.8%) responded that proficiency testing gets them to apply rather than just recall information. More elementary students (74.3%) than secondary students (63.1%) reported that proficiency testing Buckle Down books are helpful in preparing for tests. According to the survey results, proficiency testing has not resulted in a majority of secondary students (37.7%) paying more attention to their teacher. However, a majority of elementary students (64.3%) reported that proficiency testing makes them pay more attention to their teacher. For 84.2% of the elementary students and 62.6% of the secondary students, proficiency testing is viewed as a good way to measure what they know about particular subjects. Only 56.3% of secondary students, compared with 82.3% of elementary students, reported that proficiency testing has allowed them to know how well they are learning.

There is strong agreement among elementary students (73.1%), compared with slightly more than half of secondary students (52%), that proficiency testing causes teachers to help students who need extra attention. Elementary students (62%), compared with only 50.3% of secondary students, reported that proficiency testing is a way to select students into gifted and talented programs. Overall, these findings depict the contrast between the more negative or critical stance of secondary students toward proficiency testing compared to the more favorable, uncritical stance of elementary students.

In relation to the negatively-worded survey statements about proficiency testing, a large number of secondary students (75.4%) reported that proficiency testing has created excess stress in their school day, while fewer elementary students (65.2%) attribute excess stress to proficiency testing. A slight majority of secondary students (53%) reported that proficiency testing has increased the amount of homework they have to do. Less than half of the elementary respondents (43.6%) agreed that proficiency testing has increased their homework load.

Secondary students (59.2%) reported more nervousness about proficiency testing affecting their academic performance than did elementary students (43.9%). Secondary students also seemed to be more concerned than elementary students about the fairness of proficiency testing. To illustrate, 60.6% of secondary students compared with 46.8% of elementary students reported that proficiency testing is unfair to students who do not test well. Both elementary (71.5%) and secondary (60.2%) students reported that proficiency testing is too hard for students with learning problems. Regarding fairness associated with proficiency testing, secondary students (59.3%) report more concern than elementary students (45.8%) that proficiency testing is unfair because one might just be having a bad day.

Both elementary (70%) and secondary (62.1%) students responded that proficiency testing has forced teachers to teach to the test. In response to whether proficiency testing has resulted in their teachers acting more stressed out in class, neither the findings from secondary (43.9%) nor elementary (31.5%) students exhibited a 50% majority of agreement. Both secondary (72.2%) and elementary (61.5%) students reported that proficiency test results do not tell them how good their teachers are. As revealed by the contrasting percentages, however, the findings suggest that proficiency testing results seem to carry more weight in the thinking of elementary students than that of secondary students.

Similar results were obtained from both elementary and secondary students regarding whether proficiency testing has speeded up the pace of how fast students learn. Only a slight majority of elementary (51%) and secondary (51%) students reported that proficiency testing has speeded up the pace of learning. However, both secondary (59.9%) and elementary (52.3%) students mildly agree that proficiency testing covers a lot of material they never had in class. Both secondary (74.7%) and elementary (72.5%) students also responded that proficiency testing has put too much pressure on students.

Moreover, both secondary (68.5%) and elementary (65.2%) students reported that proficiency testing requires too much preparation just for the tests. Secondary (77.5%) and elementary (68.7%) students also agreed that proficiency testing places too much emphasis on a single test. The higher percentage reported by secondary students reveals greater concern on their part about proficiency testing placing too much emphasis on a single test measure. However, more secondary students (65.6%) than elementary students (53.3%) reported that proficiency testing requires too much cramming of material during class. A majority of secondary students (60.3%) reported that proficiency testing has limited the number of creative classroom projects that they do, whereas less than half of the elementary students (49.8%) responded that proficiency testing has hindered creative projects in the classroom.

Greater agreement exists among secondary students (64.5%) than elementary students (54.8%) that proficiency testing scores do not show how well teachers have been teaching students. The secondary student respondents are more reluctant to link students' proficiency test scores to teacher effectiveness. Another major difference was exhibited between secondary and elementary students regarding whether proficiency testing just makes students want to get them over with rather than to do their best. For a slight majority of secondary students (52.6%), proficiency testing makes them want to get them over with. Only 30.5% of elementary students reported feeling this way. This finding seems to suggest the seriousness with which elementary students approach proficiency testing.

Both elementary and secondary students reported that proficiency test scores mean more to them than to their parents. To illustrate, 59.1% of elementary students and 51.3% of secondary students disagreed that proficiency testing scores meant more to their parents than to themselves. Neither a majority of elementary (45.1%) nor a majority of secondary (46%) students responded that proficiency testing has increased competition among students and schools.

Overall, the findings from this study reveal that elementary students are consistently more in favor of proficiency testing than secondary students.

## Comparing the Four School-Based Constituent Groups

What follows are the findings from the 13 survey items common to the four school groups (elementary students, secondary students, teachers, and support/administrative staff). The percentages that follow constitute the aggregate percentages (that is, the percentage of the group that agreed, strongly agreed, *and* very strongly agreed with a particular survey item).

## Motivation

Over eighty-three percent of elementary students agreed, strongly agreed, or very strongly agreed that proficiency testing has helped motivate students to take their studies more seriously. Although no administrators/support staff chose the category "very strongly agree", 63.7% of administrators responded that proficiency testing has motivated students to take their studies more seriously. In contrast to elementary and administrators/support staff groups, only 50.8% of teachers and 45.2% of secondary students agreed, strongly, agreed, or very strongly agreed that proficiency testing motivated students to take their studies more seriously.

## Stress

Although percentages differ between the four groups, all groups responded that proficiency testing has created excess stress in their job. The group reporting the highest percentage of excess job stress as a result of proficiency testing is teachers (80.7%), followed by secondary students (75.4%), administrators (72.7%), and elementary students (65.2%).

## Teaching to the Test

Although all four groups responded that proficiency testing has forced teachers to teach to the test, teachers (89.9%) felt the strongest about this, followed by administrators (78.8%). Regarding students, 70% of elementary students reported that proficiency testing has forced teachers to teach to the test, while 62.1% of secondary students believe this to be the case.

## Workload

Over eighty-one percent of administrators and 75.1% of teachers reported that proficiency testing has increased their own workload. More secondary students (53%) than elementary students (43.6%) responded that proficiency testing has increased their workload.

## Parental Involvement

Of the four groups, elementary students (70.1%) felt the strongest that proficiency testing has encouraged parents to become more involved in Perrysburg schools. Only 48.5% of administrators, 36.7% of teachers, and 36% of secondary students reported more parental school involvement as a result of proficiency testing.

## Comfortabilty with Experience

Although all four groups reported percentages above 50%, there are striking differences between students, faculty, and administrators in relation to who feels the strongest about their increasing comfortability with proficiency testing over time.
An overwhelming 80.4% of elementary students reported that they have become more comfortable with proficiency testing as they have gained experience compared with 62.1% of secondary students. Over sixty-one percent of administrators reported agreement, strong agreement, or very strong agreement with this survey item. Only slightly more than half of the teachers (54.5%) reported that they have become more comfortable with proficiency testing as they have gained experience.

## Learning Differences

All four groups reported concern that proficiency testing is overwhelming for students with learning difficulties. Specifically, 86.7% of teachers, 75.8% of administrators, 71.5% of elementary students, and 60.2% of secondary students responded that proficiency testing is overwhelming for students with learning difficulties.

## Pressure on Students

All groups agreed that proficiency testing has put too much pressure on students. To illustrate, 75% of administrators, 74.7% of secondary students, 72.5% of elementary students, and 72.4% of teachers reported that proficiency testing has placed too much pressure on students. Of the 33 administrator respondents, only six disagreed that proficiency testing has put too much pressure on students. No administrator chose strongly disagree or very strongly disagree to the survey statement.

## Apply Knowledge

Major differences can be found between faculty, administration, and students regarding whether proficiency testing has increased students' ability to apply knowledge. An overwhelming 81% of elementary students reported that proficiency testing has increased students' ability to apply knowledge, whereas only a slight majority of secondary students (54.9%) ascribe this benefit to proficiency testing. The results from administrators (45.5%) and teachers (33.2%) reflect more skepticism. The findings raise questions regarding the degree to which students are more impressionable at younger ages and the degree to which they have become acclimated to the proficiency testing environment.

## Math and Science Emphasis

All four groups reported similar percentages in relation to whether proficiency testing has placed greater emphasis on math and science curricula. Specifically, 68.8% of administrators, 66.7% of secondary students, 66.7% of elementary students, and 63.1% of teachers agreed, strongly agreed, or very strongly agreed that proficiency testing has placed greater emphasis on math and science curricula.

## Critical Thinking

It is questionable as to the degree that proficiency testing has helped students' ability to think critically. Only a majority of elementary students (75.7%) agreed that proficiency testing has helped students' critical thinking. Respondents from the other groups reported lower levels of agreement. Specifically, 50.1% of administrators and 50% of secondary students reported that proficiency testing has helped students' critical thinking. Only 38.9% of teachers responded that proficiency testing has helped students' ability to think critically.

## Single Test

Although the percentages differ somewhat among the four groups, the majority of respondents in each group agreed that proficiency testing places too much emphasis on a single test. Notably, teachers (89.9%) and administrators (87.9%) reported concern about proficiency testing placing too much emphasis on a single test. Only four of 33 administrators disagreed. No administrator strongly or very strongly disagreed with the survey item. Regarding students, 77.5% of secondary students and 68.7% of elementary students reported that proficiency testing places too much emphasis on a single test.

## Self-Esteem

There were major differences found between elementary and secondary students regarding whether proficiency testing has increased students' self-esteem. A majority of elementary students (61%) reported that proficiency testing has increased students' self-esteem, whereas secondary students (31.9%) were less inclined to agree. Only 18 of 187 teachers (9.5%) reported that proficiency testing has increased students' self-esteem. Likewise, only one of 30 administrator (3.3%) respondents agreed that proficiency testing has increased students' self-esteem. No administrator chose strongly or very strongly agree to the survey item.

## SUGGESTED POLICY RECOMMENDATIONS

The following suggestions are made in the spirit of continuous quality improvement. They are intended specifically to help the Perrysburg School District, but have implications for state officials. Perrysburg schools were chosen for this study because of the record of excellence they have achieved not only in their reputation for educational quality, but in the relative level of excellence their students have achieved on the proficiency tests. The analysis of survey results should be sobering when one of the best districts in the state of Ohio registers as much concern as is evident in the survey results.

1.  The impact of proficiency testing on school morale and climate, stress on faculty and staff, and increasing pressure on students, brings the cost-benefit equation of proficiency testing into question. Policy makers should not assume that state-mandated requirements necessarily lead to improved educational policy. This study suggests that such improvement should evolve out of a continuing dialogue with all constituencies impacted by such testing.
2.  The relationship between state education officials and local educators needs to be strengthened through a greater sense of advocacy for and trust of local educator capability by state officials in evolving standards of proficiency as well as implementation and improvement of policies.
3.  Despite the agreement that proficiency testing has helped align curriculum, the level of collaboration between teachers needs to be addressed because of its impact on establishment of learning outcomes and the continuity in preparing students for the tests.
4.  Since so few constituencies agreed that proficiency testing is a valid way of measuring student learning or in evaluating teacher performance, the issue of

improved assessment within the district needs to be addressed with a proactive approach determined by those constituents closest to the implementation of evaluation policy.

5.  The potential for proficiency results to be misinterpreted by the public and misused in rating students, teachers, administrators or whole districts suggests that all such comparisons are not beneficial to improving education or the public's view of it.

6.  The profound impact proficiency testing has had on the work of guidance counselors should be further analyzed with regard to what necessary functions have been adversely affected and at what costs to the counseling needs of school children.

7.  The apparent level of negative critique regarding proficiency testing found at the higher grade levels suggests that students' attitudes, as well as aptitudes, must be taken into consideration in preparing them for proficiency testing.

8.  There is a need to reconcile the potential conflict between the moral and legal rights of students with learning difficulties and the need to maintain consistent standards of performance. The issue of fairness does not necessarily align itself with standardization of process when the needs of the individuals are not served through such process.

9.  The assumption that proficiency testing leads to greater accountability to the public was not confirmed through this study and, therefore, such assumption must be brought into question.

10. Finally, the quantified proficiency testing results must be viewed as only part of the way in which the quality of student learning should be measured and educational process reformed.

# Chapter 2

# MARKET-BASED REFORMS OF PUBLIC SCHOOLING: RE-EXAMINING THEIR UNDERLYING RATIONALE

*Nick Adnett and Peter Davies*

Centre for Economics and Business Education,
Staffordshire University Business School, UK

## ABSTRACT

We examine the economic theory underlying the international trend towards increasing the role of market forces in educational decision-making. We argue that these reforms have often utilised a naive analysis, neglecting the complexity of the operation of market forces and the unique nature of schooling markets. We concentrate upon measures to increase parental and pupil choice and examine their consequences for behaviour in local schooling markets. Our analysis indicates the importance of designing and publicising performance indicators and providing incentives for schools that minimise dysfunctional responses.

## INTRODUCTION

Broadly similar critiques of state schooling systems emerged in Australia, Britain, Canada, the US, New Zealand and parts of Europe in the 1970s and 1980s (OECD, 1994 and Lauder et al., 1999). These critiques were often based upon low pupil attainment levels in standardized international tests. When combined with the public choice-based critique of state schooling, they popularized the view that national economic competitiveness was being threatened by the failures of the schooling system. It was argued that the state schooling system in these countries lacked the characteristics perceived as necessary for efficiency: consumer choice, competition, incentives and performance-related teacher pay (Fels, 1995). The solution adopted by many Western governments was greater reliance on the market mechanism in the delivery of education and upon the ideology of consumership (Cookson, 1992), particularly policies that increased consumer choice and voice.

Economists since Adam Smith have analyzed education as an investment in human capital that both directly generates productivity gains and higher earning-power to individuals, and produces additional benefits to society as a whole. Orthodox economic analysis suggests the potential for market forces to efficiently allocate resources between alternative uses. Relying upon the self-interest of producers and consumers can, under certain conditions, lead to socially optimal outcomes. Market choice theorists have used this analysis to justify market-based reforms, arguing that parents and pupils have incentives to choose both the type and duration of schooling which best suits their abilities and the needs of the economy. These incentives are assumed to be signaled via the structure of labor market earnings, as orthodox analysis interprets schooling decisions as predominantly concerning investments in human capital. Where these incentives are strong enough, resources permit and market structures allow, consumer preferences in a competitive market can, it is argued, motivate schools to respond to perceived parental needs.

Whether such conditions can be generated in educational markets is much disputed (Vandenberghe, 2000). Most educational markets have restricted competition, remain highly regulated and produce multiple outcomes that are difficult to quantify. Furthermore, consumption and investment elements are here closely interlinked, uncertainty and asymmetric information problems abound and equity considerations often appear to conflict with issues of efficiency. These complications have caused many to question the appropriateness of orthodox market choice analysis in this area, and others to resist all economic analyses of schooling issues.

In the following analysis we reassess this economic rationale for increasing the role of market forces in educational decision-making. Initially we explore the market choice critique of public schooling, establishing the mechanisms that are thought to cause under-performance in public schooling systems. After this discussion of government failure in educational provision, we turn the arguments around to consider the requirements for the efficient operation of schooling markets and likely sources of market failure. Here we explore the characteristics of schooling which give rise to externalities that so complicate any assessment of the need for, and consequences of, market-based reform. The fear of significant market failure has so far led to reforms of state schooling that generally fall short of a full-market solution. Emphasis has largely been upon increasing schooling choices and devolving more decision-making powers to individual schools. The term 'quasi-market' has been used to describe the type of market organization where open enrolment prevails, but government remains the purchasing agent and retains control of curriculum, school entry and exit and the occupational licensing of teachers (Glennerster, 1991). We discuss the nature of these quasi-markets in the following section. Here we review what we have learnt about the operation of this form of schooling market. We concentrate initially, upon the reasons for the dominant role of the state in the provision of elementary and secondary education. Next we examine the role of assessment and signaling of relative school performance in these markets, and address the origins and consequences of cream-skimming and polarization. Finally in this section, we consider the consequences of positional competition and the impact of schooling quasi-markets on student attainment and the diversity of educational provision in local markets. We conclude by identifying the key remaining questions which researchers into market-based reforms need to address.

## THE CRITIQUE OF PUBLIC SCHOOLING

The market choice critique of state schooling which developed from the work of Friedman (1955), combines a belief in the potential effectiveness of the market mechanism with a belief in the intrinsic inefficiency of public provision based upon public choice theory. As Shleifer (1998) explains, the case against the prevailing system of state schooling is not just that governments allow schools a captive market where they have no need to innovate or to respond efficiently, or sometimes at all, to consumer preferences. An important element of the original Chubb and Moe (1988) critique was that state education systems had effectively allowed educational decision-making to be subverted to serve the interests of educational administrators and teachers. In the US, the apparent absence of a relationship between school inputs and student performance, the secular rise in per student teaching and administrative costs, and the poor relative performance of schools in metropolitan areas have all been attributed to the effectiveness of teacher unions in determining public policy (Hoxby, 1996a and Peltzman, 1993).

These sources of government failure can be given an agency theory interpretation (Rapp, 2000). The principal-agent problem arises when a principal (parents, taxpayers and the government in the case of public schooling) delegates some decision-making authority to an agent (teachers). For parents the objectives of state-schooling is human capital creation, whilst taxpayers are motivated by the benefits of a more educated populace. Parents and taxpayers delegate responsibility for achieving these outputs to government. Information asymmetries arise since the teachers are more knowledgeable about the actual efforts they make and the composition of educational outputs they are seeking to generate. Hence, the agency problem is how to ensure that teachers do not exploit their informational advantages to lower and distort educational outcomes away from those desired by the principals. Bureaucratic failures also reflect asymmetric information problems. Local providers have little incentive to refrain from spending up to their set budget. They learn that any savings are likely to return to central budget-holders and that their future budgets are likely to be revised downwards. Hence, information flows are distorted and schooling expenditure patterns have a 'ratchet' effect over time (Milgrom and Roberts, 1992).

A key argument against public provision of education is the inefficiency of centralization as a means of addressing these agency problems. Lack of direct accountability results in an over-regulated and non-diversified provision. The different needs of local markets, schools and individual pupils are neglected in favor of a common curriculum and assessment system designed in part to enable the monitoring of school performance. Commitments to both an occupational licensing system and wage bargaining at the national level for teachers further limits flexibility and prevents the design of effective incentive mechanisms to motivate teachers.

Market choice critics advocate school privatization, often combined with some system where students can use publicly-funded vouchers at any school of their choice. Such a combination of vouchers and school choice are perceived to have several advantages over publicly-provided schooling (Shleifer, 1998). First, private schools have more incentive to reduce costs and innovate, potentially leading to both more efficient and higher quality education. Second, private schools will be more able to resist the attempts of teacher' unions to distort provision in favor of their members' interests. Finally, competition between schools, both existing and potential, ensures that the 'exit' threat constrains the ability of private schools to undertake quality-reducing cost reductions. Reputational considerations strengthen this market discipline, whilst the presence of many not-for-profit private schools also curbs the ability of schooling-providers to exploit their market-power.

## SCHOOLING MARKETS

### Requirements for an Efficient Schooling Market

For an efficient schooling market, output needs to be maximized for the given utilization of resources. Efficiency can be improved if more output is achieved for the same resources or alternatively if the same output can be achieved for less resource use. Differing uses of the term 'efficiency' in discussions of schooling markets have been a cause of some confusion. We follow the classification used by Hoxby (1996b). She argues that the ultimate function of an educational system is to create an environment that induces people to make socially optimal investment decisions. Within this framework, she argues that equity is about ensuring that this standard of optimality is applied to all groups, regardless of family background or wealth. The problem of allocative efficiency, whether society is making best use of its resources, concerns the standard, type and amount of schooling provided, whilst productive efficiency concerns minimizing the costs of that provision (the 'value for money' or 'cost-effectiveness' dimension). According to the market critique, the absence of market forces and the behavior of self-interested pressure groups caused homogeneous and, in relation to the resources provided, mediocre schooling throughout the state system. The system had failed on each of the efficiency and equity criterion identified above.

Conventional economic analysis argues that there are three main sets of conditions that are necessary if market forces are to promote a socially optimal level of educational provision. Firstly, consumers need to have a choice of schooling and access to the appropriate information to assess alternative provision, together with an ability to change schools should circumstances require. The constituents of 'appropriate information' according to the investment emphasis explicit in the conventional economic analysis of human capital are both complex and numerous. Unlike most consumption decisions, investment decisions require information about the future consequences of the decision taken. Since it is the role of the labor market in this framework to ensure that the educational needs of the economy are reflected in the structure of labor market earnings, pupils/parents require information about the labor market consequences of their different schooling options.

Different schooling decisions also imply different costs for pupils and their families in terms of travel and effort and different risks of non-completion. These costs and risks again need to be assessed in comparison with the expected lifetime labor market income associated with the alternative potential schooling attainment levels, where the latter comprise of academic, vocational and personal skills and qualifications. To even begin to estimate the probability distribution of the latter, pupils/parents need information about their absolute and relative position in the ability range and comprehensive data on the past performance of every school in each of these areas.

A second precondition for markets to generate socially optimal outcomes is that consumer preferences are efficiently communicated to schools who are able and motivated to respond. In most markets consumer preferences are communicated through purchasing decisions with firms able to adjust prices and output to maximize their profitability. How to mimic such mechanisms in schooling markets, if the government retains the purchasing role, has led to much discussion about the advantages of vouchers.

Equally problematic is how to model the objectives that motivate schools in markets. A pupil's education is a joint-product, dependent upon the contribution of several teachers, the prevailing school's culture and contextual factors, such as peer groups. It follows that the degree of co-ordination and the efficiency of intra-organizational behavior are critical determinants of schooling outcomes. Successful schools are likely to be those that achieve the right balance between co-ordinating teachers' activities and respecting their professional autonomy (Vandenberghe, 1999). Levin (1994) argues that this optimal balance has five key attributes. First, schools must be clear about their objectives and these have to be measurable, and both agreed and accepted by all participants. Second, teachers and principals must have incentives, pecuniary or otherwise, which are related to their success in meeting these objectives. Third, information systems within the school must be designed and utilized to encourage systematic assessment of current practices and innovations. Fourth, schools must continually evolve to reflect their changing economic and social environment and the particular requirements of their current pupils. Finally, schools must be able to choose the most efficient teaching technology within their budget constraints. The key question is therefore whether these attributes can be encouraged by market-based reforms and associated changes in school governance structures.

The third set of conditions necessary for markets to produce socially efficient outcomes require that consumer preferences are themselves consistent with social welfare maximization over time or that the regulatory regime adjusts market behavior to achieve this outcome. These conditions raise issues concerned with the objectives of parents and pupils in schooling markets and whether they internalize into their decision-making all the consequences of their behavior. These issues concerned with spillovers and externalities are addressed in the following section.

## Market Failures and Schooling

We have seen that the conclusion that competitive markets can promote the public interest rests upon certain assumptions about the behavior of parents, schools and governments. We now need to explore the nature of potential schooling market failures, that is circumstances where the market will fail to produce optimal outcomes. Apart from equity considerations, we can identify several types of market failure which may be present in schooling markets:- ill-informed and irrational consumers; inadequately and inappropriately motivated providers, and the presence of externalities. We now consider these individually.

*Consumer Behavior*

There is ample evidence from other markets than when consumers are faced with complex decisions they rely upon simple signals and employ heuristics which generate systematic deviations from that behavior implied by conventional economic analysis (Conlisk, 1996). As Levin (1991) originally argued, schools are too complex to portray their quality effectively to parents and pupils. Most parents make infrequent, but closely-spaced, schooling decisions and the consequences of those decisions are only revealed, if at all, in the long term. Moreover, education is an 'experience good' in that the costs of identifying the quality of provision are higher before admission than after pupils and parents have spent time at the school. There are also significant switching costs should pupils and parents wish to change schools. In such markets Klemperer (1987) has shown that consumers are reluctant to exercise their 'exit' threat and consumer voice may be less effective at influencing school behavior.

Mainstream economists are beginning to acknowledge that the failure of the labor market to provide cheap and/or appropriate signals to educational decision-makers may lead to greater reliance upon peer group and role-model behavior (Pratten *et. al.*, 1997). Key educational decisions, such as those influencing staying-on rates and applications for higher education, may therefore be subject to bandwagon effects rather than the incremental changes implied by conventional economic analysis. In addition the emphasis upon the investment nature of education in economic analysis, neglects the consumption element of those decisions and may further weaken the link between consumer preferences and social welfare. Recent work by Frank (1997), synthesizing psychological and economic research, indicates that consumer satisfaction depends heavily upon their consumption relative to other consumers. Thus individual payoffs from schooling decisions may differ sharply from the benefits to society. As Ball (1993) argued, exclusivity may itself be desired by participants in schooling markets, hence parents may be willing to pay a premium to buy a house in the catchment area of a 'good' school, but unwilling to collectively fund the leveling-up of standards. We discuss the implications of the positional demand for schooling below.

*School Behavior*

Where schools face little existing or potential competition then they are not subject to market pressures and may have little incentive to respond to consumer preferences. Naïve applications of market analysis often ignore two important characteristics of schooling markets: they are local and a clear hierarchy amongst current providers often exists. The degree of actual competition in schooling markets reflects the locational mobility of parents and schools and the extent of economies of scale in schooling provision. In many local markets schools have substantial monopoly power, with high barriers to entry preventing new entrants. That is the degree of contestability is often low. Thus in many local markets there are no, or very weak, entry and exit threats to encourage efficient school behavior. However, technological developments and changes in labor market behavior are beginning to challenge such inertia. These forces have already caused major changes in access to schooling at the tertiary level with the growth of distance learning and intensive study (Heyneman, 2000).

The existence of an, often well-established, hierarchy amongst local schools also constrains their response to market-based reforms. Local market leaders with excess demand for their places may have little incentive to improve their own performance, since they can expand market share and benefit further from any scale economies and positive peer group effects (discussed in the following section). Those schools lower down the rankings face the prospect of losing market share, especially amongst the more able in their intake. Even the most efficient amongst them will therefore have difficulty in maintaining the absolute level of attainment of their pupils. We discuss the consequences of such processes below.

*Externalities*

Society benefits from increased education not just through the higher earning power that accrues to the individual. A higher average level of education in the workforce creates faster economic growth and promotes both social and political inclusion (Vila, 2000). As a consequence, externalities or spillovers occur in schooling markets since the decisions of parents and schools influence the well-being of those not a party to the original decisions. Since these, in this case, beneficial consequences to others are not internalized in the original decision-making then unregulated markets may generate socially sub-optimal outcomes. For example, modern theories of economic growth emphasize the benefits of a more educated workforce in raising the rate of success, and therefore the level, of research and development, resulting in a faster rate of productivity growth (Crafts, 1996). Along similar lines, other economists have argued that economies which lack an adequate supply of vocationally educated and skilled workers may generate insufficient incentives for employers to create or sustain high technology production (for example, Snower, 1996 and Acemoglu, 1996). A consequence is that economies can get stuck in a 'low-skill, bad-job' equilibrium, whereas seemingly similar economies maintain a 'high-skill, good-job' equilibrium. A common element of these approaches is that relative earnings in labor markets may provide inadequate signals to individual educational decision-makers. In such circumstances we cannot rely upon schooling reforms based upon strengthening consumer power to produce socially desirable outcomes, even when the latter is measured solely in terms of international competitiveness and economic growth.

Peer group effects mean that some externalities occur during the process of education itself. Able, well-adjusted pupils create positive spillover effects for their fellow pupils and their teachers. In particular, the knowledge a pupil assimilates at school depends directly upon the ability and behavior of their classmates. Summers and Wolfe (1977) initially found positive peer group effects in the US and Argys et al., (1996) also found small net positive effects, while Robertson and Symons (1996) and Feinstein and Symons (1999) provide recent UK evidence. Questions remain as to the strength and precise functional form of peer group effects, as well as to whether their estimation may be subject to bias due to endogeneity in peer group selection (Evans *et al.*, 1992; Betts and Shkolnik, 2000). Feinstein and Symons find evidence of strong peer group effects and do not reject exogeneity of the peer group. Their results confirm the 'parents and peers' theory of educational attainment of Robertson and Symons. Parents select the peer groups of their children in ways associated with their social class, educational background and family structure. Peer group factors together with parental involvement in their child's education, rather than other background variables, appear to largely determine educational attainment. It follows that given heterogeneous pupil ability and peer group effects, the pattern of allocation of individuals across different schools influences aggregate educational attainment (Vandenberge, 1998). A free schooling market, since it fails to internalize these externalities, would therefore be unable to generate the socially optimal allocation of pupils between local schools.

## Summary

In a world where schooling markets contain no sources of market failure, equity considerations apart, market-based reforms must improve overall performance. However, our discussion of both government and market failures indicates that no general conclusion can be made as to the optimal degree of government involvement in education. The theory of the second-best explains how in the real world of imperfect markets, movements towards more competitive behavior cannot be assumed to be beneficial. Equity considerations may require some minimum mandatory years/levels of education to be enforced, whilst capital market imperfections may also necessitate government funding for such requirements to be met. The presence of externalities also provides a rationale for welfare-improving government intervention, though not necessarily for public provision. As to government involvement with curriculum, schooling funding and teacher accreditation and pay then theory provides no clear rules. It follows that it is important to assess how successful have been recent quasi-market experiments.

## EVALUATING QUASI-MARKET REFORMS

In most current schooling quasi-markets, a central agency still provides funding and tries to impose constraints on:- the quality and variety of schooling offered; the ability of schools to expand or contract, and the structure of decision-making within schools. This high degree of regulation retained can be viewed as responding to the diversity of purchasers and providers in the schooling quasi-market and the asymmetry of information between them, which together preclude a more contractually-based system of controlling standards (Challis *et. al.*, 1994). Currently the UK has a quasi-voucher system in which parents and pupils exercise choice and with money following pupils under an age-weighted, pupil-number formula. Little formal information is generally available to schools about consumer preferences apart from pupil registrations. The increase in inter-school competition following the creation of quasi-markets itself reduces cross-school co-operation and creates further information asymmetries (Power *et al.*, 1997). For most schools it follows, that discovering the preferences of existing and potential consumers is expensive in the current quasi-market structure, much more accessible are the preferences of Government and their regulators.

The informal information on preferences that is available to schools may be distorted by the quasi-market process. By strengthening market forces, the reforms make schools more responsive to the perceived needs of the more visible and potentially mobile consumers. This bias when combined with unit funding may limit the ability of school managers and government to cross-subsidize between different groups by allocating resources on the basis of their judgements rather than those of consumers. Whilst this may result in equity problems (Edwards and Whitty, 1994), it may also be inconsistent with dynamic efficiency, a proposition we consider below.

### Public Provision

A key question within quasi-markets concerns whether public schools should dominate educational provision. Brown (1992) provides a rationale for the dominance of public provision of schooling based upon the economics of risk and uncertainty. He argues that since parents all seek a similar provision in terms of curriculum and socialization, private schools have few niches to exploit. Most that do survive offer a characteristic unavailable in the public sector: such as religion or responding to idiosyncratic demands, largely based upon income or positional considerations. The reason for this outcome is that parents are initially uncertain about the ability and career preferences of their children and wish to avoid premature specialization that restricts future options.

Gradstein (2000) provides a further rationale for the dominance of public provision. A common problem with government financing and/or provision of private goods and services is that typically the time horizon of their decision-making is short-term, related to the electoral cycle. This problem is related to a further one: time-inconsistency.

Government may take decisions to influence the future behavior of teachers, trading-off high salaries against the desired changes in teacher behavior, but once behavior has changed they often have incentives to renege on the higher salaries. Similar considerations concern their funding of education through taxation. Gradstein argues that it is just this impossibility of a government to commit to future taxation that, perversely, explains the widespread phenomenon of uniform public schooling. It is parents' fear of future high redistributive taxes that causes them to under-invest in their child's human capital in a private schooling market.

Though there may be reasons for the dominance of public provision, our previous discussion indicates that a degree of competition from alternative providers may be beneficial. Several American studies have analyzed whether competition from private schools improves student performance in neighboring public schools (for example, Dee, 1998 and Hoxby, 2000). In general, these studies find a positive relationship between increased competition from private schools and the high school graduation rate of neighboring public schools. Though, Hoxby finds that competition from neighboring public schools also improves student outcomes.

## Standards, External Exit Exams and League Tables

US debates on educational reform have recently focused on policies that would make educational standards more homogeneous across schools. Costrell (1994), Bishop (1996, 1997) and Somanathan (1998) have developed the case for curriculum-based external exit exams (CBEEE's) justified by the resulting improved signaling to the labor market of relative academic achievement. The absence of mandatory CBEEE's has been argued to contribute to a large variation in school quality in the US. Somanathan (1998) develops this argument to show that where informational asymmetries prevent employers observing the quality of school attended by an applicant, greater school diversity can lead to inefficient human capital decisions. Somanathan advocates CBEEE's to correct this inefficiency, since they improve information flows and reduce the distortions favoring college entry. CBEEE's in quasi-markets are also likely to influence the pattern of demand for schooling and may through this channel increase the diversity of schooling outcomes in a local market.

In the absence of a price for schooling, quasi-markets encourage parents to respond to measures of the quality of schools' outcomes. Choosing an appropriate measure is problematic since these schooling outcomes are necessarily uncertain and disparate (e.g. average level of academic outcomes, distribution of academic outcomes, vocational preparation, socialization). Yet, as explained above, consumer behavior in all markets relies on the application of simple heuristics. Parents will tend to gear their decision making to one or two key signals which provide partial, biased, information about the full set of outcomes with which they are, in principle, concerned. However, suppliers only have an incentive to provide information which they believe will encourage consumers to demand their service. Information on quality, using criteria that can be applied to all providers, more commonly results from government intervention or the activity of consumer groups. Therefore, it is not surprising to find the government acting on behalf of consumers to determine measures of quality which schools must disclose. An inevitable consequence of this government intervention is a sublimation of diverse parental criteria of quality by a uniform government criterion.

In the UK, experience gained from the regulation of privatized utilities encouraged the application of competition by comparison policies (Vickers, 1995) to the schooling market. The government sponsored the compilation and publication of school league tables that currently consist largely of measures of the proportion of pupils obtaining good passes in national curriculum-based exams at ages 16 and 18. Thomas and McClelland (1997) found that school league table performance has now become an important influence in parental decision-making, a finding consistent with US evidence that consumer choice is highly sensitive to relative test scores (for example, Murray and Wallace, 1997). Goldstein and Thomas (1996), and Goldstein and Spiegelhalter (1996) analyze the specific UK indicators currently published. In common with the analysis of Meyer (1997), they argue that average unadjusted examination results obscure information and are inferior to value-added measures of pupil attainment. The consequences of such biased signaling are explored in the following sections.

## Quasi-markets, Cream-skimming and Sorting

In the UK, the removal of local government's right to manage the allocation of pupils in a local market, led to schools being required to accept as many pupils as their physical capital allowed. Parental preferences have in general to be respected, including cross local government-boundary preferences. This change appears to have produced a greater segregation of pupils within local schooling markets.

Where formula funding rewards expanding schools and the school 'league tables' are based upon unadjusted pupil performance, then there are only indirect financial incentives for schools to raise levels of pupil attainment and maximize value-added. There is evidence for England (Taylor and Bradley, 2000) that in the face of these financial incentives, schools increase their capacity utilization rate to lower unit costs. Schools with an excess demand for their places can 'cream-skim'. Here, school managers recruit those 'cheapest' to educate (high raw mean ability) and concentrate resources on those pupils able to register in the league tables. Oversubscribed schools select on this basis, whilst those schools wishing or needing to increase market share or improve their league position target the 'active' middle-class parents. Schools seeking to respond to these 'consumerist' parents by providing a traditional academic schooling do not fear alienating their existing 'passive' working class parents, since they are predominantly choosing on the basis of location (Whitty et al., 1998).

The present system of formula-funding in the UK encourages other forms of opportunistic behavior by school-managers anticipated by economic analysis (Williamson, 1985). Almost uniquely, in this market providers by excluding disruptive and less able pupils can improve the public perception of their own performance and worsen those of competitors who may be required to enroll those excluded (Blyth and Milner, 1996). Additionally, most common funding formulae generously fund pupils in post-compulsory schooling. Barrow (1996) reports that some schools have established, often very small, sixth forms for such pupils to exploit this funding and the immobility of their pupils, whilst also gaining the prestige associated with such schooling.

One major weakness of much recent analysis has been the neglect of peer group effects and other externalities, including voluntary donations from parents, which cause there to be potential social benefits from having integrated schools. Epple and Romano (1998) include peer group effects as one of the determinants of school quality in their analysis of the impact of vouchers on the competition between private and public schools in a market with open enrollment. While public and private providers are assumed to be equally effective at delivering education, a strict hierarchy of school qualities characterized by two-dimensional pupil sorting with stratification by ability and income typifies equilibrium in their model. In certain circumstances, ability segregation can lead to under-performance and under-investment in terms of effort and resources by parents, pupils and teachers in the lower-ranked schools (Adnett et al., 2001). An outcome that is both inefficient and inequitable. Greater social integration can however produce a trade-off between the short-run costs borne primarily by rich/active parents and the long-run benefits of faster economic growth felt by everybody.

There is some supporting evidence for this analysis. Over-subscribed schools are required to follow published admission criteria. Though these criteria rarely explicitly included pupil ability, research suggests that schools increasingly targeted the children of the active middle class parents in the local market with increased stratification by social class resulting (Gewirtz et al., 1995, Whitty et al., 1998 and Woods et al., 1998). Aggregate studies have attempted to validate the results of these local case studies. As we noted in above, the exam attainment of pupils is heavily dependent on contextual factors, and it therefore becomes problematic to distinguish statistically the impact of educational reforms on the level and distribution of pupil performance. Gorard and Fitz (2000) challenge the conclusion that at the national level quasi-markets have created more stratification than the previous zoning system. Gibson and Asthana (2000) and Bradley et al., (2000) dispute the validity of this finding. The latter provide an analysis of the consequences quasi-market reforms for pupil allocation and school performance in England. They find further substantial evidence to support the conclusion above that the number of new admissions is positively related to a school's exam performance and negatively to those of its local competitors. These effects were strengthened by the quasi-market reforms and have resulted in 'good' schools achieving a faster growth in their pupil numbers. They also find some evidence of increased polarization of schools with respect to family background.

Comparative studies of the consequences of increased school choice suggest the importance of historical, institutional and societal differences. In the Netherlands strict streaming and increased diversity between schools has meant that increased choice has only been associated with slight increases in social differences between schools (Teelken, 1998). In neighboring Belgium, quasi-markets in the French-speaking community have exacerbated 'ability' segregation: the less concentrated the local schooling market the more dramatic the interschool integration (Vandenberghe, 1998). In New Zealand, published details of the socioeconomic mix of pupils appear to be used by parents to infer school quality, even when at the secondary level data on the performance of students in national tests is also available (Fiske and Ladd, 2000). As a consequence polarization both in terms of ethnicity and social class has been strengthened by the market-based reforms.

## Quasi-markets and Positional Competition

Previous debates concerning the impact of parental behavior in schooling markets have included some discussion of the consequences of education being viewed as a positional good (e.g. Jonathan, 1990 and Tooley, 1995). It has been argued that a characteristic of positional goods is that the total level of welfare or benefits to be derived from such goods in a market is fixed. An increase in the benefits from 'consumption' for one individual must therefore be at the expense of benefits to others. This follows since parents are presumed to be concerned with the educational attainment of their children **relative** to other children in the cohort, not with their absolute level of attainment. An underlying rationale for such behavior can be provided via fixed hierarchies of employment opportunities and social status linked to educational attainment and sustained across generations by the distribution of cultural capital. Jones and Hatcher (1994) argue for the existence of a fixed hierarchy of employment opportunities. While Bourdieu and Passeron's (1977) analysis of cultural capital's role in perpetuating a hierarchy of social standing has formed a crucial part of many sociological analyses of recent educational policy (e.g. Ball *et al.,* 1996).

In conventional economic analysis, the utility gained from a good or service is an increasing function of its present and future consumption. For Hirsch (1976), the value of education depends upon **both** absolute and relative levels 'consumed', with many consumers seeking status based on exclusivity or scarcity. These latter considerations lead to positional competition, where individual parent's attempts to improve their child's relative position encourages imitation, and can result in both low private and social marginal returns to increases in the resources devoted to schooling.

Noting that consumer behavior will be based upon the expected, rather than the actual, consumption and investment benefits of a high 'relative' consumption, Frank (1985, 1997) extended the analysis of positional consumption. Utility from consumption depends upon context, each individual's consumption behavior affecting the frame of reference with which others evaluate their own consumption behavior. He argued that this frame of reference effectively becomes a public good influencing the subjective well-being generated by individual behavior. The uncoordinated decisions of individual parents cannot produce an optimal output of this or any other public good. In his analysis of 'local' status, individuals are largely concerned with within-group comparisons. He argued that positional considerations were particularly important when choosing for one's child and educational decisions were identified as an example where interpersonal comparisons were particularly important. As Mason (1998) points out, both Hirsch and Frank viewed demand for positional goods and services as being consistent with standard economic theory's assumption of the rational pursuit of self-interest, though they did differ as to the main implications of the consequences of widespread positional behavior. Whereas Hirsch's main concern was the absence of any strong relationship between economic growth and social welfare, Frank's was the bias against saving and leisure in competitive markets and the consequential need for regulation to promote social welfare. In the context of local schooling markets, Frank (1997) argued that the tendency for families to seek to buy houses closer to 'better' schools reallocates family expenditure away from retirement savings and inflates certain house prices without raising social welfare.

Frank argued that 'prisoner's dilemma' effects in combination with the prevailing frame of reference would cause this wasteful competition to persist over time. In contrast, Congleton (1989) pointed out that the social desirability of such status-competition depends crucially upon the net size of the externalities or spillover effects generated. Transferring Congleton's argument to the schooling market, what matters overall is whether those demanding highly-ranked education for their children, have the effect of raising or lowering the general quality of education in society. There are both consumption and investment externalities to be examined: one individual's consumption and investment of schooling affects the consumption and investment returns available to other individuals. For example, the inclusion of a disruptive child in a class may affect the level of educational attainment of their peers. However, such externalities are not inevitably negative. For example, one parent's decision to invest in more schooling eventually increases the supply of educated workers and raises the probability that an employer can fill a vacancy for a 'good' job. As a consequence more 'good' jobs are created as we noted previously.

Previous discussion of market-based reforms has often implicitly assumed that positional competition is inevitably economically wasteful and socially undesirable. Since positional competition can generate both positive and negative externalities, a more cautious assessment is required. Where positional considerations apply then several conventional economic policies to influence demand may be counter-productive. For example, applying the logic of Corneo and Jeanne (1997) to schooling markets, punitive taxes on private school fees can in certain circumstances actually stimulate demand for private schooling. Further, the 'poor' may prefer the continued presence of private schooling, although its effect is to increase inequality. This follows, as Biggs and Dutta (1999) argue, if state schooling suffers from congestion and though the rich partly pay for state schooling through taxes they do not use it. In general, positional considerations may make it difficult for governments to generate voter support for policies to reallocate educational resources to 'unsuccessful' inner-city or high-cost rural schools (Kozol, 1991). Suburban voters do not wish to create stronger competition in post-compulsory education and the labor market for their own children. Even with the presence of beneficial externalities from such a re-allocation, it is likely that these benefits will be too diffuse to influence local decision-making. Voters will therefore sustain allocations of public educational expenditures that may be inefficient in terms of overall national levels of educational attainment. Market-based reforms therefore need to mould the frame of reference of parents in a socially beneficial way, whilst also discouraging individual parents from participating in positional competition. In Frank's terms, what policy needs to encourage is the universal adoption of a frame of reference in parental decision-making that stresses private net benefits and positive externalities and abhors negative externalities.

## Quasi-markets and Educational Attainment

In quasi-markets, open enrolment appears to create financial incentives for schools to respond to the strengthening of exit and voice mechanisms by striving to raise the attainment levels of their pupils. The survey by Lamdin and Mintrom (1997) indicates that evidence supporting the accuracy of this argument remains scarce, though recently Zanzig (1997), Hoxby (1998) and Marlow (2000) have drawn more positive conclusions. Zanzig found that greater competition between school districts was associated with improved student achievement. Marlow, also using California data, concluded that the greatest benefits associated with increased choice in education arose during the formative years of schooling.

Particularly relevant are those studies that have sought to address market-based reforms with models incorporating peer group effects. Initially, Arnott and Rowse (1987) and Brueckner and Lee (1989) concentrated upon the implications for the optimal allocation of students and educational expenditures within schools. De Bartolome (1990) showed how peer group effects together with the presence of locally financed input differences and migration, may lead to market inefficiencies. Adnett et al., (2001) develop a simple model of competition within a specified quasi-market structure which illustrates that increased parent and pupil choice may not generate sufficient incentives for individual schools to improve their productive efficiency. Good schools may be unable to signal their quality, while under-performing ones with high-ability pupils may have no incentives to improve. This model can reproduce the observed reinforcing of local school hierarchies (Gewirtz et al., 1995, Whitty et al., 1998 and Woods et al., 1998) and the apparent widening of the gap between the performance of 'successful' and 'unsuccessful' schools in both the English (Audit Commission, 1999) and New Zealand (Lauder et al., 1999, Fiske and Ladd, 2000) quasi-markets.

## Quasi-markets and the Diversity of Curriculum

One of the main advantage of a market-based school system was that it would produce greater diversity of provision, as schools were forced to provide the type of curriculum desired by parents in that segment of the market within which they operated. Levin (1991) summarized this argument as follows: "the advantage of a market approach is the ability to satisfy a wide range of preferences by encouraging individual schools to differentiate their offerings to appeal to a particular set of clientele.... this.... must necessarily create a diverse system of education, rather than one that converges on a common educational experience" (p. 148). The economic rationale for such a claim remains unclear, since only recently has economic analysis begun to formally examine the conditions under which competitive markets promote innovation rather than inertia and produce diverging rather than converging producer behavior.

Parents and schools contemplating a switch from their current pattern of consumption or production face costs in gathering information and making a change which must be weighed against uncertain future benefits. Parental and school behavior which seeks to minimize these costs and uncertainties encourage curriculum conformity, at least in the short term. As discussed earlier, Brown (1992) argued that where parents are uncertain about the abilities and future employment preferences of their children, they will opt for a common, broad curriculum as a means of shedding risk. This suggests that curriculum diversity should increase as pupils progress through the schooling system, because the uncertainty of outcome decreases. If this argument is combined with the 'active consumer' argument outlined earlier we should expect to find all schools initially seeking to provide a curriculum broad enough to encompass the options potentially desired by middle class parents.

Curriculum conformity may be gradually undermined by school choice reforms due to the uneven distribution of pupils likely to achieve high academic outcomes. Schools with an above average initial quota of such pupils will, when quasi-market forces are introduced, attract more pupils. As schools change in size in response to these movements of pupils, the breadth of the curriculum that it is possible for them to offer also changes. However, the costs of change and innovation mean that schools are likely to initially resist these pressures. Schools are constrained in responding to consumer choice by the specificity of the human capital of their teachers (House, 1996). Teacher's investments of time and effort into designing and delivering the existing curriculum, their sunk costs, inhibit the speedy initiation of major curriculum change as markets evolve. Often inertia can only be overcome by the threat of closure or staffing changes amongst senior management. This transaction cost approach suggests a gradual adjustment of curriculum by schools to the increase in competition generated by the creation of the quasi-market. In addition, it suggests that minor curriculum changes are more likely than major ones, and that the latter are more likely to be found amongst schools persistently losing market share. Levin and Riffel (1997) make similar conclusions utilizing an organizational analysis of Canadian experience.

Modern analysis of consumer and producer behavior, noting the presence of fads, fashion leaders and herding phenomenon, has developed models of information and network externalities relevant to our analysis (Liebowitz and Margolis, 1994, Bikhchandani *et al.*, 1998). Schools find it difficult and expensive to accumulate their own information about market conditions whilst the consequences of their decisions are dependent upon the behavior of others. For example, in part, the marketability of a new qualification, depends upon sufficient other schools and pupils choosing this qualification that employers have an incentive to assess the relative capabilities of those acquiring the qualification. Given that both acquiring market information and curriculum innovations are costly, schools over rely on the signals provided by other schools. That is, the presence of these externalities encourages conformity and schools are likely to 'free-ride', relying on gaining knowledge from those schools losing market share who are forced to innovate. This 'externalities argument' also suggests a gradual adjustment by schools to the quasi-market, with major curriculum changes being concentrated in schools seeking to increase market share.

Together our analyses suggest a staged response by schools to the introduction of a quasi-market. Costs and uncertainty will cause schools initially to avoid change in the curriculum, preferring to devote resources to persuading parents of the benefits of their current curriculum. A second stage is ushered in by the effects of the willingness of middle class parents to move their pupils, and the introduction by the government of a criterion on which parents are encouraged to choose schools. The criterion chosen for England and Wales, the publication of unadjusted examination results in the form of school league tables, reinforces the movement by middle class parents. In this phase all schools have an incentive to conform their curriculum to a broad menu dictated by the preferences of middle class parents. This stage will begin to crumble in competitive local school markets if the effects of pupil movement upon school size make sufficient impact on schools' finances to encourage them to take on the costs and risks associated with substantive change. Adnett and Davies (2000) provide some evidence supporting this sequence of responses in UK schooling markets.

An associated problem resulting from increased parental choice is that active searchers determine market norms, even when their tastes are not those of the more passive parents. Gewirtz (1998) shows how the undersubscribed and 'unsuccessful' schools in local markets, even those effectively targeting the needs of their existing clientele, may seek to 'improve' by changing their provision to attract middle class parents. If it is the case, as Lauder *et al.* (1999) argue, that middle-class parents take a longer-term perspective to educational decision-making than working-class ones, then this bias produced by the marginal, active parents may be thought to be desirable. However, this presupposes that the type of schooling that produces the highest return is the same for all pupils, an assumption previously questioned (Davies and Adnett, 1999). As argued above, if segmentation, by ability and parental cultural capital, concentrates positive peer group effects in high-ranked schools then existing rankings are reinforced, as we observe the simultaneous convergence on traditional academic schooling in local markets.

## CONCLUSIONS

Schooling quasi-markets are recent phenomenon and it should not be surprising that at the end of our analysis we are left with more questions than answers. We concentrate upon three inter-related key issues. Firstly, we question whether rewarding success and penalizing failure is an appropriate mechanism for schooling markets. Secondly, we ask whether the increased use of incentives must harm beneficial co-operation both between and within schools. Finally, we consider whether market-based reforms inevitably lead to increased polarization.

## Should Resources be Re-allocated Away from 'Unsuccessful' Schools?

Market forces promote efficient behavior when incentives are created for agents to promote social welfare. They are less successful in raising welfare when some agents have substantial market-power or when efforts are not reflected in rewards. Market-based reforms of schooling markets need to ensure that incentives are generated which encourage all schools and teachers to raise educational value-added. Appropriate performance indicators to assess the extent of "success" in schooling markets need to be constructed and publicized, if the market mechanism is to be successfully employed.

The difficulties of promoting entry and exit in local schooling markets and constraints upon the ability of 'successful' schools to expand create further complications. The quasi-market rewards success and therefore re-allocates resources to expanding schools. However, it is not clear that in schooling markets the marginal net benefits from additional expenditure on expanding schools exceeds that spent on declining schools. Indeed, the conventional economic logic of diminishing returns suggests that under these constraints, resources should be re-allocated to the weaker schools. In several of the quasi-market systems 'failing' schools are indeed allocated additional funding, being closed only in extreme circumstances. Such perverse incentives have no place in the market choice model given their effects upon dynamic efficiency, but their survival requires a deeper analysis.

## Do Increasing Incentives have to Jeopardize Co-operation?

Market-based reforms seek to strengthen incentives for individual schools and teachers to improve their relative performance in local schooling markets. One way to achieve this outcome is to co-operate with other schools and teachers only when the benefits from such actions are distributed in one owns favor. The logical consequence of such selectivity is that beneficial co-operation between schools largely disappears with a local market. Information flows deteriorate, inertia and duplication increase and the overall quality of decision-making falls over time.

A similar process can occur within schools, when individual performance related pay is introduced (Holmstrom and Milgrom, 1991). Remunerating teachers in this way encourages them to make decisions about the reallocation of their time and effort. They are encouraged both to neglect those aspects of their duties that are not monitored and to no longer internalize the consequences of their behavior for fellow teachers and overall school performance. Hence the benefits gained from increased motivation need to measured against the cost of reduced co-operation. More positively incentive mechanisms need to be designed which reduce these dysfunctional responses. Rewards need to target absolute rather than relative, and collective rather than individual performance.

## Is Increased Polarization Inevitable?

Different policies have been introduced to try to address the issue of increased polarization. In some local school markets in New Zealand, over-subscribed schools in order to promote social mix are required to select intake via ballot, instead of academic merit or proximity (Lauder, *et al.*, 1999). In Finland, some local authorities have paid the bus fares of those opting for specialist academic provision in schools outside of the neighborhood (Ahonen, 2000). Policy in the Netherlands rather than trying to fight social segregation directly, focuses on providing a high quality education for all by weighting funding towards schools with high proportions of pupils from disadvantaged backgrounds (Ritzen, *et al.*, 1997). Social inclusion considerations have also led to a similar skewing of funding in the UK. In addition, the British government has introduced Beacon schools and 'superhead' initiatives as a way of imitating desegregation without requiring the same degree of short-run costs to be borne by the parents of those in highly-ranked schools. In these initiatives 'successful' schools in local markets are encouraged to assist other local schools to raise overall performance. Value-added league tables which provide information relevant to all parents, regardless of the ability of their children, are a further mechanism to try to encourage a diversity in the frames of reference employed in schooling choices and a less-polarized outcome.

## REFERENCES

Acemoglu, D. (1996), A Microfoundation for Social Increasing Returns in Human Capital Accumulation. *Quarterly Journal of Economics*, **111(3)**: 779-804.

Adnett, N., Bougheas, S. and Davies, P. (2001) Market-Based Reforms of Public Schooling: Some Unpleasant Dynamics, *Economics of Education Review (forthcoming)*.

Adnett, N. and Davies, P. (2000) Competition and curriculum diversity in local schooling markets: theory and evidence, *Journal of Education Policy*, **15(2)**: 157-67.

Ahonen, S. (2000) What happens to the common school in the market? *Journal of Curriculum Studies*, **32(4)**, 483-93.

Argys, L., Rees, D. and Brewer, D. (1996), Detracking America's schools: equity at zero cost? *Journal of Policy Analysis and Management*, **15**: 623-45.

Arnott, R. and Rowse, J. (1987), Peer Group Effects and Educational Attainment, *Journal of Public Economics*, **32**: 287-305

Audit Commission (1999), *Local Authority Performance Indicators 1997/8: Education Services*, (Abingdon UK.: Audit Commission).

Ball, S. (1993), Education Markets, Choice and Social Class: the market as a class strategy in the UK and the USA. *British Journal of Sociology of Education*, **14(1)**: 3-19.

Ball, S., Bowe, R. and Gewirtz, S. (1996) School choice, social class and distinction: the realization of social advantage in education, *Journal of Educational Policy* **11(1)**: 89-112.

Barrow, M. (1996), The reform of school funding: some case study lessons, *Environment and Planning C*, **14**: 351-66.

Betts, J. and Shkolnik, J. (2000) The effects of ability grouping on student achievement and resource allocation in secondary schools, *Economics of Education Review*, **19**: 1-15.

Biggs, M. and Dutta, J. (1999) The distributional effects of education expenditures, *National Institute Economic Review* **July**: 68-77.

Bikhchandani, S., Hirshleifer, D. and Welch, I (1998) Learning from the behavior of others: conformity, fads, and informational cascades, *Journal of Economic Perspectives*, **12(3)**: 151-70.

Bishop, J. (1996), Signalling, Incentives, and School Organization in France, the Netherlands, Britain and the United States, in E. Hanushek and D. Jorgenson (eds.) *Improving America's Schools: The Role of Incentives*, (Washington D.C.: National Academy Press).

Bishop, J. (1997), The Effects of National Standards and Curriculum-Based Exams on Achievement. *American Economic Review*, **87(2)**: 260-4.

Blyth, E. and Milner, J. (1996), Unsaleable Goods and the Education Market, Ch. 3 of Pole, C. and Chawla-Duggan, R. (eds.), *Reshaping Education in the 1990s: perspectives on secondary schooling,* (London: Falmer Press).

Bourdieu, P. and Passeron, J-C. (1977) *Reproduction in Education, Society and Culture,* (London: Sage).

Bradley, S., Crouchley, R., Millington, J. and Taylor, J. (2000) Testing for Quasi-Market Forces in Secondary Education, *Oxford Bulletin of Economics and Statistics*, **62(3)**: 357-90.

Brown, B. (1992) Why Governments Run Schools, *Economics of Education Review*, **11(4)**: 287-300.

Brueckner, J. and Lee, K. (1989), Club Theory with a Peer-group Effect, *Regional Science and Urban Economics*, **19**: 399-420.

Challis, L. Day, P Klein, R. and Scrivens, E. (1994), Managing quasi-markets: institutions of regulation. Ch. 1 of Bartlett, W. Propper, C. Wilson, D. and Le Grand, J. (eds.) *Quasi-Markets in the Welfare State: the emerging findings*, (Bristol: SAUS Publications).

Chubb, J. and Moe, T. (1988) Politics, Markets and the Organization of Schools, *American Political Science Review*, **82(4)**, 1065-87.

Congleton, R. (1989) Efficient Status Seeking: Externalities and the Evolution of Status Games, *Journal of Economic Behavior and Organization*, **11**:175-90.

Conlisk, J. (1996), Why Bounded Rationality? *Journal of Economic Literature* **34(June)**: 669-700.

Corneo, G. and Jeanne, O. (1997) Conspicuous consumption, snobbism and conformism, *Journal of Public Economics*, **66**: 55-71.

Costrell, R. (1994) A Simple Model of Educational Standards. *American Economic Review,* **84(4)**: 956-71.

Cookson, P. (1992), The Ideology of Consumership and the Coming Deregulation of the Public School System. *Journal of Education Policy* **7(3)**: 303-11.

Crafts, N. (1996), Post-Neoclassical Endogenous Growth Theory: what are its main policy implications? *Oxford Review of Economic Policy* **12(2)**: 30-47.

Davies, P. and Adnett, N. (1999) Quasi-market Reforms and Vocational Schooling in England: an economic analysis, *Journal of Education and Work*, **12(2)**: 141-56.

de Bartolome, C. (1990), Equilibrium and Inefficiency in a Community Model with Peer Group Effects, *Journal of Political Economy*, **98(1)**: 110-33.

Dee, T. (1998) Competition and the Quality of Public schools, *Economics of Education Review*, **17(4)**: 419-27.

Edwards, T. and Whitty, G. (1994), Education: Opportunity, equality and Efficiency. Ch. 2 of Glyn, A. and Miliband, D. (eds.) *Paying for Inequality: The Economic Costs of Social Injustice*, (London: Institute for Public Policy Research).

Epple, D. and Romano, R. (1998) Competition Between Private and Public Schools, Vouchers and Peer-Group Effects. *American Economic Review*, **88(1)**: 33-62.

Evans, W., Oates, W. and Schwab, R. (1992) Measuring Peer Group Effects: A study of Teenage Behavior, *Journal of Political Economy*, **100(5)**: 966-91.

Feinstein, L. and Symons, J. (1999) Attainment in Secondary School, *Oxford Economic Papers*, **51**: 300-21.

Fels, R. (1995), Making U.S. Schools Competitive, Ch. 5 of Becker, W. and Baumol, W. (eds.) *Assessing Educational Practices: The Contribution of Economics*, (Cambridge, Mass/New York: MIT Press, Russell Sage Foundation).

Fiske, E. and Ladd, H. (2000), *When Schools Compete: A cautionary tale,* (Washington D.C.: Brookings Institution Press).

Frank, R. (1985) *Choosing the Right Pond: Human Behavior and the Quest for Status,* (Oxford: Oxford University Press).

Frank, R. (1997), The Frame of Reference as a Public Good. *Economic Journal* **107(445)**: 1832-47.

Friedman, M. (1955) The Role of Government in Education. In Solo, R. (ed.) *Economics and the Public Interest,*(New Brunswick: Rutgers University Press).

Gewirtz, S. (1998) Can all schools be successful? An exploration of the determinants of school 'success', *Oxford Review of Education* **24(4)**: 439-457.

Gewirtz, S., Ball, S. and Bowe, R. (1995), *Markets, Choice and Equity in Education,* (Buckingham: Open University Press).

Gibson, A. and Asthana, S. (2000),What's in a number? Commentary on Gorard and Fitz's 'Investigating the determinants of segregation between schools'. *Research Papers in Education*, **15(2)**: 133-53.

Glennerster, H. (1991) Quasi-markets for education? *Economic Journal*, **101**, 1268-76.

Goldstein, H. and Spiegelhalter, D. (1996), League Tables and Their Limitations: Statistical Issues in Comparisons of Institutional Performance. *Journal of Royal Statistical Society A*, **159(3)**: 385-443.

Goldstein, H. and Thomas, S. (1996) Using Examination Results as Indicators of School and College Performance. *Journal of Royal Statistical Society A*, **159(1)** 149-63.

Gorard, S. and Fitz, J. (2000), Investigating the determinants of segregation between schools. *Research Papers in Education*, **15(2)**: 115-32.

Gradstein, M. (2000) An economic rationale for public education: The value of commitment, *Journal of Monetary Economics*, **45**: 463-74.

Heyneman, S. (2000) Educational qualifications: the economic and trade issues, *Assessment in Education*, **7(3)**: 417-38.

Hirsch, F. (1976) *Social Limits to Growth*, (London: Routledge).

Holmstrom, B. and Milgrom, P. (1991) Multitask Principal Agent Analyses: Incentive Contracts, asset Ownership, and job Design, *Journal of Law, Economics and Organization*, **7(sp)**: 24-52.

House, E. (1996) A framework for appraising educational reforms, *Educational Researcher*, **25**: 6-14.

Hoxby, C. (1996a) How teachers' unions affect education production, *Quarterly Journal of Economics*, **111(3)**: 671-718.

Hoxby, C. (1996b) Are efficiency and equity in school finance substitutes or complements? *Journal of Economic Perspectives*, **10(4)**: 51-72.

Hoxby, C. (1998) What Do America's "Traditional " Forms of School Choice Teach Us About School Choice Reforms? *Federal Reserve Bank of New York Economic Policy Review* **4(1)**: 47-60.

Hoxby, C. (2000) Does competition among public schools benefit students and taxpayers? *American Economic Review* (forthcoming).

Jonathan, R. (1990), State Education Service or Prisoner's Dilemma: The 'Hidden Hand' as Source of Education Policy. *Educational Philosophy and Theory*, **22(1)**: 16-24.

Jones, K. and Hatcher, R. (1994) Educational Progress and Economic Change: notes on some recent proposals, *British Journal of Educational Studies*, **42(3)**: 245-260.

Klemperer, P. (1987), Markets with Consumer Switching Costs. *Quarterly Journal of Economics*, **102(2)**: 375- 94.

Kozol, J. (1991) *Savage Inequalities: Children in America's Schools*, (New York, Crown Publishers).

Lamdin, D. and Mintrom, M. (1997) School Choice in Theory and Practice: taking stock and looking ahead. *Education Economics*, **5(3)**: 211-44.

Lauder, H., Hughes, D., Watson, S., Waslander, S., Thrupp, M., Strathdee, R., Simiyu, L. McGinn, J., Dupuid, A. and Hamlin, J. (1999) *Trading in Futures: Why Markets in Education Don't Work*, (Buckingham, UK: Open University Press).

Levin, B. and Riffel, J. (1997) School system responses to external change: implications for parental choice in schools, in Glatter, R., Woods, P. and Bagley, C. (eds) *Choice and Diversity in Schooling: perspectives and prospects*, (London: Routledge).

Levin, H. (1991), The Economics of Educational Choice. *Economics of Education Review*, **10(2)**: 137-58.

Levin, H. (1994), Economics of school reform for at-risk students. In Hanushek, E. et al. (eds), (Washington D.C.: The Brookings Institution).

Liebowitz, S. and Margolis, S. (1994) Network externality: an uncommon tragedy, *Journal of Economic Perspectives*, **8(2)**: 133-50.

Marlow, M. (2000), Spending, school structure, and public education quality. Evidence from California, *Economics of Education Review*, **19**: 89-106.

Mason, R. (1998) *The Economics of Conspicuous Consumption: Theory and Thought since 1700*, (Cheltenham: Edward Elgar).

Meyer, R.(1997) Value-added Indicators of School Performance: A primer, *Economics of Education Review*, **16(3)**: 283- 301.

Milgrom, P. and Roberts, J. (1992) *Economics Organization and Management*, (Englewood Cliffs, NJ: Prentice Hall).

Murray, M and Wallace, S. (1997) The Implications of Expanded School Choice. *Public Finance Review*, **25(2)**: 459-73.

Organisation for Economic Co-operation and Development, Centre for Educational Research and Innovation (1994) *School: a Matter of Choice*, (Paris: OECD).

Peltzman, S. (1993), The Political Economy of the Decline of American Public Education. *Journal of Law and Economics*, **36(2)**: 331-70.

Power, S., Halpin, D. and Whitty, G. (1997), Managing the State and the Market: 'New' Education Management in Five Countries, *British Journal of Educational Studies*, **45(4)**: 342-62.

Pratten, C., Robertson, D. and Tatch, J. (1997), A Study of the Factors Affecting Participation in Post-Compulsory, Full-Time Education and Government Supported Training By 16-18 Year Olds in England and Wales. *University of Cambridge, Department of Applied Economics, DAE Working Papers*, No. 9711.

Rapp, G. (2000) Agency and Choice in Education: does school choice enhance the work effort of teachers? *Education Economics*, **8(1)**: 37-63.

Ritzen, J., Van Dommelen, J. and De Viljder, F. (1997) School Finance and School Choice in the Netherlands, *Economics of Education Review*, **16(3)**: 329-35.

Robertson, D. and Symons, J. (1996) Do Peer Groups Matter? Peer Group versus Schooling Effects on Academic Attainment, *Centre for Economic Performance, Discussion Paper 311*, (London: London School of Economics).

Shleifer, A. (1998), State versus Private Ownership. *Journal of Economic Perspectives* **12(4)** 133-50.

Snower, D. J. (1996) The low-skill, bad-job trap. In Booth, A. L. and Snower, D. J. (eds.) *Acquiring Skills: market failures, their symptoms and policy responses*. (Cambridge: Cambridge University Press).

Somanathan, R. (1998) School Heterogeneity, Human Capital Accumulation and Standards. *Journal of Public Finance*, **67**: 369-97.

Summers, A. and Wolfe, B. (1977) Do Schools Make a Difference? *American Economic Review,* **67**: 639-52.

Taylor, J. and Bradley, S. (2000) Resource allocation and economies of size in secondary schools, *Bulletin of Economic Research*, **52**: 123-50.

Teelken, C. (1998) *Market Mechanisms in Education: A Comparative Study of School Choice in the Netherlands, England and Scotland*, (Ph.D. Thesis).

Thomas, G. and McClelland, R. (1997), Parents in a market-place: some responses to information, diversity and power. *Educational Research*, **39(2)**: 184-94.

Tooley, J. (1995) Markets or Democracy for Education? A reply to Stewart Ranson, *British Journal of Educational Studies* **43(1)**, 21-34.

Vandenberghe, V. (1998) Educational quasi-markets: the Belgian experience, in Bartlett, W., Roberts, J. and Le Grand, J. (eds.) *A Revolution in Social Policy. Lessons from developments of quasi-markets in the 1990s*, (Bristol: The Policy Press).

Vandenberghe, V. (1999) Economics of Education. The Need to go Beyond Human Capital Theory and Production Function Analysis, *Educational Studies*, **25(2)**: 129-143.

Vandenberghe, V. (2000) Combining Market and Bureaucratic Control in Education: an answer to market and bureaucratic failure? *Comparative Education*, **35(3)**: 271-82.

Vila, L. (2000) The Non-Monetary Benefits of Education, *European Journal of Education*, **35(1)**: 21-32.

Vickers, J. (1995) Concepts of Competition. *Oxford Economic Papers*, **47**: 1-23.

Whitty, G., Power, S. and Halpin, D. (1998) *Devolution and Choice in Education: The School, the State and the Market,* ( Buckingham: Open University Press).

Williamson, O. (1985) *The Economic Institutions of Capitalism: Firms, Markets, Relational Contracting* (New York: The Free Press).

Woods, P., Bagley, C. and Glatter, R. (1998), *School Choice and Competition: Markets in the Public Interest?* (London: Routledge).

Zanzig, B. (1997) Measuring the impact of competition in local government education markets on he cognitive achievement of students. *Economics of Education Review*, **16(4)**: 431-41.

# Chapter 3

# TEACHERS' PERCEPTIONS
# OF ADMINISTRATIVE CHANGE

## *Chris and Gary Easthope*
School of Sociology and Social Work
University of Tasmania, Australia

## TEACHERS ' PERCEPTIONS OF ADMINISTRATIVE CHANGE

## ABSTRACT

In this article we describe the impact of systemic administrative change on the perceptions of a specific group of teachers of Behavioural Studies subjects in Tasmania, during the period 1984-1996. We look at the multiple dimensions of change and how these changes are interrelated. How have these teachers' views about teaching changed? In what ways has teaching, for them, changed as professional work? How differently do these teachers relate to one another and to their administration?

## METHODS

To answer these questions we draw upon accounts collected as part of a more extensive study of changes experienced by teachers in Tasmania, Australia, from 1984-1994 (Easthope 1998). The aim of that research, was to gain an understanding of teachers' responses to the changes in education over a period of ten years.

The teachers in the study taught in Tasmanian State Secondary Colleges and in private Secondary Schools (Years 11 and 12, students aged 16-18 approximately). They were all Behavioural Studies teachers who, like the first author, taught a range of subjects including pre-tertiary Sociology and Psychology (subjects recognised for university entrance) and non pre-tertiary subjects such as Introduction to Sociology and Psychology and a range of Child Development subjects.

The teachers' responses were elicited either by in-depth interviewing (I) or focus groups (FG).

Four teachers responded to in-depth interviews, a male teacher in the Catholic system who had previously taught in a state college, a female teacher in a private school, a male teacher in a college and a female teacher in a college. All teachers who attended the annual meeting of TTOBS (Tasmanian Teachers of Behavioural Studies) in 1994 were invited to take part in the focus groups. Sixteen teachers took part in the three focus groups. The teachers represented all the Behavioural Studies courses. They came predominantly from state colleges, and were drawn from different localities and schools with students with different rural/urban and socio economic status. Some worked part time and some taught in other curriculum areas in addition to Behavioural Studies. The twenty participants constituted about one in three of all Behavioural Studies teachers in the state at that time.

This particular group was chosen for two reasons. The first author had been a Behavioural Studies teacher for many years, had an understanding of their position, and easy access to them. Second, they were a diverse teaching work force: they had diverse discipline backgrounds and they taught classes ranging from pretertiary level to the less academic level.

In the interviews 'flashcards' with words such as 'students', 'workload' and 'administration' acted as an initial projective device and then each teacher was invited to select some key words to discuss in greater depth.

In focus groups teachers were asked to talk about 'the changes you have seen in teaching in the last ten years'. The focus groups were video-recorded and analysis took into account non-verbal cues.

Using grounded theory, major themes were generated. Grounded theory operates as a mode of analysis by iteration. The interviews and focus groups were coded using the teachers' own language and memos, notes, questions, insights, comparisons and summaries were made. Issues brought up in the interviews and focus groups were given a separate file and the transcripts and tapes were again scanned for these themes.

For each extract multiple coding was used. Placing extracts into several appropriate codes at the same time meant that at the end of the process the relative importance of each of the codes was signified by the number of pages printed out under each heading.

Each theme was then colour coded and hard copy printed out. Then, using the walls of a study to stick on the sheets - and coloured twine to show relationships- the themes were analysed, diagrammed and mapped. Links between categories were ascertained by comparing and contrasting themes (Cicourel, 1974:124-125). This increased the level of abstractness and clarified the development of the theory (Glaser, 1978).

A preliminary analysis of the data was presented to groups of Behavioural Studies teachers at the state subject meeting in 1996. This "member check" (Fine, 1994: 44) produced general consensus that their situation was described correctly and their opinions reported accurately.

Theory was generated by constant interaction between the interviews, focus groups, the observation and experience of the first author as a teacher, the literature and the diagramming and mapping of themes. As Glaser (1978:2) explains: 'Grounded theory methodology explicitly involves generating theory and doing research as part of the same process.'

In this article we use what Atkinson (1995: 122) calls the 'devices of contrastive rhetoric' to examine the key themes of managerial ideology[1] and professional ideology. Contrastive rhetoric is a device to highlight and contrast differing viewpoints. It is a somewhat simplistic but powerful method of distinguishing between the competing ideologies of management and teachers.

We contrast the managerialist rhetoric of the systemic administrators with teachers' stories of *their* perceived realities .

## RESULTS

Collins (1991: 138) has pointed to the danger that system administrators will 'become trapped within managerial fantasies and ideologies' and lose sight of 'chalk-face reality'. Teachers were often critical of administrators. They delighted in pointing out their 'fantasies and ideologies' and in telling how they, the teachers, perceived the situation. They gave many examples of how the 'fantasies and ideologies' which we call the 'rhetoric' of management compares with teachers' understandings, which they saw as 'reality'.

We accept that both administrators and teachers produce 'rhetoric' and experience them as their own versions of 'reality' but in this article we privilege the teachers' realities. The management version of 'reality' is very powerful. Managers control resources of time, money and promotion. By privileging the teachers in this article we are giving them a voice, a voice that is rarely heard outside the staffroom and, even there, is often muted.

'Administration' must be seen in context. Generally, when teachers talked of their administration they were referring to the principal, assistant principals and, sometimes, Advanced Skills Teacher level 3s (AST3s). We call this administration the school administration. Tasmanian teachers generally call these positions 'the administration', rather than 'management'. They are aware that these senior staff members are carrying out the requirements of the Education Department, which we call the system administration. Therefore the 'administration' can sometimes include superintendents and others from the Education Department. Teachers also sometimes include the Senior Secondary College Assessment Board (previously the Schools Board) in their description of administration.

---

[1] The managerialist ideology derives from the ideology of economic rationalism which is defined by Waters (1994:56) as "the theory that human beings have individualised material interests [and that] these interests take precedence over commitments to such general values as justice or welfare, personal development, intellecvtual stimulation, aesthetic appreciation, and pursuit of comunity".

Education is a state responsibility and in the state of Tasmania education has been the object of funding cuts and rationalization whether Labor or Liberal parties have been in power. Both parties support the ideology of economic rationalism and want to reduce the cost of education to the government.

The major changes in system administration that impacted on these teachers were:

1. Change in the administrative structure.
2. Change in the curriculum and the assessment of learning.
3. Change in the terms of employment, specifically the operation of involuntary transfer and promotion.
4. Change in working conditions, specifically the introduction of the idea of multi-skilling and an increase in workload.
5 Change in gender issues. The system wide policy on gender equity will be examined as it throws into sharp relief the disjunction between rhetoric and perceived reality.

We examine each of these in turn.


## CHANGE IN THE ADMINISTRATIVE STRUCTURE

These teachers generally favoured reduced administration and supported the idea of a 'flatter' administrative structure. They knew of the findings of the Cresap Report (1990: 3) which found that Tasmania had almost twice the national level of out-of-school staff. Generally teachers felt that there were too many out-of-school staff and they do not know, or concern themselves with, what many of these out-of-school staff did and generally would have been unconcerned by reduction in out-of-school staff.

However, in practice, the rationalisation, as it affected the schools, was one that reduced the overall number of heads of subject departments. Within the schools and colleges the Education Department reduced administration by removing the position of Senior Master or Mistress (SM) of a subject and replacing them with fewer Advanced Skills Teacher level 3 (AST3) positions. The new AST3s were seen as senior managers. The reality of abolishing heads of subjects was that the 'buffer' between the teachers and the principal was withdrawn. Teachers now report to AST3s who are no longer necessarily long-standing teachers of subjects. These AST3s have responsibility for several subjects and/or can be responsible for a cross-college administrative area. Appointments to AST3 are based on administrative rather than teaching criteria. Teachers are appointed to these positions on the basis of their management potential and their teaching ability and relationships with students are taken as given. It is presumed they are good teachers. For promotion they have to show initiatives in management. The perception is increasing that subjects are not as important because there are no specific subject heads and AST3s are responsible for several subjects and for cross-college activities. These cross-college activities are seen as increasing in importance while subjects are seen as declining in importance. Redican (1988: 155) observes the effects of reducing the power of heads of subjects; subject knowledge is devalued and there is a reduction in the 'psychic rewards gained from classroom success for those teachers'. Cross-college responsibilities include student services, computer services, student activities/recreation, community education, school liaison, student administration, resource management, professional development, financial management, curriculum, marketing and publicity. It is interesting in that these cross-college activities are often listed and mentioned first when describing the portfolios of AST3 teachers. Previously, these cross-college activities were carried out by SMs and APs (assistant principals) and sometimes teachers on release from some classroom teaching duties but they were not considered as important as teaching subjects to students. Rather they were seen as activities to support the primary activity of teaching. However, with increased workloads (see Easthope and Easthope, 2000), teachers became more reluctant to carry out non-teaching activities and therefore they became incorporated into the job descriptions of AST3s. As management structures are no longer closely related to responsibility for subject areas, so teachers are now more likely to deal directly with the administration of colleges rather than with subject senior colleagues, thus increasing the chance of developing what Ball (1990: 97) calls an 'us and them' orientation.

RUTH:      Us and them, unfortunately.
CE:        So even in the colleges where you feel the administration will support you there is still and us and them?
RUTH:      I think so to a certain extent.
BRIAN:     More than in the past and that has partly got to do with the way that teachers have picked up a fourth line[2], but AST3s haven't always picked up a third line. (FG1)

## CHANGING CURICULUM AND ASSESSMENT

The rhetoric is one of serving the clients. The perceived reality is that decisions are made for administrative expediency. For example, the number of subjects and the level of difficulty of those subjects used to be an academic decision for the benefit of the individual student. This is no longer the case:

CE:        How does the change in year 11 and 12 work out? You know, it used to be that if you were bright you did pretertiary subjects in year 11 and now there is a limit, usually, to how many pre-tertiaries you do in grade 11. How is that working out?

---

[2] A line is one class of students for a week. It should be five hours of teaching. Teachers taught three lines and then had three hours other contact with students for pastoral care, sport and recreation. This has now increased for most teachers to four lines plus pastoral care and sport and recreation.

BRIAN: In the beginning we were counselling kids heavily away from pretertiary in grade 11, but we have relaxed, well the uni matric regulations allow kids to do more than one pre tertiary subject anyway. So quite often the very able students are doing three or even four in grade 11.

ROS:    Yes and I'm finding, because we are doing enrolments now, I'm finding that kids who are planning on doing medicine now are probably doing a night pretertiary as well. (FG1)

The rhetoric is that the colleges provide education for all students. The reality is that economic and managerial decisions drive the curriculum. When teachers were paid for the number of students they had in college then the number of courses the average student could study was four. Now that payment is made on the number of hours taught the average student studies five subjects or their equivalent. Teachers now tell students that decisions are made according to staffing requirements and this might be, as Joan (below) suggests, one reason for decreased commitment from the students:

CE:     Yes, that is the other thing. At one time it was normal to do five subjects and now it is four subjects?

ROS:    No not for us, we are trying to enrol at 750 (hours) minimum now per year, if not more.

JILL:   That is ours now.

BRIAN: The funding has switched again last week, it was based on number of students, now it is number of hours.

ROS:    We have some students doing 900 hours.

JILL:   See you have got Cs, Bs and As.[3]

BRIAN: So it is quite a shambles really, in that students are being counseled quite radically between one year or other on how many subjects to do based entirely on the way the funding operates, not really at all a kind of educational decision for students.

JOAN:   The focus has changed hasn't it? Money and centralised what looks good, away from what kids, from what is really going to benefit students, and I think they know they have been short changed...that might be something to do with their lack of commitment as well.

ROS:    We explain to them too, we require you to do so many hours because it fits our staffing.

JILL, RUTH and BRIAN:        Yes.

RUTH:   And it certainly went the other way this year, you can't do X and Y because we haven't got the staff to cover it. Like a lot of the humanities things, Studies in Religion and World Literature and Ancient Civs. those humanities things, just went down the tubes because we didn't have the staff. (FG1)

---

[3] C courses are 150 hours, B courses are 100 hours and A courses are 50 hours. So although C courses run throughout the year A and B courses can start and finish at different times. For example it is possible to have a 'fat B' which is completed in half a year whilst a 'thin B' will take the whole year to complete.

The introduction of the Tasmanian Certificate in Education to replace the Higher School Certificate is one of the numerous changes introduced during the ten years 1984-1994.

> MICHAEL: Change from HSC to TCE. My attitude, it is simply another one of those copied experiments from overseas and it is an idea that arrived at exactly the wrong time with educational budgets declining rapidly and that was obvious to everyone five years ago. It was no time to organise a scheme which is phenomenally expensive, which is extremely demanding of teachers' time into an education system that was looking at poverty in the future.

The TCE has been introduced at a time of a national push for increased retention rates. The reasons for retention rates being increased are open to debate. The mission statement of the Department of Education and the Arts (Tasmania Department of Education and the Arts1994: 4) is to provide the Tasmanian community with high quality educational, youth and cultural services so that young people can develop in all aspects of their social, intellectual, physical, emotional and moral life. It also refers to the expectation that young people will make a contribution to the economic and social life of the state. Cynical teachers at the time pointed out that increased retention rates would also help the unemployment figures[4]. As Collins (1991: 137) writes:

> From the outside, much of what has already happened looks like the achievement of a national schooling retention target. On the inside, in many places (not all) it looks like a herding operation of the most manipulative kind in which those to whom the dole has been refused must have their attendance at a place of incarceration recorded in order to receive the financial means to survive.

At this time of increased retention it was necessary to change the ideology of the Matriculation Colleges. Their names were changed. The 'Matriculation' in their title was dropped as the majority of students did not, in fact matriculate.[5]

The result of increased retention has led to the necessity of a review of the curriculum; a 'watered down' academic curriculum was not suitable for divergent ability levels. However, curriculum policy was not left to teachers or other educationalists but undertaken by government appointed bodies: the Finn and Mayer committees. Both Finn and Mayer, who chaired the committees, are businessmen, the Finn committee had no teacher representation and the Mayer committee only had teachers on it after union pressure. The reality is that educationalists, including teachers, have lost much of the power to manage the curriculum.

---

[4] Students are required to attend college to receive Austudy, a government means tested allowance for full time students. Since the completion of the research the government now requires all young people to attend school or a training course to receive "Youth Allowance."

[5] Matriculation was the term given to obtaining the requirements for university entrance.

All subjects have a neighbouring, less difficult subject. If a student fails to reach the standard required they are assessed on the neighbour, thus making it difficult to fail outright. All subjects have a number, the higher the number the higher the difficulty. Some subjects are designated 'pretertiary' and they are the highest level. The ideology is that the abilities of all students should be celebrated. In the extract below teachers are explaining the reality of an ideology that says that all students should be rewarded for what they can do. They would agree with that sentiment, but the reality is that some students do little work and are 'evaluated on the neighbour':

SUE:      That is the other thing wrong with the TCE, they don't allow the kids to fail enough, as in:- if you can not be assessed here, they will give you know like a compensatory prize.

NANCY:   That is the whole philosophy of it.

SUE:      There seems a big focus not to let them fail, whereas I learnt more when I failed than I did when I ever-

NANCY:   But then you were a successful student.

SUE:      I don't know if you would say that.

NANCY:   Well you must be to be here now, you must have been to be here now. Whereas the philosophy of the TCE is that they all have to succeed at some level.

SUE:      But life isn't like that!

NANCY:   Oh that is not my argument, that is the argument of the TCE.

SUE:      Yes I know, but that is what I am saying, if you don't let them fail and to know it is okay to fail and to learn more about yourself when you fail and know what you can do. Most people fail because they haven't put in, not because it wasn't suited.

JO:       But that depends if you have got people in the right places and in the right courses.

SUE:      That's right.

JO:       I mean some kids try their little hearts out and they just can't do it. It is beyond their capacity.

SUE:      Then they should not be there.

JO:       I know, but good grief that could apply to half our Behavioural Studies classes!

SUE:      That is right.

JO:       I mean we have kids, in English this year I had a couple of kids.

SUE:      But shouldn't you not let them show that they can't do it?

JO:       No, I don't see any point in that.

SUE:      You don't think you should say 'You can't do this?'

JO:       No they shouldn't have been there.

SUE:      But they still think they can to a certain degree because you have just given them the neighbouring syllabus. So they will never really know.

JO:       These kids were not even capable of getting the neighbouring syllabus. They were in the wrong course. They should not have been there.

SUE:      My point is just that!

JO:       They should have been counselled into a course that was appropriate to their ability. (FG2)

The underlying problem is that, with increased retention, the administration has to provide courses that are relevant to the abilities of the students. These students include 'special needs' students who were previously in special schools.

Teachers in colleges find it difficult to understand the intricacies of the TCE and consider there is even more confusion among parents and employers.

SUE: And the people out in the community don't understand.

SARA: No they don't.

CE: Employers as well of course?

JO: Oh heavens no!

SUE: They have no idea, so you have got all these kids who are really quite cunning, who are getting an SA (Satisfactory Achievement) at the higher neighbour, say in Intro and they will say

'Oh will you assess me at the neighbouring syllabus?' So they will come out with say an OA (Outstanding Achievement) or HA (High Achievement) and the people will say

'Oh this one has an HA in one of their subjects while this one only has an SA in theirs!' So they know that they'll get that.

NANCY: That is if they know what a SA and a HA are.

JO: And the only difference on the paper is that one says BH 716 and the other says BH 715.

SUE: And they don't know that there is a, you know?

SARA: Supplementary.

SUE: For those who didn't get it. (FG2)

In other words, some students know how to 'play the system' to the disadvantage of other students in a climate of the worst youth unemployment in Australia. The sad point is that it is doubtful that the administrators are even aware of the situation; teachers would perceive this lack of knowledge as another example of managerial 'fantasy'.

There are other unintended consequences of the TCE, other realities as perceived by the teachers. For example, as a result of the emphasis on those students who do not intend to go to university, time and attention has been devoted to these students and their educational requirements to the disadvantage of more academically inclined students. The results of the Tasmanian Certificate of Education (TCE) for 1996 show that of the twenty two students scoring the maximum 100 points only three were from state schools. When the numbers of students in each system are taken into account–in 1994 there were 6,652 students in years 11 and 12 in state schools and 2,436 in non government schools (Rogers 1996: 115)–then these figures have serious repercussions in terms of life chances and social inequality. To some extent this concentration on the majority of students who will not attend university is completely understandable and is justified. However, in an attempt to accommodate these students, there is the risk that the more academic students are marginalised. Certainly, as far as the teachers are concerned, to be called an 'academic' teacher is now a derogatory term that implies lacking the ability to accommodate teaching to suit all students.

Also, although the system is intended to celebrate what all students can achieve some teachers in this research report that the TCE restrains creativity and encourages conformity.

JO:        And that's it too, I mean TCE has done nothing for creativity in terms of rewarding it.

CE:        It hasn't?

SUE:       It was meant to but it doesn't.

CE:        But the theory is that is does, but it hasn't?

JO:        No I don't think so.

SUE:       Not in our area.

JO:        In fact I have had situations where I have had conversations with kids saying 'This is brilliant, but if you do this in the exam you will fail'.

SUE:       The other thing with TCE is I have found coming through is, for some strange reason I have found coming through we have to give them the direction. Have you found that? There are not many of them... They need to be told all the time. They sit there; there is no initiative to do anything. Unless they are told to do it and it has to be step by step.

JO:        All the way along though.

NANCY: (private school teacher): Do you mean with tasks when you give them tasks?

JO:        With anything. They just sit there, they are nice and placid and they just sit there. Well once upon a time the kids would be doing all these other things. (FG1)

The imposition of marking to criteria is one of the reasons for reduced creativity. Teachers are used to the freedom of making informed, professional decisions. Now that freedom has been withdrawn from them and, as Jo describes, functionally illiterate students can be awarded a High Achievement at the highest level of English at high school:

JO:        Or particular criteria, like one funny anomaly in English, with my English C class which is predominantly year 11 and you find out what the kids' backgrounds are and all of them who are year 11 came through with an HA or OA at 417 which is the extended English. Now an HA or OA you would think would prepare them very well? Now some of these kids were functionally illiterate!
          Now I am thinking to myself 'Now hang on a minute, now how can this happen? ' And these aren't stupid kids, it has nothing to do with their intelligence or their ability. They just don't have the skill, but one of the problems has been in the English syllabuses that being able to write, communicate effectively, is not an essential criteria. They can get an HA by passing all the other criteria very well, so investigating, everything else apart from communication, they could get "As" on. They just might not be able to write it very well, and they can get an HA .....
          it is the way the syllabus has been written. (FG2)

Before the introduction of TCE, it is unlikely that teachers would or could have given high marks to somebody who was functionally illiterate.

With the TCE has come a form of assessment called Criterion Based Assessment (CBA). All subjects have to use CBA as their assessment method. The criteria are different for each subject and each level of a subject. Teachers are required to mark according to the criteria laid down for their subject and level.

CBA, as a form of criterion referenced assessment, has a long history in education. It provides an alternative to norm referenced and self referenced assessment and has been used in the USA since the 1960s.[6] The TCE is based on the Victorian VCE, and the Victorian Institute of Secondary Education said in a discussion paper (VISE 1984: 10) that 'all year 12 subjects from 1987, VISE [should] move towards approaches to assessment which are criteria-based, or standards-referenced, or work required'. The rationale is one of descriptive assessment which is 'goal based' and 'work required' rather than competitive. It satisfies the need for all students to be recognised for the work they can do, but it is an idealist administrative fantasy. Teachers often support the thinking behind CBA, since they want students to have their skills and achievements acknowledged. However, teachers in this study experienced problems with the reality of CBA which has been introduced without consultation with the teachers and with very little training. Teachers ask, 'If I evaluate a criterion more than once, and the results are different, which result should I take?' Some teachers average their results; for example, if a student scores an 'A', 'B' and a 'C', some teachers will give a 'B' mark. Others argue that if the student can demonstrate 'A' level once then they should receive an 'A' as the final score. The work on which the student scored an 'A' might have been a fifteen minute exercise at the beginning of the course, but towards the end of the course she could have a 'C' or 'D' for the same criterion for a major piece of work. Some teachers argue that work done towards the end of the course should have more weight. The policy of CBA has been introduced by the administrators but they have not negotiated with or convinced teachers that it is appropriate.[7] In time, teachers adapt and accommodate to the implementation of CBA, but the lack of planning and consultation which accompanied its implementation as part of the TCE has created difficulties for teachers.

The ideology of economic rationalism emphasises the economic value of education and requires that learning can be transferred to other educational and work situations. Many writers have explained some of the disadvantages of this concentration on the economic aspects of education, for example, Ball (1990), Dale (1989), Clark and Ramsey (1988), Hargreaves and Reynolds (1989), Lingard, Knight and Porter (1993), Marginson (1993) and Pusey (1991). As far as present day management is concerned, it seems that economic has become synonymous with 'skills', 'criteria' and 'competencies'. The danger is that skills, criteria and competencies will not be seen as a useful addition to the education of young people, but as the main function of post-compulsory education and this could have long lasting effects upon the quality of education in Australia. As Degenhardt (1989: 99) points out:

---

[6] See Hambleton et al (1978) and TenBrink (1974) for a more detailed discussion of the place of CBA as a form of assessment.

[7] Hodgman (1994) has found, in a controlled experiment, that students who use CBA perform statistically significantly worse on problem solving and evaluation skills.

'Technicism' denotes a mode of thinking that restricts our understanding and judgement as to how we conduct our lives in general, or education in particular, by reducing everything to working out efficient means to pre-determined ends. Everything becomes a matter of achieving a technical fix, and no scope is allowed for reflection on either the worthiness of the ends pursued or the moral legitimacy of the means employed.

Degenhardt is echoing Bertrand Russell (quoted in NBEET 1992: 22) who as early as 1930 said:

It is one of the effects of modern higher education that it has become too much a training in the acquisition of certain kinds of skill, and too little an enlargement of the mind and heart by an impartial survey of the world.

Economic rationalists seem to believe that the ability to manage is transferable to all management situations, the ability to teach is transferable to all teaching situations and the competencies and skills that are examined by CBA are transferable to any job which requires those skills. This reduces the need for specialisation and differentiation, but it tends to homogenise management, teachers and ultimately students. These forms of rationalism are not supported by many teachers. They want to be treated as individuals and they want their subject and age group expertise recognised. They want to be able to see and treat their students as individuals. They want to care for their students and they in turn expect care from their principals. They want personal not just institutional interaction.

The increasingly impersonal nature of teaching is demonstrated by the new method of marking the TCE. The TCE has three pass ratings; Satisfactory Achievement (SA), High Achievement (HA) and outstanding Achievement (OA)[8]. Therefore, students' results are banded into three categories. The ideology is one of not distinguishing too closely between students as would be the case if numerical assessment was used. The reality is incredibly complex. Marking is done on ten criteria with internal and external assessments for the pretertiary subjects. The results can only be worked out by complex algorithms.

The teachers in this study do, however, have increasing control over their subject, over writing new courses, over moderation of assessment and over the content of the syllabus. They have to mark according to criteria, but they can suggest changes of criteria to the Tasmanian Secondary Assessment Board (TSAB). The reality is that this control has been given to the teachers for many of the decisions concerning the implementation of subjects because subjects themselves have declined in importance. This decline in the importance of subjects is evinced by the larger number of, predominantly non-pretertiary, subjects. Non-pretertiary subjects are seen as less academically rigorous and are more likely to be taught by multiskilled teachers with no background in the area. The situation is that many subjects are taught by non-specialists and AST3s are increasingly likely to

---

[8] University entrance requirements allocate numbers to these categories so that, for example and OA would receive a mark of 19 or 20.Entrance into medical school (an undergraduate course in Australia) requires a total Tertiary Entrance Score of about 95.

be responsible for subjects they know little about. This means that the AST1s have to shoulder the everyday administration of subjects.

The rhetoric is that pretertiary subjects and their examinations are important. The perceived reality is that increased workloads and increased administration coupled with the increased complexity of the pretertiary exam and the rigours of marking to criteria means that it is difficult to find enough Behavioural Studies teachers to mark the exam. Marking the pretertiary exam no longer gives kudos and marking takes longer - most sections have to be assessed by reference to at least two different criteria, and has to be done collegially. Furthermore, it is increasingly likely that teachers will be encouraged to mark in more than one subject area and as many now also teach non-pretertiary classes (which are internally marked), there is a large increase in workload.

Although changes in the exam are generally welcomed by these teachers they do not have the time to do the marking. At one time the external marking of the pretertiary subjects would be of major importance and most people would give it priority over everything else. The period after exams is now even busier than when teachers are teaching. Time is taken up by compulsory meetings as this part -time teacher describes

> MEG: During this period of productivity, or whatever other colleges call it, since the students have left, I actually have not been able to take that whole day off since the students have left and I was struggling to take the whole day off beforehand. (FG3)

'Period of productivity' is an interesting use of managerialist language. The period of productivity, in at least one college, is the official name given to the time when all the students have left and the teachers remain. As far as I know, there is no equivalent name for the period of the term when teachers teach.

The teaching year has increased by five days as a move to more efficient use of resources, but this has been accompanied by compulsory in-service training. Marking the external exam is not compulsory and, therefore, teachers are electing not to do it.

Pretertiary subjects now appear to have been devalued, in a relative sense, since the administration has emphasised the non-pretertiary subjects, especially work related subjects. This devaluing of subject and professional expertise is echoed by the University's reduced role in marking. The TCE seems to have reduced status when compared to the Higher School Certificate (HSC).

Government initiatives and funding have encouraged the development of work related courses. In the following extract, Gwen points out the reality of these courses–that in her college, the brighter students do these courses because the college wants the courses to succeed. It is then more difficult for these students to matriculate because of timetabling difficulties caused by them being required to do work experience placements for one day a week. She points to the cost in terms of staffing and then points out that the students the courses were meant for are even further away from getting jobs because they have not had the training of their brighter peer group (and anyway there are still too few jobs). However, this is not the 'reality' which the administration want to hear. They want these programs to be successful.

I can't see a really big future for a lot of the work related courses because I mean if the jobs aren't there, no matter how well trained they are, no matter how well intentioned the teachers are, no matter how much on the job training they have, if the actual positions aren't there for the students I think you have done something; I mean you hand pick your class, to start off with right? So you can't be that surprised that half of them get jobs of that hand picked lot. But when you are talking of a class of only twelve and of that twelve only six get part-time jobs. You are looking at a fairly poor return for one third of a teaching load. When you are looking at twelve students and the other six don't actually qualify enough to get their diploma or get 'satisfactories' or stuff and I'm not necessarily...So you know that what they are hoping to do is actually make the selection process even more stringent which to me seems ridiculous, because surely, these are the kids who basically will get a job anyway. So they are looking at the cream and what they are going to do is train the cream so they become la creme de la creme, but you see, some of them don't really want to go and work in somewhere like Purity. Surely the aim should be looking at the kids who are marginal and trying to get them into a situation where they become employable and I'm not talking necessarily about the special kids, but I'm looking at the ones we can often tell often, this kid, you know, providing we give them this, this and this. They are more likely to stick with a job like that. The creme de la creme aren't. How many weeks are they going to stay with Kentucky or Macdonald's or places like that? I think, it sounds really good, but when you actually have a look at the number of teachers involved in this and the number of teacher hours involved in this and the number of actual students involved in this and the outcomes; I think you know 'Phew!' They are doing this because it sounds great to be doing a new course at Tasman[9] which bla bla bla but if you actually look at the kids who get a job at the end of the course, it is very, very, small. So I don't know, as I say nobody knows, but that is the way they have got to look at it simply because that is where the money is going to be; because that is where the government is going to put the money in; training courses, work related stuff; year 13 is muted isn't it? But it is really to keep the kids out of the dole queues for as long as possible. Getting a bit more like Tech I suppose, you know the TAFE sort of stuff. We are starting two more work related courses next year...but again all those hand picked kids who are limited in what they can do elsewhere. They are limited by them needing every Thursday off to do their work experience, they are limited to two, only usually a couple of other subjects which means if they decide that retailing is not what they want to do they have wasted, not exactly wasted, but you know what I am saying? They have spent, I mean they can not matriculate for a start if they do this, or they can but it is very, very difficult, the constraints on which line they can do the, I think there is actually only one full line that they can do, they probably could matriculate but I think they limit their options a lot, so I would like to see it happen to the kids who need it more if you like.

If work related programs are used inappropriately then students at the bottom of the hierarchy become even further behind in the race for employment.[10] Seddon and Deer

---

[9] Names of colleges and schools are false to preserve anonymity.

[10] There has been a marked increase in work related courses in the colleges since 1994 and now the less able students routinely include work related courses in their studies. However some of the less able and disaffected students cause embarrassment to teachers and dissatisfaction to employers when they approach work situations with either very limited ability to work or

(1992: 196) point to the rhetoric and the reality of the situation: 'firstly, while post-compulsory curricula are comprehensive in the sense of bringing a wide range of knowledge to students, that full range of knowledge is not accessible to *all* ' (italics in original).

Schools are able to write glowing reports on work experience courses, especially when 'successful' schools will get increased funding and save teacher jobs. Furthermore, those teachers espousing such courses will improve their promotion prospects.[11] Therefore the state and federal administration could believe that they were tackling the unemployment situation. The school administration know that they had successfully implemented the innovations of work experience courses, some teachers would have a strong investment in these courses, students on the courses feel confident that they would be more likely to obtain a job. A college handbook states that the Australian Vocational Training System (AVTS) 'will provide easier access into the workforce'. Students' parents are delighted and employers feel they will acquire skilled and motivated employees. Few hear the voices of caution from some teachers, and those students for whom the courses were originally envisioned would know nothing of what they had missed.[12]

---

negative attitudes towards work.

[11] The lack of awareness of the administration continues to this day. While writing this we read, in the local paper, a column written by Graham Harrington, a senior educational administrator . In it he refers glowingly to a curriculum developed at Dover, a local fishing port, that is he considers "an excellent example of a joint school/local industry program". He then goes on to say "at the moment there are only two students who actually atternd the Dover campus" (another 10 are doing the course through distance education and a further 20 employed in the industry are using aspects of the program).The irony of a program set up in conjuction with local industry that only recruits two local students appears to escape him. Later in the same article he writes "The demand for teachers to operate ouside their subject areas is occuring on two fronts. At the senior secondary level, more and more teachers are becoming involved in vocational programs.. [and] at the junior secondary level many teachers are participating in... programs where the emphasis is on reducing the number of teachers that students react with ...As a result teachers are often operating across a number of subject areas. According to reports in the...press this practice is drawing some criticism...This surprises me, as teachers who are involved in either vocational or middle school programs... are most enthusiastic about what they are doing" (Mercury July 8th 2000). It does not surprise us as, we have argued, teachers must express enthusiasm in such courses to maintain their positions and/or to gain promotion.

[12] In Britain, John Clare, the Education editor of the Telegraph, writes 'The national system of vocational qualifications set up by the Government 10 years ago at a cost of more than 100 million [pounds] has achieved almost nothing.' (*Weekly Telegraph* 9.10.1996-15.10.1996 : 10)

## CHANGING CONDITIONS OF EMPLOYMENT

### Involuntary Transfer

There has always been some involuntary transfer of teachers in colleges. Students from year eleven going into year twelve did not receive their Tasmanian Certificate of Education results until mid January,[13] therefore enrolment into year twelve took place in early February and it was common for classes not to be finalised until the start of first term. It was also usual for some teachers to be moved to other schools at the beginning of first term.

With the adoption of the rhetoric of economic rationalism, and the desire to be seen to be saving money, teachers were seen as multiskilled and interchangeable. The rhetoric of involuntary transfer became a reality for some teachers. Even if teachers were not moved, in practice all teachers thought there was a strong possibility of them being involuntarily moved. Therefore, we have a situation where, as a result of economic rationalist thinking, most of the teaching profession in Tasmania has been unsettled.

This situation has been further exacerbated by three factors:

- Falling numbers of students: this is the result of a decline in the population of young people aged 16-18. Tasmania has a declining population.
- The increase in teacher workload so they teach more classes with more students in each class.
- The policy to consider moving teachers after five years in a school.

All these factors interrelate to make involuntary transfer a major issue for these teachers.

Graph 1 demonstrates the rise, followed by the decline, in student numbers.

---

[13] Since 1996 results have been made available before Christmas and colleges are provisionally enrolling students in November.

**Graph 1**: Number of Full Time Equivalent Students in Colleges in Tasmania 1984-1994

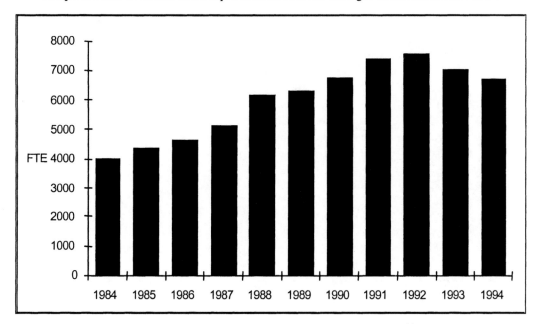

(Source: Ed Dept Tasmania and Australian Education Union (AEU))[14]

Until 1992 enrolments increased each year so there was little pressure to transfer teachers. However in 1993, a drop in enrolments, continuing into 1994, meant that teachers either had to be fired or transferred to areas where there were vacancies due to either retirements, resignations or the unattractive nature of the school or its environs, the so called 'hard to staff schools'.

This fall in numbers has resulted in an increase in workload for teachers in two ways. Firstly, in 1993/1994 the teaching load of college teachers was raised from 3 to 4 'lines',[15] effectively reducing demand for teachers by one quarter. Secondly, there were increases in class sizes, also reducing the demand for college teachers. A fact sheet issued by the Australian Education Union (June 1994) reports that 'senior secondary classes have experienced an almost 500% increase in class sizes of greater than 25. In 1988 7% of classes had more than 25 students. In 1994 this figure has skyrocketed to 33%'.

The response of teachers to the new involuntary transfer situation is a perception that involuntary transfer is a means of control.

SARA:     And I suspect it is political. I think people are being moved for pretty shabby
          reasons. (FG2)

---

[14] These figures are based on the February enrolments and during recent years there has been a large 'drop-out' rate amongst students (The state total full time equivalent students in February 1994 was 7773.4; the state total equivalent full time students in August 1994 was 6744.2).

[15] A 'line' is all the contacts a teacher will have with one class, usually five hours a week.

Brian describes the rhetoric and the perceived reality of the transfer policy.

BRIAN:   It is a brilliant invention. I think, it was originally presented as a way of shifting teachers out of hard to staff areas of the state who had been there so many years, but in fact it has gone way beyond that because they only needed to move a relatively small number of teachers but the entire teaching profession is basically now on this five year assignments or will be.
Fifteen[16], it is going to be ten, ultimately five year assignments. So there is no sort of, no certainty any more you can, practically all of us will be on sufferance really within an institution. (FG1)

The fact that teachers know they are 'on sufferance' makes it much easier for the management to subtly control teachers. The rhetoric is one of fairness for all teachers, but the reality for some teachers is that even in the execution of the policy the administration has been unfair.

SUE:    Then you get some people who go and then someone says 'I am not going!' and they stayed.
SARA:   Yes that's right.
SUE:    And then these other people did the right thing and went along with the Department and you know they had to sell their house and buy a new one and some people stayed because they said 'Oh no I can't do that! I can not go! (FG2)

This sort of activity means that teachers no longer trust the Department. Previously there had been a fair amount of goodwill between teachers and the Department, but now the teachers feel they have to 'examine the fine print'.

Teachers suggest less threatening alternatives such as providing incentives to moving to hard to staff schools and also point out the reality of the unintended consequences of labeling schools as 'hard to staff'.

SUE:    But that is really stupid because they are working from the other end as usual. This is another thing in the Ed Department, they, when we go to uni and do our training they say 'reward anyone who does everything good' and ignore the bad as best you can. So they don't say to all those brilliant teachers in those hard to staff schools, and there are some brilliant ones, we are going to give you $ 2,000 more, and they do this in England. If you are in a hard to staff school in a real tough borough they pay you extra and they will pay your costs to get there because often you don't live in that area.
SUE:    ...Like I have this friend who suddenly; like she didn't realise her school was hard to staff. She has been given a classification on her school. She loves her school.
SARA:   In Tasmania?

---

[16] It was proposed that the education department started by moving teachers who had been fifteen years in one school, then ten years and so on.

SUE:     In Tasmania, she loves her school, she loves where she is at Southerton and she has been told.

JO:      She is category A ? (a teacher in a difficult to staff school.)

SUE:     Yes and she thought. Oh well this has put a downer on this school! All the kids now know they are in category A and they are fairly you know, you have just stereotyped and labelled a whole school and you have done it throughout the whole state haven't you really?

SARA:    Indeed.

SUE:     And if the employers get hold of this. 'Oh that kid came from that school, it is even worse than the initial labelling. Oh that was a tough school! But now it is written down, the Education Department has labelled them and instead of saying to this person who loves that school, she probably won't move, but she will have to because of the transfer policy, because she has been there for fifteen years, and they have to get her out of this hard to staff school because she has been there for fifteen years and she has had a hard time. She thinks she has had a wonderful time!

JO:      ...it is a big percentage of the work force that has been dislocated and it is going to have significant impact on the culture of all schools because in some schools you have no continuity at all operating and you have, particularly I think in one sense yes, but five years, it is not very long, and it is a bit like, well I think we will end up like politicians, which may or may not be a good thing, that the people don't really have an investment in the school any more.

SUE:     Yes I can't be bothered doing anything because I know I will be moved in a year.

JO:      So why should I bother?

SUE:     Why should I bother? (FG2)

The unintended consequence of this transfer policy, is that teachers will feel that it is not worth bothering because they will soon be transferred. For example, it can take a year or more from the initial ordering of a text book to it appearing in the library. Teachers might be unwilling to spend time researching their subjects if they do not know that they will be teaching that subject next year.

Sue, quoted below, explains the importance of understanding the levels of internal assessment given by the feeder schools and the importance of consistency in staffing.

SUE:     ... So their moderation process I suppose isn't working. So we know which feeder schools mark easier in maths and which mark harder, but that takes a couple of years to realise that and you have a couple of kids going through that failing. (FG2)

This observation is supported by the research of Gudmundsdottir (1995: 28):

research focusing on experienced teachers demonstrates that this group of teachers know their subject matter differently than their less experienced colleagues. ...Their knowledge is practical, it has developed over the years through accumulated 'wisdom of practice'.

Teachers are not able to easily substantiate claims to 'wisdom of practice'. The Education Department in Tasmania believes that all its teachers are good teachers, that they all have the relevant 'wisdom of practice'. The administration concedes that teachers have specific skills, but they argue that those skills are transferable to any teaching situation. This assumption of the transferability of skills appears to be a fundamental tenet of economic rationalism in education, which is then used to justify multiskilling and the involuntary transfer policy.

The 'burnt earth policy', where some teachers are leaving no notes or teaching materials behind when they are transferred, will mean that in place of the help and encouragement traditionally given to new teachers in an area, help will be considerably reduced. Teachers new to the area may soon have to be formally inducted into the subject by management directive rather than be able to rely on informal help and guidance.

As it stands now, the administration appears to maintain the position that 'a teacher is a teacher is a teacher' and, as such, teachers can be moved to teach any age group in any subject.

The administration recognised that teachers would feel undermined if promotion positions went to those who spent time on administration and they recognised that good teachers should be rewarded. Therefore the position of Advanced Skills Teacher level 1 (AST1) was introduced. The job description for AST1 teachers from the Tasmanian Education Department (undated) is as follows

> The significant role of this position is an instructional one, being classroom based with some additional curriculum and administrative duties. The position has been developed to enable recognition in the teaching service award of the possession of 'advanced' teaching skills.

The term 'senior manager' was initially used for middle level administrative positions but it was short lived, and teachers in this management position were soon described according to their official designation: Advanced Skills Teacher level 3 (AST3.) The term Advanced Skills *Teacher* may be misleading since AST3s are appointed to the position for administrative skills rather than for their teaching ability. They no longer necessarily have the expertise to organise the day to day running of the subject departments as they are now responsible for several subject areas. When I went to enrol my daughter at a college I was surprised to see a teacher in the Humanities enrolling students for Mathematics. She told me that she was Head of Mathematics. She taught three classes in the Mathematics area (none of them pretertiary) and a class in another non Mathematics area. There were not enough students for her to teach a class in her Humanities area this year.

The reality is that the AST1s had to take over much of the management of their subjects. The reality is that someone has to run subject departments, allocate classes, order books, attend curriculum meetings, organise internal and external assessment and so on. Thus the rhetoric of reduced administration at senior levels becomes the reality of increased administration for AST1s, reducing their time for teaching at a time when the teaching load for an AST1 increased from three to four lines. AST1 teachers are expected to undertake the administration of their subject(s) as part of their normal workload and there is thus an increasing gap between the teaching loads of AST1s and AST3s.

> RUTH: Some AST3s teach two lines and some teach three and do their administration and some teach two and do their administration and I think, because I have been an acting AST3 I have had a foot in both camps this year. I think from what I can perceive from the general staff, administration is not 'real' but being in front of twenty five kids teaching Behavioural Studies or Child Studies is far more real and therefore you are working 'harder' than someone who has got to ring up and organize work place placements or whatever and for me, although the administration was not as stressful as perhaps being in the classroom or as time consuming, it still took up a lot of time and it is a different sort of pressure. So there is always going to be inequity between a person who is on two lines doing two lines of admin compared to some one who is teaching five different classes on four lines (FG1).

The reality of promotion is that

- it is more difficult to obtain as there are fewer promotion positions.
- promotion rewards administration rather than teaching.
- promotion protects teachers from involuntary transfer. The number of years a teacher has been in a school *in that position* is the basis of transfer policy. The policy has only been introduced for assistant principals and above since 1996.
- promotion does not necessarily go to 'good' teachers because the administration does not choose to evaluate teaching quality[17]. System administrators do not necessarily want 'good' teachers to become administrators.
- whilst keeping good teachers in the classroom, the system fails to reward good teaching as much as it rewards the ability to be seen as 'administrative material'. This further undermines the value of teaching as it is the perception of many teachers that concentrating on teaching, which takes time and effort, may disadvantage them in the promotion quest.

As in the work of Gitlin and Margonis (1995: 387), who report on situations where 'everyone has a job that creates work for others ...career ladder teachers create work for teachers and limit their decision making authority', teachers in this research were angry because of all the work they were expected to do which often arose from the career aspirations of ambitious teachers.

---

[17] The majority of the teachers in this study are AST 1 teachers. This classification does require teaching ability. These teachers are talking of promotion past this first rung of the promotion ladder.

SUE: I go home very angry often because of everything extra we have to do.I also get very angry at those people who are climbing up the ladder who create things so they can be recognized and you go home and you have all these other things to do and you never have time to do what you need to do and your life is just so narrow. The only satisfaction I get is being in the classroom. I love being in the classroom because I know no-one is going to come and bug me ask me for my help: ask me to do five hundred and fifty things to help this person get Principal somewhere or whatever and never get any feedback on it. (FG 2)

Promotion is seen to be the result of convincing the selection panel that you satisfy the criteria for promotion. Teachers see 'really good people' being 'knocked back', not because they would not be excellent at the job but because they cannot write convincing 'essays' which satisfy the criteria.

CE:      Now you were talking about promotion. What is the promotion situation like now?

BRIAN: It is an essay contest. The kids don't write essays any more, but we have to, to get promotion.

AVRIL: And if you say the right thing, I think on one hand the department is saying, you need these qualities, and I think on the other applications are looked at and if the person has written down a good enough essay as Brian said and dealt with those particular things in their essay then they will get the positions.

RUTH: If they are cold and calculating.

AVRIL: Yes!

BRIAN: And you have to mention the right people, and the right programs and the right professional development.

RUTH: And read the right books.

BRIAN: All the things the students don't have to do any more in the exam.

RUTH: I think promotion makes people very cynical, I know in our, particularly in our college, you will see really good people say 'Oh stuff it'.

JILL:    Exactly!

ROS:    Some people are happy to go on just the level.

RUTH: It is just not worth it.

JOAN:  Gradually get themselves to the point were they can start going part timing and go backwards and backwards and backwards and ease themselves out. (FG1)

Soon teachers realised that there were desired responses to the questions asked at interviews for promotion. Then cognitive dissonance (Festinger 1957) comes into play as teachers, through many interviews, reiterate answers that conform to the answers required by the administration. Then, for their own internal consistency, teachers may change their thoughts to bring them into line with what they say.

There is also a growth in mentoring, that is, senior staff coaching their friends into the intricacies of applying for promotion. The managerialist ideology is therefore reinforced by group membership. Such group membership is achieved in several ways, with one of the most important in Tasmania being ascription. In a small state with a history of few institutions of higher education (and now only one), many teachers share links that are multifaceted in a manner that is more often seen in small pre-industrial tribes than in modern states. In a state with a relatively small middle class, teachers are often related through family or marriage. Many teachers in Tasmania have teachers as parents, as brothers and sisters, or as husbands and wives. It is not unusual to have related people on the same staff of the colleges and, if previous and defacto familial relationships are taken into account, the interweaving of relationships is complex and widespread. Add to this the interactions generated by common membership of sports and social clubs and the networks of people with whom they went to university or with whom they have taught and it becomes apparent that such links are powerful. The after hours drinking activities of college staff may also be significant. These tend to be male dominated although increasingly with some female members. Such cliques, unlike those derived from ascription, can be penetrated by non-Tasmanians but they tend to be less influential than the ascriptive links because they are much more localized, usually confined to one college.

In recent years 'sisterhoods' have emerged who support each other in the 'promotion game' and they have had considerable success in a context where gender equity has been a policy priority. The process of mentoring is also a process of anticipatory socialisation where those aspiring to promotion are groomed into the world of managerialism. This role playing eventually is likely to become, in Goffman's (1959) terms, 'internalised'.

The rhetoric for those who are appointed to promotion positions is one of collaboration rather than authority:

> BRIAN: All of these changed values tend to be built into the promotion system so you tend not to get APs and principals who are authoritarian, they simply wouldn't get to the top any more.
> JOAN:   Very much to do with substantial value changes impinging on the whole picture. ( FG1)

The reality is, however, one of control through subtle means:

> BRIAN: Ten years ago if the principal in our college said 'Wouldn't it be a great idea if we did so and so ?'A lot of people would say 'Phew, pathetic idea, you know, forget it!' Now you have to look at what the principal and the other leaders in the college are suggesting and you have to say 'Yes there is something good about that' because otherwise what are you going to be doing? You are not going to be part of the plan, the program, the change that is going on in the college, you get marginalised and the next stop is out of the college perhaps in some way. (FG 1)

These teachers are aware that despite the rhetoric of administration not being so authoritarian, the reality is that teachers are controlled more than ever before. Collins (1991: 140) writes 'Why stay in a system which rewards controllers rather than those with professional knowledge and skills?' This sort of undermining of teaching is one of the reasons for teacher dissatisfaction and contributes to teacher withdrawal.

Yeatman (1990) and Blackmore and Kenway (1993) point to the colonisation of 'feminine' traits by managerialism. Increasingly principals are expected to have affective and personal interpersonal skills. As Blackmore and Kenway write (1993: 44) 'This is most evident in the ways the nature of school principalship has been reconceptualized. Principals are now expected to be facilitators, communicators, team leaders, instructional leaders, and so on'. The rhetoric is of the caring and consultative manager. Teachers, however, remain unconvinced by this veneer of caring.

## CHANGING WORKING CONDITIONS

One of the greatest causes of concern for teachers is the application of the policy of multiskilling. Multiskilling, a major feature of the economic rationalist ideology, means teachers being able to teach over a wide range of subjects to a wide age group of students. This is desirable for the administration, and it could be advantageous to the teachers. However, this policy has been introduced without adequate retraining. The teachers moved to date have had no retraining. They are arbitrarily told to teach out of age group and out of subject area with no training. Some teachers who have had their time at colleges extended for a year or two have been told that in those two years they can take advantage of the in-service training available to their own colleges. This hardly provides sufficient training for those teachers who, for example, are to be reassigned to teach in primary schools when they have had no experience at all with that age group. Teachers are now seen as endlessly interchangeable.

Increasingly teachers and system and college managers have not communicated well. Teachers have just been told, 'You will teach such and such next year'. Managers often do not understand the situation of teachers, and Freedman (1988: 143) argues that, this lack of communication and understanding is undoubtedly a factor in teacher stress and burnout:

Burnout, however, does not come from overtaxing one's intellectual and mental capacities. Burnout comes from not being able to use those abilities to handle difficult emotional and managerial problems. These problems are often the result of administrators' analysis of a situation far removed from their personal and immediate responsibility.

Teachers and their unions have been unable to communicate effectively with senior management of the Education Department. In some cases, the Union has played into the hands of the administration. For example, during the 'Special Case' hearing[18] in 1991 for improved pay for teachers, the Senior Secondary Colleges Staff Association (SSCSA) in an unpublished information sheet, argued that teachers deserved more pay because they had increased the value of their work by teaching outside their subject areas. The SSCSA conducted a survey to establish how many of its teachers were teaching outside their areas of expertise. At the time, in late March 1991, there were 548 EFT (equivalent full time) teachers in the colleges. There were 324 responses, with 128 of the teachers

---

[18] The teacher unions in Tasmania argued that teachers should receive increased pay on the grounds of increased productivity. This was during a period of pay restraint when unions were working with the federal Labor government to limit pay increases to 'special cases'.

indicating that they were teaching at least one subject outside the area for which they were trained. This increased productivity was used to argue for a salary increase that was obtained. However, the repercussions for the teachers were that the administration took the flexibility of teachers as a given and were free to expect increased 'multiskilling' and 'involuntary transfer' which have both been causes of stress for teachers. In economically rational terms, multiskilling became part of award restructuring.[19]

With hindsight the teachers could have argued that, when they taught outside their subject specialism, it was because they had negotiated with the administration. Usually it was the case that there were not sufficient classes in their subject so they had to teach another subject or be involuntarily transferred. In such cases some teachers chose to teach outside their area of expertise: they may have been offered a selection of subjects which had been oversubscribed and had voluntarily agreed to the change. They usually knew about the change in plenty of time to prepare and often had a colleague on the staff to guide and advise them in the materials needed and in teaching the subject.

In some colleges this is still the case but there have been changes in others:

RUTH:	And the other thing which has changed in the last ten years is dumping on teachers the day before school starts, it happened to me and saying 'You have to teach pretertiary C English. That is it, move out of your subject area, wphee.
CE:	And the expectation is that you don't have to teach in your subject area?
AVRIL:	Yes.
RUTH:	Very definitely.
JILL:	Multiskilled. Teach wherever.
CE:	Now how does this multiskilling affect you?
RUTH:	Just more work.
JOAN:	I think it disadvantages kids too.
AVRIL:	Yes.
JILL:	Very definitely.
RUTH:	It is stressful when you are teaching a pretertiary C and you have never taught it before, and everyone, and every one is too busy to help you and it is just grrr. (FG1)

Teachers are only mentioned three times in the Departmental Strategic Plan (Tasmania. Dept of Education and the Arts, 1994: 11) which covers the period July 1994 to June 2004 (one mention is about staff housing, another is about the pre-service training of teachers), but a priority task for completion by June 1995 was 'The establishment of a policy to increase the multiskilling of teachers'. Note that it says nothing of retraining. The reality is likely to be that increasing numbers of teachers will teach outside their area of expertise. This is despite the fact that in Tasmania, since 1984, there has been on-going research, by Abbott-Chapman et al, into government Senior Secondary Colleges which found, as Holloway et al (1992: 1) writes, 'mastery and enthusiasm for subject and the skill communicating this to students to be central to effective teaching'; also, 'The

---

[19]  See also Ashenden (1990) and Bluer & Carmichael (1991) for further discussion of the rationalisation of teaching.

teacher/student relationship was found to be of central significance to the whole teaching/learning experience'. Abbott-Chapman et al (1989: 191), in part of the same longitudinal research, found that when students were asked about how secondary teachers influenced them, 46% said that the teachers' 'enthusiasm for subject' was most influential. This research indicates that mastery of subject and teacher/student interaction is extremely important.

The policy of the Education Department chooses to ignore this research on their own senior secondary colleges and views 'flexible' teachers, who teach across the board, as 'more valuable' than 'elitist' subject teachers. Such teachers allow flexible staffing and more subject choice to the students (or 'clients' as they are now called). The expertise of teachers to teach the new subjects, or subjects which they had been 'encouraged' to teach, is never questioned.

> SUE: I don't think they ever become adequate, you know? They don't stay there. If we lost our whole department when Jo leaves then, if I had left and Ned had left there would be nothing left in that department. No one to teach them, but they are saying anyone can teach this subject, so they should be able to get our physics and chemistry teachers to come over and teach that subject. Now certainly I couldn't teach physics and chemistry and I don't want to, I don't even want to try to do that. If I had wanted to do that I would have done my training. (FG2)

There is thinly hidden acknowledgment that some non-pretertiary classes are there to keep students 'amused' and 'off the streets' and off the lists of the unemployed. To achieve this, there has been a proliferation of what both teachers and students call 'Mickey Mouse' courses. With a huge range of courses and a declining number of teachers the fact that the teacher may not have the expertise to take those classes is ignored. The reality is that management imperatives are more important than educational expertise.

The rhetoric is one of teachers being multiskilled. The reality is a devaluing of the education given to students, especially the less able students, which has grave implications for social equity:

> JO: Even some administrators though, I mean some subjects get branded as 'Oh well anyone could teach that!' At times you hear principals or whoever, it is not only principals, but a lot of other people too, who say to you, the perception for example with Intro [Introduction to Sociology and Psychology] is they, really, if you read the *Woman's Weekly* you can teach the course.
> SUE: So it becomes a dumping ground for these teachers who need one more line to fill. So really, I get all these teachers, really. (FG2)

Therefore this AST1 teacher, who has responsibility for all the non-pre tertiary classes in Behavioural Studies in her school, also has to induct non Behavioural Studies teachers into the subject.

In 1994, teachers decided to use one text book for the non-pretertiary Behavioural Studies Course. This book does not satisfy all the requirements of the syllabus by any means but their workload, and the necessity to spend time helping teachers 'drafted in' to teach the subject, resulted in teachers deciding to give up on trying to make their teaching current and interesting.

The significance of this shift is far-reaching. The less academic students are no longer able to receive the expert teaching which was the case ten years ago. It is fallacious to argue that just because they are less academic they do not need the expert teaching of teachers trained in their area. Less able students often do the non-pretertiary course in year 11. If they are taught by a teacher with expertise in the subject, that teacher can note if the student has potential in the subject and can coach them so that they can attempt the pretertiary subject in year twelve. If the course is taught by a teacher who does not perceive the links between the *Woman's Weekly* and topics covered by the pretertiary course (indeed is unlikely to know even the subject matter of the pretertiary course) then a learning and nurturing opportunity is lost. This is an issue of equality of opportunity. Teachers have lost their intellectual authority because they have lost their subject departments and even lost their subjects through multiskilling. They should, then, be left with their professionalism as teachers, but even their teaching is undermined when recognition and promotion are dependent on administrative rather than teaching ability.

## Change in Gender Issues

Blackmore and Kenway (1993: 43) have noted that the administration is able to appropriate currently 'politically correct' thinking:

the hegemonic potential of corporate culture lies in its ability to readily subsume and appropriate social justice and affirmative action strategies into its corporate planning, under the guise of representation and participation.

The awareness of gender issues has changed the expectations of women teachers
CE:       How do you find the administration?
BRIAN:  Do we like doing it?
CE:       I don't want to ask you a leading question.
RUTH:   Male dominated in our college that is how we find the administration!
AVRIL:  Male dominated in our college that's how we find the administration!
JILL:     And ours as well!
BRIAN:  We have just had two people, two males, assigned to our college and that means
             now we have three male APs (assistant principals) and a male principal.
RUTH:   And we have one woman on the senior management.
JILL:     And the males listen to the males.
BRIAN:  It is a male club really.
CE:       So although earlier on you were telling me that knowledge, and you knew about
             sexism and it came into promotion. It still exists at the minute?
BRIAN:  It depends on the college, X is quite different from Y.
CE:       Do you think they are trying to change it? You said about this promotion that
             people who wanted promotion had to be aware of SES [socio economic status)]
             and

BRIAN:  Yes I think there is a change coming, but it is going to take a long time to get through to the top in the colleges.
RUTH:   It is not necessarily coming from within the colleges, but coming from within the Department.
ROS:    We have got this strategy on at the moment, equal opportunity, equity program, but the males I think are resistant.
JILL:   The females run these programs, the males ignore them!
ROS:    I have got a male partner, and he is really good, we are running it together and he is terrific. (FG1)

Women are disillusioned that despite the rhetoric of gender equity, the reality is that there is much hidden resistance. As the 1994 report on Women in the Teaching Profession (NBEET, 1994) found 'on balance, women remain heavily under-represented in school leadership and promotional positions, and the improvement in their positions is very slow'.

Blackmore and Kenway (1993: 27) point out that 'the "taken-for-grantedness" of the division of labour in education in which men administer and women teach is still evident in educational research'.

AVRIL:  Can we put Professional Development on the list?
CE:     Oh yes, sure. How has that changed Avril?
AVRIL:  Well we went to the workshop on gender and there was reporting back to the staff and that was reasonable and then the next Professional Development night that we had, the whole staff, the greatest joke was made of the construction of gender. That was brought up
ROS:    So you wasted time?
AVRIL:  Yes it was a waste of time.
CE:     I know some colleges are talking about sexual harassment as well, is that one of these issues?
ROS:    That was last year's.
CE:     So this year is there an issue?
AVRIL:  Construction of gender .
ROS:    And looking at the curriculum, equal attention given to both sexes and the deconstruction of the sexes.
CE:     And is this coming from the Department?
ROS:    Yes.
CE:     They didn't used to do that did they ten years ago?
AVRIL:  No.
CE:     So this is a change. Is it the Department telling the colleges what to do in professional development?
AVRIL:  Well it is the whole system, not just the colleges, it is a priority that they have established in the gender area up until '97, there is going to be something each year. (FG1)

Although the gender issue is a Departmental priority there is resistance from some males. In one college where a male teacher was running a gender equity committee little was said whilst the principal was present, but when the principal left some males voiced their resistance. The rhetoric is one of gender equity but the reality is of some male teachers resisting gender equity and some woman teachers being disillusioned that gender equity is treated 'as a joke'. As Yeatman (quoted in Blackmore 1993b: 43) comments 'Equal opportunity ....comes to be reframed in terms of what it can do for management improvement, not in terms of what it can do to develop the conditions of social justice and democratic citizenship'. These examples also indicate the difficulties of 'top down' policy initiatives. Blackmore et al (in press: 2) show that for the administration 'The assumption is, that once policy is written, that it is passively and unproblematically received by those it targets, and that the failure of policy can be attributed to teacher resistance, poor implementation or inadequate leadership, usually at the level of the school'. Senior staff are reluctant to tell the system administration of their problems in colleges since it may be seen as their failure. Hence, resistance is hushed up, teachers worry that they may be involuntarily transferred and there is fictitious implementation of innovation[20] with a rise in the appearance of participation but in reality a decline in free speech. Yeatman (1990: 134) describes the situation as one where corporate management

> co-opts the language and ideas of equity (and social justice) into techniques – sets of variables to be managed, either on the margins of organisational life, or swallowed into the organisational mainstreams – while discarding the underlying principles and values. In this process of equity management, women become policy targets, objects of policy rather than empowered by policy.

The rhetoric is one of gender equity, but the reality is more likely to be the colonisation of gender equity into the ideology of economic rationalism as is so convincingly argued by Henry and Taylor (reported in Lingard et al 1993: 153-175). Of the eight senior secondary colleges in Tasmania at the end of October 1995:

- One has a female principal. One has an acting female principal.
- Each of the eight colleges also has three assistant principals.
  Two of those colleges have three male assistant principals.
  The other six colleges have one female assistant principal and two male assistant principals each.
- The top three positions in education are held by men: Deputy Secretary of Education, Deputy Secretary of Corporate Services, Secretary of Education.

---

[20] Shipman coined this phrase as reported in Esland (1972 : 110).

## CONCLUSION

In this article the discontinuity between the rhetoric of educational change and the reality as perceived by teachers is highlighted. This article has concentrated on the way teachers perceive their situation. However, a recent newspaper article about parents' concern with the education system indicates that they, too, are likely to see a dysfunction between the rhetoric of the administration and their own perception of reality. As this editorial in *The Sunday Tasmanian* (23.2.1997: 16) points out:

> It may be the case, as far as the Education Department is concerned, that there is no crisis in Tasmania's public schools...Parents are confused and concerned. They are confused because reassurances issued by the department run contrary to their day-to-day experiences with the education system...Many teachers and parents are convinced that there are serious problems with Tasmanian education.

Generally teachers in this research were dissatisfied with administration. They felt that senior staff in colleges were administratively rather than educationally orientated. During the process of member checks, teachers seemed to agree with our findings overall but one teacher, married to a principal of a senior secondary college, quite justifiably put forward the point that principals have a very difficult time. She drew word sketches of some of the situations he has to deal with and made the point that teachers do not understand the situation of principals. In the meeting I (CE) agreed with all she had to say, but pointed out that the research was on teachers and teachers generally were dissatisfied with their school administrations. I acknowledged that other research on senior staff in colleges would have different results.

It is the case that at least one principal in a Tasmanian high school is also dissatisfied with the systemic administration as this item in the (*Mercury* 2.5.1996: 25) indicates:

> A Tasmanian high school principal has called on the State Government to abolish much of the Education Department bureaucracy...describing the bureaucracy as an outdated, wasteful and ineffective means of delivering quality education.

We can summarise the findings of the research in a diagram where we associate the 'fantasies and ideologies' of managers with the ideology of economic rationalism and the 'chalk face reality' with the professional teacher ideology. The management and the teachers have differing discourses (see Figure 1).

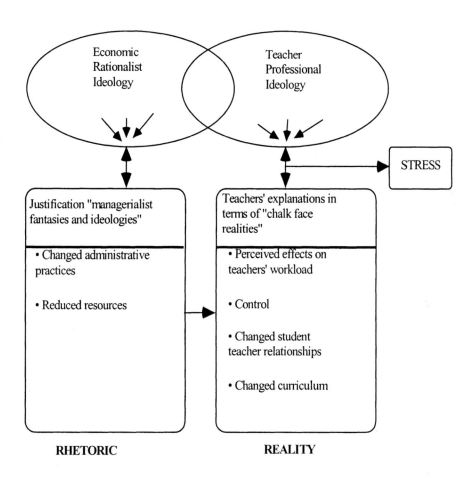

**Figure 1:** Competing Discourses: Economic Rationalism and Teacher Professionalism

The effects of changes in administrative structure, the curriculum and modes of assessment, terms of employment, workload and the imposition of a policy of gender equity is increased teacher stress. Stress is a second order consequence, a reaction to changes in workload, interaction with students, feelings of conflict, uncertainty and powerlessness.

The rhetoric is of improved managerialism and cost saving. For many teachers in this research the reality is a reduced ability to teach well and a decline in the quality of their interactions with students. The rhetoric of improved education becomes the reality, for the teachers, of more control of teachers. The rhetoric of less authoritarianism becomes the reality of more accountability. The rhetoric of a more economically responsible education system becomes the reality of increased workload (see Easthope and Easthope, 2000). The rhetoric of a more efficient system becomes a system where the students are the last people to be considered.

## REFERENCES

Abbott-Chapman, J., Hughes, P. and Wyld, C., 1989, *The Identification and Development of Intellectual Ability,* vol. 3, Centre for Education, University of Tasmania.

Ashenden, D. 1990, 'Award restructuring and productivity in the future of schooling', *Victorian Institute of Educational Research Bulletin,* vol. 64, pp. 3-32.

Atkinson, P. 1995, *Medical Talk and Medical Work,* Sage. London.

Australian Education Union, Tasmanian Branch, 1995/96 Budget Submission to the Tasmanian Government from the Australian Education Union Tasmanian Branch March 1995.

Ball, S. 1990, *Politics and Policy Making in Education, Explorations in Policy Sociology,* Routledge, London and New York.

Blackmore, J. and Kenway, J. (eds) 1993, *Gender Matters in Educational Administration and Policy: A Feminist Introduction*, Falmer Press London.

Bluer R. and Casrmichael L. 1991, 'Award restructuring in teaching', *Unicorn* 17, 1: 24-29.

Cicourel, A. 1974, *Cognitive Sociology,* Free Press, New York.

Clark, E. and Ramsay, W. 1988, 'Government policy and higher education: seeing more colours in the educational rainbow than red and white', *Youth Studies,* vol. 8, no. 2, pp. 31-36.

Collins, C. 1991, 'Effective control of post compulsory education or effective post compulsory education?' in H.F. McKenna, and J.R. Nethercote (eds), 'Educating the clever country', *Canberra Bulletin of Public Administration.* no. 67 pp. 135-144.

Cresap Report 1990, Review of the Department of Education and the Arts, Tasmania, *Foundations for the Future, a Focus for the Administration of Tasmanian Education and the Arts,* CRESAP, Melbourne.

Dale, R. 1989 *The State and Education Policy*, Open University Press, Milton Keynes.

Degenhardt, M. 1989, ' "Curriculum" As Fraud', *Unicorn,* Vol. 15, No. 2, pp. 96-99.

Easthope C. 1998, Teachers' stories of change: an interpretive study of teachers's stories of change in Tasmanian schools and colleges 1984-1994, PhD Thesis, Deakin University.

Easthope C. and Easthope G. 2000, Intensification, extension and complexity of teachers' workload British Journal of the Sociology of Education, 21, 1: n43-58.

Esland G. 1972 'Innovation in the school,' in P. Seaman, G. Esland and B. Cosin (eds) *Innovation and Ideology*, Open University Press, Buckingham.

Festinger, L. 1957, A *Theory of Cognitive Dissonance,* Stanford University Press, Stanford, CA.

Fine, M. 1994, 'Dis-stance and other stances: Negotiations of power inside feminist research', in A. Gitlin, (ed) *Power and Method, Political Activism and Educational Research,* Routledge, New York.

Freedman, S. 1988, 'Teacher 'burnout' and institutional stress', in Ozga, J. (ed), *Schoolwork: Approaches to the Labour Process of Teaching,* Open University, Milton Keynes.

Gitlin, A. and Margonis, F. 1995, 'The political aspect of reform: Teacher resistance as good sense ', *American Journal of Education, vol.* 103, pp. 377-405.

Glaser, B. G. 1978, *Theoretical Sensitivity: Advances in the Methodology of Grounded Theory,* Sociology Press, Mill Valley, CA.

Goffman, E. 1959, *The Presentation of Self in Everyday Life,* Doubleday Anchor, Garden City, New York.

Gudmundsdottir, S. 1991, 'Story maker, story teller: Narrative structures in curriculum', *Journal of Curriculum Studies* vol. 23, pp. 207-218.

Hambleton, R., Swaminathan, H., Algina, J. and Coulson D. 1978, 'Criterion-referenced testing and measurement: A review of technical issues and developments', *Review of Educational Research*, vol. 48, no. 1, pp. 1-47.

Hargreaves, A. 1994, *Changing Teachers, Changing Times: Teachers' Work and Culture in the Postmodern Age,* Teachers' College Press, New York.

Hargreaves, A. and Reynolds D. (eds) 1989, *Education Policies: Controversies and Critiques,* Falmer Press, NY, Philadelphia, London.

Hodgman, J. 1994, An evaluation of the effects of the criterion-based assessment on design outcomes and student performance, paper presented to the Annual Conference of the Australian Association for Research in Education University of Newcastle 27 November-1 December.

Holloway, G., Abbott-Chapman, J and Hughes, P. 1992, *Identifying the Qualities and Characteristics of the Effective Teacher, Report 2, Normative Dimensions of Teacher/Student Interaction,* Youth Education Studies Centre, University of Tasmania.

Lingard, B., Knight, J. and Porter, P. (eds) 1993, *Schooling Reform in Hard Times,* Falmer Press, London.

Marginson, S. 1993, *Education and Public Policy in Australia,* Cambridge University Press, Melbourne.

National Board of Employment, Education and Training, 1992, *The Australian Vocational Certificate Training System,* Employment and Skills Formation Council.

National Board of Employment, Education and Training, 1994, *Women in the Teaching Profession*, Commissioned Report no. 32, Canberra.

Pusey M. *1991, Economic Rationalism in Canberra; A Nation-Building State Changes its Mind, Cambridge University Press, Cambridge.*

Redican, B. 1988, 'Subject teachers under stress', in Ozga, J. (ed), *Schoolwork. Approaches to the Labour Process of Teaching,* Open University, Milton Keynes.

Rogers, D. 1996, *Tasmanian Year Book.* Australian Bureau of Statistics, Canberra.

Tasmania. Department of Education and the Arts. 1994, *Strategic Plan,* Hobart, Tas.

TenBrink, T. 1974, *Evaluation: A Practical Guide for Teachers,* McGraw-Hill, New York.

Victorian Institute of Secondary Education (VISE), 1984, 'Towards a revised policy on curriculum and assessment in the Victorian Year 12 HSC program', Discussion paper, VISE, Melbourne.

Waters M. 1994, *Modern Sociological Theory*, Sage, London.

Yeatman, A. 1990, *Bureaucrats, Technocrats, Femocrats: Essays on the Contemporary Australian State,* Allen & Unwin, Sydney.

*Chapter 4*

# Dealing with Constant Demands for School Change: A Temporal Perspective for Understanding Teacher Behavior in Urban School Organizations

## *James E. Bruno*
Professor of Education
University of California, Los Angeles

## Abstract

American public schooling practices over the last several decades have been affected by wave after wave of proposals for school change and reform. Most of these school reform efforts were not initiated by classroom teachers, but by politicians, private sector executives, professional educators, and parents. It has been especially difficult to affect change, and more importantly to get all classroom teachers on the same "page" with regard to participating in school change activities, in large urban school district settings. To have an impact and to be educationally effective, changes that deal with the inputs of the schooling process (students, teachers, facilities), the processes of schooling (new curriculums, multiculturalism, computer technology), and the outputs of the schooling process (test scores, social promotion, accountability, equal educational opportunity), have to be accommodated by all classroom teachers in the school organization. While there are wide variations associated with teacher participation in school change activities, a large portion of this variation can be explained by the temporal orientation of the teacher. In turn, temporal orientation of teachers can impact on how well a they can accommodate to constant demands for school change and how effectively they can incorporate these changes into actual classroom teaching practice.

## INTRODUCTION

The ability to adapt to change is essential in the lifetime of individuals as it is in the lifetime of work organizations. Examining how constant change impacts on human behavior is extremely important to study since efforts at a global economy and New World economic order will tend to accelerate change even further. What happens to individuals and work organizations when there are wave after wave of changes and the cumulative effect of these changes begin to exceed the capacity of individuals to incorporate these changes into their work and home life? Living under conditions of constant change is like watching a TV program with someone using a remote control and constantly changing the channel. Constant change tends to force individuals to live in a state that is best described as an "extended now" , to ignore the future altogether, and to find life fulfillment in the present. Dealing with constant change in an organization also tends to lessen the sense of personal urgency or need for change, thus making one develop a resistance to any type of change. As one researcher noted, "a market driven culture with accelerating rates of change takes the waiting out of wanting and the distance between desire and fulfillment narrows". (Brand, 1999). In many instances attitude towards change in life, reflects itself in attitude towards change in the workplace.

Constant demands for change in private sector work organization, such as high technology, science, law, and medicine, force individuals to keep up with these changes in order to secure their employment at a market-clearing price (salary). In most instances after work time or the use of "discretionary time" (8 hours per day and 16 hours per day on the weekend) is used by these professionals to keep up with these changes at work. In most instances these work centered time investments are taken at the expense of (in order) entertainment time, personal development time, and time for social relationships. Of course these time stressed individuals can always leave an organization and find another less time demanding position (usually at less salary) in a similar, but less change oriented work organization. Another alternative, that is typical of a mid life crisis career change, is to change professions to those that are less discretionary time demanding. In fact many doctors, lawyers, and engineers shift careers at midlife precisely because they want more control over their time in their life and desire more time for their relationships and self-development.

School organizations are unique in the world of work because of the way they compensate teachers, the way the teaching profession is protected by tenure, the influence of strong teacher unions over school work policies, and the way teaching assignments are organized in a repetitive, yearly format. To be effective educational change requires an adoption of the change effort by all classroom teachers in the school organization. This is because schooling is a process whereby students advance through sequential grade levels, where each level dependent upon the quality of the previous level. There would be little overall school effectiveness if half the teaching faculty adopted the school change and the other half opposed or ignored the change.

Getting all teachers on the same page with regard to school change and reform is particularly difficult for educational leadership and requires an understanding of teacher behaviors with regard to how they value their time and by extension how well they can accommodate to change.

Change in education is far different today than it was years ago, is much more constant with regard to yearly changes, and is far more radical in terms of the types of change recommended. For example, each year the legislature of many states mandate dozens of school reforms which when added to the reforms already proposed by educational professionals (usually university professors), private foundations, parents, and private sector work organizations creates a situation of change overload. Modern educational change has required time consuming and radical changes in curriculum (phonics, new mathematics), structure and governance (charter schools, school based management), and workload responsibilities (whole child responsibility). Even if a teacher's discretionary time is compensated by the school organization, time has to be taken from their important social relationships in life and their own personal development activities. Both types of time erosions tend to lower overall lifestyle satisfaction, which might have an impact on the behavior classroom teachers at school. In short, constant demands for change in school organizations typically impacts on the behavior of teachers and can cause dropout, burnout in addition to a degradation of their own personal and professional life quality.

School organizations are not ideally suited for adapting to constant change demands because they employ a fixed step salary schedule. This type of compensation scheme only recognizes classroom contract time, college credits, and classroom experience for purposes of determining salary levels. Work in the classroom and teaching assignments are also cyclical in nature such as teaching at the same 3dr grade level or the same algebra I class each year. In addition, tenure of classroom teachers guarantee their employment by the school organization regardless of their extra discretionary time investments outside of school to service the demands for school change. All three conditions of cyclical time, fixed step salary schedule, and tenure create little financial incentive for teaching professionals to use their discretionary time for supporting constant change efforts at school. In addition classroom teachers also have to accommodate to major time consuming changes in their own life that are personal (psychological and physiological health), environmental (the quality of home and school geographical space), and social (divorce, substance abuse).

From a leadership perspective, getting all teachers to be on the "same page" with regard to classroom change requires a greater understanding of how classroom teachers respond to and can accommodate to the change process- especially with regard to time investment preferences at school. For example, it is not uncommon for senior teachers at urban school settings to not desire yearbook or school newspaper assignment and to leave such after school time-consuming activities to younger teachers.

Actually ensuring that all changes as designed and interpreted by school administration and others are actually carried out or delivered in classroom practice is another particularly problematic, time related issue for school leadership. It used to be that the career path of school administration was a natural mechanism for classroom teachers who wished to pursue a professional career in education. School leadership, specifically the principalship, has now become so overwhelmed by the needed time commitments to affect constant demands for school change that fewer teachers desire to go into school administration. Similarly put, large numbers of teachers are not interested in making the enormous time commitment to school change largely because they have other time demands in life that are outside of school that have more lifestyle value.

Enormous time consuming change at a school site runs the gamut from those advocating a return to phonics, arithmetic drills, memorization of facts, and constant testing, to those recommending more school prayer. Additional time-consuming changes in curriculums centered on multiculturalism, social justice, whole language, and cooperative learning are also being proposed. In essence some recommended educational change requires a total rethinking about the delivery of instruction, is enormously time-consuming, and more importantly requires that all teachers at a school site participate. Naturally some classroom teachers, over the course of their career, develop a comfort zone with their teaching and become reluctant to accommodate to any type of school change that might affect their present, time efficient, teaching practices. In short, there is a great amount of variation in the way teachers are able to respond and accommodate to constant demands for school change. This study proposes a theoretical framework of temporal orientation of classroom teachers as a mechanism to explain a part of this variation. Specifically, the pattern and use of discretionary or non-contract, outside of regular school hours time and characteristics that describe a teacher's temporal orientation are proposed as a model for understanding the ability of teachers to accommodate to constant demands for school reform and change.

## CLASSROOM TEACHERS AND CHANGE

As noted earlier, there are many issues that make constant demands for change interesting to examine in the context of school organizations. These include

1.  school change is qualitatively and quantitatively different than school change in previous generations and is far more radical and time consuming

2.  The amount of change and demands for change required is not only different, but is a constant year to year occurrence. Each year the state legislatures mandate numerous school reforms to public education in order to satisfy various political constituencies

3.  The amount and type of change is so vast and the time investment needed so acute that a teacher's discretionary time is impacted. This time investment overload might affect teacher behavior at a school site and result in burnout and dropout

4.  The school organization itself is not conducive to satisfying the demands for constant change because of characteristics such as tenure, fixed step salary schedule, cyclical clock for the teaching assignment, and strong teacher unions.

5. Because of the way schooling is organized in America, for maximum educational effectiveness all teachers have to participate in the change effort. If part of the faculty is involved with the change effort and the other part resists change, then the change effect will eventually fail in the school organization.

6. The educational attitudes of children that teachers have to teach in their classrooms have changed dramatically over the last several decades. Time investments by parents in their children have declined and there is also a higher incidence of single parent homes. Both social henomena have made the degree of difficulty of teaching much higher.

Part of the individual variation of a classroom teacher's ability to accommodate to school change has to do with their motivation for and resistance to change. Both conditions are highly related to the personal characteristics of an individual teacher-especially personality, age, marital status, children at home, and their temporal orientation. By temporal orientation is meant time investments, view of past, present, and future, the perceived value of time with age, and the perceived satisfaction to perceived time effort ratio (to be discussed later).

With regard to personality, research has found that there is a strong relationship between Myers-Briggs type and individual preferences for organizational change (Burt,1997). The effects of change on religious organizations, specifically the Mormon Church and the changing role of women roles has also been examined with the expected findings that there was increased participation among younger and less experienced members and less participation among older members. (Iannaccone and Mikes, 1990).

From the perspective of an aging classroom teacher, time has an increasing value or worth that tends to make it a very scarce resource to be invested wisely. For example, time outside of classroom contract time can be invested in other competing time-consuming activities in life in order to obtain more "lifestyle" objective such as playing more golf, being with grandchildren, etc.

The essential problem associated with American public school change efforts has been that they are heavily time laden, extremely disjointed, and have come in a yearly, piece-meal waves of change. All of these characteristics tend to lessen the sense of urgency for change and ultimately undermine the next year's effort at school change. In addition, these change efforts are typically engaged by only a handful of teachers (usually younger) and this phenomenon tends to alienate other (usually older) teachers at the school site. While change activities at rural and suburban schools are somewhat more successful than change efforts at urban schools, both types of school settings have continuing problems with getting all teachers involved with the school change process.

Large urban school settings with strong teacher unions that recognize and value and protect a teacher's discretionary time can also be a major impediment to school change. In addition urban classroom teachers typically have a wider availability and variety of outside of school options for their discretionary time investments. Finally, nearly all efforts at change in school organizations do not appeal to a teacher's professional or idealistic values, but instead entail major materialistic and other monetary compensation. Various forms of material compensation such as released time from the classroom, extra pay, or summer stipends for their discretionary compensated time only attract those teachers (usually younger) where material compensation is more valued than time compensation for engagement in other lifestyle activities. This practice of material compensation for participation in school change efforts also tends to place additional burdens on school budgets and draws resources away from classroom instruction. In short, constant demands for school change comes at a high price to the school organization. Because school change is not fully integrated into the professional development for all teachers at a school site it stands little chance of successful integration into actual teaching practice in the classroom.

Separate school settings in urban areas, such as charter and magnet schools, have been established in order to attract teachers willing to invest large amounts of their discretionary time in change efforts thus creating a school district within a school district. Similar to their professional counterparts in the private sector, these teachers are more amenable to change, have a more professional attitude towards the need for change in teaching, and do not require extra or non-contract monetary compensation for their extra discretionary time investment. But for most urban school settings discretionary, non-contract, uncompensated time investments by classroom teachers to service the needs for school change are rare.

Because many classroom teachers are attracted to the teaching profession in public school settings precisely because they can exercise some degree of control over their work, time perception becomes part of the problem as well as part of the solution. In short, the temporal orientation of classroom teachers and the ability to accommodate to rapid and constant demands for school change are highly related. While there are large variations in teacher participation in change efforts, temporal orientation and the congruence between school time and teacher time can explain a large part of this variation.

## TIME FOR LIFE AND TIME FOR WORK IN AMERICA

Because there is only a finite amount of time available in a day or lifetime, there is always a competition for ones time and by extension the ability to accommodate to change. Life, especially in urban areas of America, is in a state of constant overdrive and people experience what has been referred to as an acceleration syndrome with regard to ever increasing change and demands on their time both at work and outside of work:

These is more information to absorb, more time consuming demands to be met, more roles in the work organization and in private life to play, the technology to accomplish everything faster is available, and there is never enough time to get it all done at a reasonable level of quality (Schwartz, 1988, p 147)

As taxpayers, breadwinners, parents, and concerned citizens, classroom teachers are part of this time acceleration syndrome in America. Temporal stability (same family) and spatial stability (same home residence) in a teacher's life also has a great deal to do with their capacity to accommodate to change. Divorce, maladjusted children, health problems, constant job, residence, and family changes, etc are also a part of the lives of teachers as they are for adults in the general population.

Because of the unique characteristics of classroom teachers, the security of their employment, their methods of compensation, and the cyclical time clock in school organizations, the acceleration syndrome has to be addressed differently for classroom teachers. Since these teachers are only paid for classroom contract time, the amount of discretionary or non-contract time provides a teacher with a wide choice of time investments outside of school. In essence, when the demands for constant yearly change in educational practices and functions intersect with a teacher time need for lifestyle satisfaction we have a problem of teacher participation in the change and reform process. In addition there are major problems associated with the delivery of the proposed school change to actual classroom practice that are also associated with time. This situation tends not to happen in charter schools, private schools, magnet schools, and other private sector work organizations since temporal orientation (demands for discretionary time investments) are part of the selection process and an important criterion for selection to the job, promotion, and salary advancement in the organization.

While many of the reforms are sensible enough when considered as isolated components, there is a threat that they will never cohere into a program of systemic reform that is truly needed to improve student performance for all California students. Fragmentation has long hampered the state's educational system, and it may do so for a long time to come.

Burr, Crucial Issues in California Education 20000: Are the Reform Pieces Fitting Together. P 2

## A MODEL FOR EXAMINING CONSTANT CHANGE AND THE ABILITY OF TEACHERS TO ACCOMMODATE CHANGE

In figure 1, a hypothetical relationship between rate of change, the average teachers' ability to incorporate change in their life, and "organizational temporal stability" or the ability to implement the change into actual classroom teaching practice is described. The y-axis shows the amount of change imposed on the classroom teacher while the x-axis shows the ability of classroom teachers to accommodate to change. In general a teacher's ability to accommodate to change by classroom teachers is linear, and highly related to their temporal orientation (letter A in figure 1). Sometimes the ability of teachers to accommodate to change is non-linear, especially for older teachers and for teachers having to deal with major changes at home, with friends, children, and health (sloping downward). The rate of change in school organizations, especially when one adds technological change and cumulative, constant, yearly, state political demands on the schools is highly non-linear (sloping upwards- letter B in figure 1). Some of these yearly changes have occurred in waves starting in the early 1980's and have included important subject matter school reform such as in math, language, and reading-changes that require enormous time efforts on the part of classroom teachers. The point of intersection between the rate of change curve and the teacher accommodation curve reveals much about the "temporal stability" of the school organization with regard to its ability to incorporate change into actual teaching practices for all the teachers at the school site. In school organizations where demands for change exceed a teachers' ability to accommodate to change we have (especially with teacher tenure, strong teacher unions, and the fixed step salary schedule), teachers working in an "extended now" or a reversion to past or time efficient and more comfortable teaching practices.    In school organizations where demands for change are less than the teachers' ability to accommodate we have teachers easily incorporating change into everyday classroom teaching practice.  Note in figure 1 that curve A is the teachers' ability to accommodate to change and might be related to personal characteristics such as age, personality, outside competing time consuming interests, health, family, etc. (see figure 7 for a more comprehensive analysis of the characteristics that might describe these curves). The curve represented by letter B is the cumulative demand for change in curriculum, pedagogy, governance, organizational structure, facilities, and personnel and the needed time investments to affect school change. Region 1 makes the school organization amenable to change (temporal stability between the time demands of the individual and the school organization), while region 2 is a school organization where change is difficult.

Ravitch (1999) proposes similar themes as she documents the diferentt waves of school reforms that have occurred in American public education. For example whole language vs. phonics, tracking vs. detracking have been seemingly contradictory waves of reform for classroom teachers to accommodate. We have also seen the progressive vs. traditionalist perspective to schooling and the child centered vs. teacher centered perspectives to curriculums come in waves to public education. These demands for constant change, especially those that seem contradictory in nature, tend to make teachers live in an extended now and revert back to their time tested and time efficienct classroom practices.

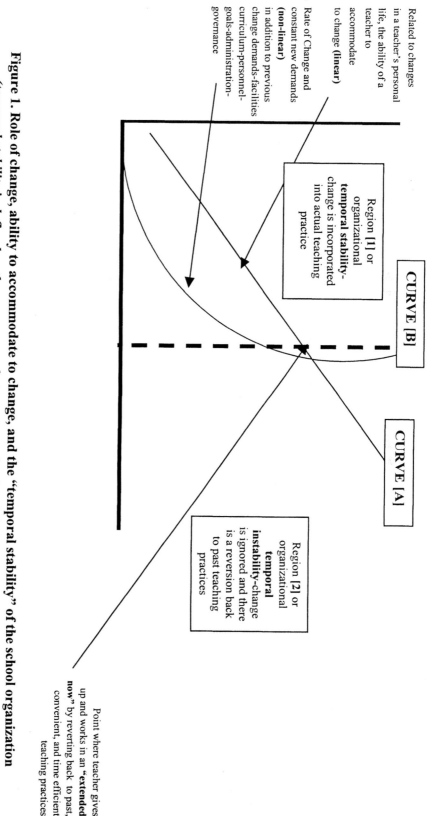

Related to changes
in a teacher's personal
life, the ability of a
teacher to
accommodate
to change **(linear)**

Rate of Change and
constant new demands
**(non-linear)**
in addition to previous
change demands-facilities
curriculum-personnel-
goals-administration-
governance

Region [1] or
organizational
**temporal stability-**
change is incorporated
into actual teaching
practice

**CURVE [B]**

**CURVE [A]**

Region [2] or
organizational
**temporal
instability-**change
is ignored and there
is a reversion back
to past teaching
practices

Point where teacher gives
up and works in an **"extended
now"** by reverting back to past,
convenient, and time efficient
teaching practices

**Figure 1. Role of change, ability to accommodate to change, and the "temporal stability" of the school organization**
*(temporal stability is defined as the congruence between organizational time and teacher personal time needs)*

School organizations and the perception of time by classroom teachers has been extensively examined in the context of urban schooling (Bruno,1999, 1998 ) with specific regard to their participation in change efforts. Research is currently under way with regard to figure 1 that specifically examines the rate of change demands and the ability of teachers with various the physical, psychological, and attitudinal characteristics to accommodate to change. Exactly how much of the variation in teacher participation or uncompensated discretionary time can be explained by temporal orientation will be the main focus of this future, more empirical, study of teacher temporal orientation. (Bauer, 2000). Naturally school administrative personnel can develop policies that change the shapes of both curves by limiting the amount of change or by increasing the capacity of teachers to accommodate to change. While the former is highly related to state and local politics of education, the latter strategy is part related to school leadership and their understanding the temporal orientation of teachers.

In the educational research literature a constant theme for both school organizations and classroom teachers involved with the urban school change process one of the scarcest of all resources seems to be "time." (Purnell and Hill, 1992, Watts and Castle, 1993, Raywid,1993).

Designing incentives for classroom teachers to engage and participate in school reform efforts require a fundamental understanding of the perception of "professional" time by classroom teachers and the importance of "personal" time to what is generally described in the literature as "lifestyle satisfaction" (Shmotkin,1991; Colarusso,1994). A sense of time limitations as one ages tends to shape our behavior away from the work organization and more towards taking care of personal needs of the self, and strengthening relationships to others.

The recognition of time limitation stimulates a redefinition of goals and channels energies and resources into obtainable objectives that enrich the lives of oneself and loved ones. Colarusso (1994) p. 241

## A MODEL FOR EXAMINING THE CHANGING TIME INVESTMENT PATTERN OF TEACHERS OVER A CAREER IN THE CLASSROOM

As noted earlier, there are many important differences in the way a classroom teacher and a school organization are "paced" by time. In essence the school organization essentially uses teacher time in a cyclical time framework while teachers' age on a linear time framework. Teachers age each year of their teaching career, and more importantly use more and more of their personal or "out of school" time to pursue personal lifestyle satisfaction goals rather than using this time to accommodate to the demands for school change. Work organizations in the private sector on the other hand, closely resemble a linear time framework and compensate their employees accordingly. Each day, month, and year in a private work organization is different in order to meet the changing demands of the market place. Extra discretionary time demands are simply part of the job. Unlike school organizations, these work organizations are not in a "monopolistic" position in society since they can "fail" and go out of business if they do not remain competitive. If an employee does not adapt and adopt a linear time clock at work, then the private sector work organization can fire, transfer, downsize, or layoff the employee. These personnel policies are designed to ensure that the organization remains competitive by getting a closer fit in time perception between the employee and the work organization.

Technological change continues to accelerate, so the speed with which obsolescence occurs also is increasing. Organizations cannot ignore developments which give advantage to competitors. This requires that employees are constantly changing and staying current in terms of their skills, jobs, and often the culture (attitudes) of the work place. Hussey (1990) p 11

In short, the basic linear vs. cyclical time discrepancy between the classroom teacher and the school organization is a major factor that makes the school change process, from design to actual implementation in the classroom, particularly difficult.

The relationship between school change and the needed time investments by classroom teachers to service the needs of school change is not new. As these educational researchers have noted:

Time has become the most limiting resource in management of the change and reform process in the schools (Purnell & Hill, 1992, p. 19).

Time is the basic dimension through which the teachers work is constructed and interpreted Huyvaert (1998) p 247

From a classroom teacher perspective, creating constant change and reform in the school organization requires that they also invest large amounts of personal time or "out of school" time to the reform process.

Creating time for reform requires investment. Teachers have to invest extra time and energy as participants in restructuring the school. The needs for time and resource are interlocking (Purnell and Hill, 1992, p. 11).

Another educational researcher has echoed a similar theme with regard to the needed "extra" teacher time investments to service the constant need for school reform.

Ask anybody involved in school reform about its most essential ingredient and the answer will most likely be time. Time has emerged as the key issue in every analysis of school change appearing in the last decade (Raywid, 1993, p. 30).

A somewhat related problem that is associated with time and the propensity of teachers to engage in school change efforts, is the problem of some classroom teachers "doing time" or "waiting until retirement" in the school organization. (see figure 2) . In essence for these classroom teachers more lifestyle satisfaction is gained by investing discretionary time in "outside of school" rather than "inside of school" time consuming activities. The transition point in figure 2 is interesting to examine because it is related to school leadership policies towards the older or doing time teacher in a school organization. In figure 1, if one plots the percent of uncompensated discretionary time outside and inside of school (100% inside-0% outside to 0% inside to 100% outside) against teacher age, a graph similar to figure 2 results..

The temporal orientation for those classroom teachers past the transition point in figure 2 is primarily aimed at merely waiting and hanging on until retirement from the profession. These teachers, because of their temporal orientation are highly unlikely to engage in school change efforts unless strong material, social, and professional incentives are offered. (see far right in Figure 2). In essence, the professional career for these classroom teachers has "plateaued" in the school organization (Milstein, 1990) or has gone beyond the transition point in figure 2 where a higher percent of discretionary time is spent on outside of school time consuming activities (golf, health, family, etc). In a private sector work organization many of these "plateaued" employees would be downsized.

For classroom teachers who are past this transition point, engagement in time consuming school change activities is particularly difficult. This is because there is no possibility of moving up in the school organization, they are at the top of the fixed step salary schedule, and because of tenure there is no possibility of moving down. In short, the "plateaued" teacher in an urban school setting remains in the classroom, but has little personal attachment to the goals of the school organization. In addition they perceive no direct pecuniary or non- pecuniary incentive to change or invest extra discretionary time (outside of contract teaching time) at school. These teachers become "locked" or "trapped" between the time demands of the school organization and the increasing "outside of school" time demands required by their own personal quest for lifestyle satisfaction. The rate of change for these teachers is way above their desire of these teachers to accommodate to these changes. (see figure 7 for an analysis of characteristics that might be used to describe figures 1 and 2)

Plateauing can be an important first step towards reassessment and growth, but if forward movement does not occur it can also lead to the perception of being trapped. Milstein (1990) p. 173

In short, in many urban school settings it is the combination temporal orientation, teacher attitudes towards change, politics of the workplace, organizational structure, and the seniority mentality of teacher unions that prevent change

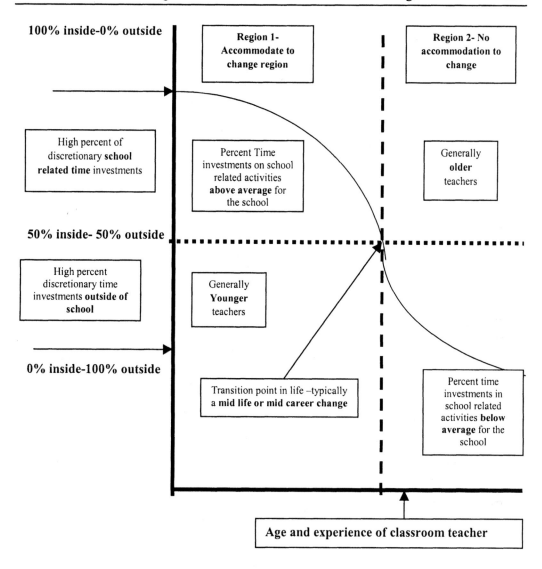

**Figure 2**
**The *inside and outside* of school uncompensated time investments as a**
**function of teacher age**


On one hand school are expected to engage in continuous renewal and change. On the other hand, the way teachers are tenured, the way schools are organized, the way the educational hierarchy operates, and the way political decision makers treat educators results in a system that is more likely to retain the status quo. Fullan(1993) p. 12

The construct of "time" therefore, in the context of an urban school setting, has important applied (school leadership) as well as theoretical (research into teacher behavior) significance. For social organizations in general (McGrath & Rotchford, 1981), and school organizations in particular (Bruno, 1997), time essentially acts as a "currency

" of exchange that is used to purchase both school organizational goals as well as individual classroom teacher lifestyle satisfaction goals.

## TEMPORAL ORIENTATION MEASURES AND THE SHAPING OF TEACHER BEHAVIOR IN SCHOOL ORGANIZATIONS

**Five** temporal orientation measures and constructs of classroom teachers are defined with regard to their significance in understanding the behaviors of classroom teachers towards change. These temporal orientations and constructs include:

*a)* the previously noted **linear vs. cyclical time** disparity between the classroom teacher and the school organization

*b)* the composition of the **time investment portfolio** of classroom teachers or how teachers invest their time both in and out of school (see Bruno, 1995 for research dealing with time investment portfolios of children and teachers (Bruno, 1999)

*c)* the **satisfaction to time effort ratio** or a concept for understanding the motivation of teachers to engage in various types of time-consuming activities that are associated with school reform (i.e. is the reform effort worth my time

*d)* **the subjective weighted hour** or how the older teacher, compared with a younger teacher, values time and how the subjective worth of time is associated with participation in school change and reform  activities (see Bruno, 1995 for more discussion of this temporal concept).

*(e)* **polychronmetric** time or a split screen approach to behavior or doing two or three things during the same unit of time i.e. going to a faculty meeting and grading papers.

### Cyclical and Linear Time

As noted earlier, the cyclical-linear time disparity relates to the type of "clock" that paces activities in the life of a school organization as well as the lifetime of a classroom teacher. In a school organization, classroom teachers have the opportunity to repeat their job tasks each year of their career. In figure 2 these are indicated by the investments of high amounts of their discretionary time early in their career in order to "get the job down" or attain teaching fluency or efficiency. These initial time investments are expected to pay a "return" in time efficiency in later career.(region 1 in figure 2). The perception of the school organizational clock is cyclical in nature i.e. the work tasks or contractual teaching obligations repeat themselves each year.[1] A cyclical time framework, also ensures that the teacher's essential job function remains stable over time and this job stability generates little in the way of direct outside incentives for school change. In fact, the development of classroom teaching job "fluency" or getting the teaching task "down" (i.e. more time efficient) creates conditions so that other activities in a teacher's life can be serviced with the "released" time (Region 2 in figure 2). One of the major reasons why change is so difficult to affect in the classroom is related to the teaching time demands and classroom implications associated with the proposed change. The major non- pecuniary benefit of working in a "cyclical time" framework can make the profession of teaching extremely attractive for some individuals. In essence, because of the element of time control in the workplace, except for formal classroom contact time, teachers can exercise nearly full control over their time in the school organization. More importantly time responsibilities in school organizations are cyclical and can be planned for over a career. In essence, once tenured, teachers have the opportunity to repeat their classroom teaching obligations each year of their career and benefit (time wise) from the cyclical time nature of the school organization.

## Time Investment Portfolios

Within the constraints of a finite amount of time in a lifetime, some teachers, especially mid career and older teachers, will tend to invest any "free" or "released" discretionary time to pursue their personal lifestyle satisfaction goals. Goals such as earning more income, athletic interests, recreation endeavors, building relationships, developing talents, etc (see figure 2- region 2) become important time consuming activities outside of school. Unlike the private sector, teacher tenure in the school organization and strong teacher unions ensure that there is no linkage between "after school" or discretionary time investments and salary. In fact, from the standpoint of a fixed step salary schedule and teacher pecuniary benefits, all that is needed for a classroom teacher to earn a living is to meet teacher contractual time obligations, accrue experience or years of service, and build college credits. Extra "after school" or extra "out of the classroom" time to engage in school reform activities is typically not compensated by the fixed step salary schedule.

The various types of time investments that teachers can make in life to pursue lifestyle satisfaction is referred to as a *time investment portfolio*. Using a time investment portfolio concept, teachers can generally invest their time into one of four main types of time-consuming activities:

---

1 Another major non-pecuniary benefit of teaching, of course, is related to the age identification with children (feeling youthful) in the classroom. Teaching young children for many teachers makes them feel younger than their actual age giving some beginning teachers the sense of cyclical (never getting old) time.

*a)* time to "**sell**" to the school organization (or other work organizations via moonlighting) for purposes of ***material*** compensation and earning a living (defined as **outer** directed time)

*b)* time to "**give**" to the "significant" relationships in life for the purpose of ***social*** compensation (defined as **other** directed time)

*c)* time to "spend" on themselves for the purpose of private or ***personal*** benefit compensation (defined as **inner** directed time)

*d)* time to "fill" or consumptive time or "non-directed" time that teachers use as a "filler," or to recover from the work day i.e., passive ***entertainment*** compensation, i.e., TV, movies, etc., (defined as **non directed** time) (Bruno, 1995).

In short, from a school leadership and management perspective time investments made by classroom teachers to promote school reform and change will generally require some form of material (pay teachers extra), social (build colleagueship), personal benefit (professional growth), intellectual (stimulate their mind and imagination), or entertainment compensation.

## Satisfaction to time effort

There is an important, but related theoretical concept called the perceived **satisfaction(S)** derived (perceived material, social, intellectual, and psychological benefits) from the school change time-consuming activity to perceived **time-effort(TE)** needed to attain this benefit (perceived convenience, frustration, time needed) for school leadership to consider.  The S/TE ratio can provide important school leadership guidelines with regard to understanding the "why" some classroom teachers invest their time in different types of outer, other, and inner directed types of time-consuming activities that are associated with school change efforts. The S/TE ratio partially addresses the question "is the school change effort "worth" the added time effort and frustration?" More importantly, this ratio can be used to describe the initial attractiveness and the continued participation and the actual engagement of classroom teachers in certain types of school reform and change efforts (see figure 2- transition point between region 1 and region 2). Finally, the satisfaction to time effort ratio can also partially explain "general" teacher behaviors in the school organization such as burnout, dropout, push out, and leadership. Active participation, minimal effort participation, and dissension with regard to the school change efforts can also be associated with the S/TE measure. [2]

---

[2] Naturally, the attraction to and repulsion from certain types of time-consuming activities by classroom teachers is highly dependent upon other competing types and amounts of time-consuming activities in their lives. For a classroom teacher with no other competing time investments in life (family, hobbies, talents, recreation, etc.), default time investments to certain types of time consuming activities in the school organization (meetings) for school

The S/TE ratio concept is most apparent in figure 2 with regard to the choice of time investments towards within and outside of school activities. In essence, the S/TE ratios are higher for school related activities in early career than in later career. Effective school administrators develop methods to shift the transition point in figure 2 to the right. The S/TE ratio can also partially describe teacher behaviors with regard to constant demands for school change and reform (See Figure 3).

From figure 3 note that row 1 is more associated with region A in figure 2 while row 2 is more associated with region B. In general, and within a linear time framework the perceived value of time increases with age thus lowering the S/TE ratio i.e. as a classroom teacher ages in the school organization and time remaining becomes scarcer. As one researcher noted;

Adults use their birthdays to review achievements and frustrations of the past and to define their hopes for the future. Colarusso (1990) p. 250

## The Subjective Weighted Hour

Hypothetically and to illustrate the concept of a subjective "weighted" hour consider the ratio of waking hours of time (16 hours per day) lived to waking hours remaining to be lived (scarcity) for classroom teachers at various ages (assume an 80-year life span).

Note in figure 4 that the subjective weighted hour difference for a 40-year-old (2.8) and 50-year-old (4.7) classroom teacher hour is extremely high when compared to a 20-year-old teacher (1.0). The difference between "actual" time and subjective "weighted" time can sometimes impact on the concept of the satisfaction to time-effort ratio, because all else being equal, time scarcity automatically increases time effort (TE). In short, all hours of passage for classroom teachers are not perceived as being equivalent. Classroom teachers have different age related temporal orientations and a different subjective sense of the passage of time, thus their propensity to engage in school change efforts also differ. A teacher's age in the school organization, therefore, might dramatically impact on their participation rates in school change activities. (see figure 2-region 2) Consider that a one-hour duration school reform meeting has the perceived subjective sense of .35 of an hour for a 20-year-old teacher and 1.66 hour meeting for a 50-year-old teacher.(see Figure 5). Using these age-time ratios one can hypothetically derive the following subjective time estimates or weighted hours for different types of time-consuming activities that might be associated with school change activities.

reform are relatively easy to accommodate.

**Figure 3**

Individual Teacher Perceived Satisfaction*/Time Effort**
Ratio and Hypothesized Association with Urban Classroom Teacher Behaviors

| | |
|---|---|
| Satisfaction  (high) / Time Effort  (low)<br>**[Leader]**<br>**high ability to cope with change**<br><br>"Commitment"<br>to Change<br>Highly effective teachers | Satisfaction (high) / Time-Effort (high)<br>**[Active Participant]**<br>**can become overwhelmed by change**<br><br>At Risk<br>Commitment to Change But<br>Burned out teachers<br>and push out<br>likely |
| Satisfaction (low) / Time Effort (low) | Satisfaction (low) / Time Effort (high) |
| **[Follower]**<br>**generally passive participant in change**<br>At-Risk or Minimum<br>commitment to change;<br>plateaued teachers<br>early retirement | **[Dissenter]**<br>**typically resistant to change**<br>Withdraw<br>or dropout teacher<br>from the change<br>process- antagonistic towards change |

\*     Satisfaction (S) compensation- salary-professional development-visibility-status-friendships-etc.
\*\*    Time Effort (TE) a combination of actual and subjective time-energy, frustration-convenience required.

**Figure 4**

Hypothesized Perceived Value of Time: The "Subjective Weighted Hour" for a
Classroom Teacher

| Teacher Age | Waking Hours | Waking Hours | Ratio | Subjective Weighted Hours |
|---|---|---|---|---|
| 20 | 116,800 | 350,400 | .35 | 1 |
| 30 | 175,200 | 292,000 | .59 | 2.5 |
| 40 | 233,600 | 233,600 | 1.0 | 2.8 |
| 50 | 292,000 | 175,200 | 1.66 | 4.7 |
| 60 | 350,400 | 116,800 | 3.00 | 8.7 |

Assuming an 80 year life span and 16 waking hours per day.

**Figure 5**

Hypothetical Time Worth (actual and weighted) for Various After School Meetings

| DZVXSchool Reform Activity | Actual Hours | Weighted 20-year-old Teacher (.35) | Weighted 50-year-old Teacher (1.66) |
|---|---|---|---|
| One-hour meeting | 1 (60 min) | 21 min.(.35 hrs) | 99.6 min.(1.66 hrs) |
| One half-day meeting | 4 (240 min) | 84 min. (1.4 hrs) | 398.4 min. (6.64 hrs) |
| Full-day meeting | 8 (480 min) | 168 min.(2.8 hrs) | 796.0 min.(13.3 hrs) |
| | | | |

## Polychronometric Time-Multitasking

Doing two tasks at one time or multitasking using the same one unit of time is a common method for dealing with time scarcity. For example working out on a treadmill while being entertained by television or jogging while listening to music on earphones or going to a faculty meeting and grading papers are some of these adaptations to time scarcity. This adaptation to time scarcity (multitasking) is especially prevalent in urban areas where there are multiple demands on a teacher's time. In addition, this type of adaptation is one method that teachers use to shift the point of intersection in figure 2 to the right since it permits one to get more tasks completed for each unit of time. Unfortunately a split screen approach tends to diminish the needed attention and deprive the full focus and attention that the task might require. The following are some examples of teacher polychronometric time use "in school" and "outside of school" discretionary time.

**Figure 6**
**Examples of Teacher Use of Split Screen or Polychronometric Time**

| Activity | Within school time | Outside of school discretionary time |
|---|---|---|
| Home-school tasks | Teacher at school can checks up on tasks to do for the day when he or she gets home | Goes to his or he child's soccer game and grades papers |
| Personal-school tasks | Taking his or her free period and working out | Making lesson plans while watching television |
| Financial-school tasks | Checking up on real estate transactions while at school | Moonlighting and then using the same materials for class assignments |

## Time in the Urban School Setting

The urban school organizational setting is perhaps most in need of change and reform because changes in student inputs have been most pronounced, shortcomings in desired school outputs have been most visible and ignorance of new teaching processes for the classroom have been most apparent. Correspondingly, the urban school organization setting is probably most impacted by lack of incentives for teachers to change because of its size, influence of teacher unions, large percentage of teachers having tenure, tendency for teacher to have plateaued in the school organization (Milstein, 1990), and the general tendency towards a bimodal distribution of teacher ages (older teacher (age >50) and younger teachers (age<30).

...the older teacher may no longer be regarded as a respectable, wise person, but a person who has lost a number of desirable qualities. Teachers no longer felt that they occupied a congenial place among pupils, but felt more remote. Prick (1989) p 372

Numerous studies, reported in the educational administration, school reform, and school leadership research literature, focus on problems that are associated with time and time expenditures of individuals in urban school organizations. Among the more relevant of these studies are those by Peretz and Bromme (1990), Watts and Castle (1993), McDonnell (1989), Watkins (1993), Raywid (1993), Bimber (1994), Hill and Bonan (1991), Hannaway and Carnoy (1993), Purnell and Hill (1992), Robertson and Kwong (1994), Blase et al. (1986), and Johansen (1984). Some research studies have specifically focused on time expenditures of educators that are needed for successful urban school restructuring efforts. Among the more notable of these studies are those by Hargraves (1992), Adelman, Eagle and Hargraves(1997), Purnell and Hill (1992), Ben-Peretz and Bromme (1990), Tye and Tye (1984), Sheive and Schonheit (1987), West (1989), and Fullan and Miles (1992).

Urban schools have attempted to change and stimulate reform by changing the "time use rules" of the school organization such as forming charter schools[3] and magnet schools. These efforts, while an excellent change and reform strategy for education are small in scope, benefit only a small number of students, and in general have a minor educational impact in comparison to the total amount of organizational change that is needed in a large urban school district. Research studies are contemplated using figure 1 and figure 2 as a conceptual framework and where charter school teachers and regular school teachers in the same school district are compared with regard to temporal orientation.

## Summary and Recommendations for Educational Leadership

A teacher's accommodation to constant change in school organizations is highly dependent upon several school and teacher related variables working in harmony with each other. One set of variables is related to the amount of change required and the other set is related to the ability to accommodate to change. (Figure 1) Overlaid on top of these variables are the life and career cycles of classroom teachers (Figure 2). Surveys that attempt to empirically examine change in a school organization have to be developed to measure variables as depicted in Figure 7

---

[3] Interestingly, the charter school type of school reform, is a reform that is intended to make the school organization more adaptable to community needs. In doing so, charter schools change the nature of teacher time from a cyclical type of time to a linear type of time. Naturally, with these types of time oriented personnel policies, a dual public school system might emerge, i.e. a school site where teachers make the time for school reform and change and another school site in a school district where teachers are unwilling to invest the time and take advantage of a cyclical time framework.

**Figure 7:Understanding the change process in school organizations with regard to temporal orientations, teacher background, and change attitudes**

| Background Characteristics Of the Teacher | Attitudes Towards Change | Types of Proposed Organizational Changes and Demands |
|---|---|---|
| Age<br>Gender<br>Present level of responsibility<br>Competing time activities in life<br>Health –Family status changes<br>Marital status and children at home<br>Personality for change<br>Present salary-compensation<br>Amount of discretionary time available<br>Career point in teaching<br>Ratios of inside and outside of school uncompensated time over the career<br>Outside interests in life<br>Ethnic-cultural affiliation | Attitudes towards school change<br>School principal support<br>Perceived value of change to career<br>Overt- covert opposition to change<br>Identification with work as a source of satisfaction and pleasure<br>Leadership ambition<br>Time investment portfolio<br>Subjective weight of time<br>Feel plateaued in the school district<br>ID with younger teachers | Working conditions with change<br>Change that increases responsibility<br>Change that increases responsibility<br>Changes in work content<br>Facilities change (classrooms-office space)<br>Personnel change<br>Policies and procedures change<br>New technology change |

Rapid and constant, wave after wave of school change has a tendency to overwhelm classroom teachers and make them live in an extended now. Constant change also develops a resistance to change and deadens the teacher's sensitivity to the urgency for change making them less likely to participate in change activities. Excluding or marginalizing some teachers from school reform and change efforts can be very divisive in a school organization and lead to resistance to all change. In essence, all teachers have to be involved in the change process in order for the change to be effective. The burden of proof of time "worth" for classroom teachers is with school leadership. Many classroom teachers can become marginalized or plateaued or pushed out of the reform and change process precisely because they remain unconvinced of the efficacy that these proposed changes will actually help them in the classroom. The traditional practice in urban areas of substituting school reform time-consuming activities for class time-consuming activities or paying substitutes to take the teachers place in the classroom can be largely ineffectual with regard to promoting teacher participation rates. See Cutler (1983) for an examination of the issues associated with buying teacher time for staff development. If a teacher has to make up the "lost" time when a substitute teacher teaches a class then nothing is really gained for the regular classroom teacher. In fact, in many instances this practice tends to place additional workloads on the classroom teacher and thus increases TE.

In summary, this study recognizes the enormous complexity of the problem associated with teacher participation in school change and offers a temporal construct for providing a better understanding of how school change as designed can be aligned to the school change as implemented in the classroom. In essence, school leadership should give far more attention and consideration to the resource of "time" as being part of the problem as well as part of the solution. Proactive school policies to increase the satisfaction (perceived benefit) to time-effort ratios of classroom teachers of the many time-consuming activities that are associated with school change efforts should be encouraged. This type of school administrative leadership challenge can be accomplished by working on both increasing the value of the numerator (S) (teacher perceived worth-satisfaction-compensation) as well as decreasing the value of the denominator (TE) (teacher perceived time expenditures, frustration, convenience, and effort).

Finally the quality of the lifetime of a classroom teacher through their various types of time investments is strongly related to a personal sense of "self", lifestyle satisfaction, and indirectly to the quality of classroom teaching and student learning. The important role that time plays in the lifetime of a classroom teacher and evolution of the school organization implies that both the lifestyle satisfaction goals of the classroom teacher and organizational legitimacy goals of the urban school organization have to attained on a win-win footing. Classroom teachers who are unhappy about their time investments in life (poor lifestyle satisfaction) will tend to convey their unhappiness to students and thus undermine any positive effects that school reform and change efforts might have on an instructional program. Understanding and appreciating the complex concept of time as a currency of "exchange" between the classroom teacher and the school organization is an important element, and a first step in the management of the change process in urban school settings.

## REFERENCES

Adelman, N.E., Eagle, K.P.W. & Hargraves, A. (Eds.) (1997) . Racing with the Clock" Making Time for Teaching an Learning in Schgool Reform. New York, NY: Teachers College Press.

Bauer, Brian (2000). Change in Urban School Settings as a Function of Temporal Orientation. Proposal for a Doctoral Dissertation, UCLA Graduate School of Education and Information Studies.Urban Studies Division

Ben-Peretz., & Bromme, R (Eds.) (1990). The Nature of Time in Schools: Theoretical Concepts, practitioner Perceptions. New York, NY: Teachers College Press.

Bimber, B. (1994). *The decentralization mirage.* Santa Monica, CA: RAND Corporation.

Blase, J. J., Dedrich, C., & Stratae, M. (1986, June). Leadership behavior of school principals in relation to teacher stress satisfaction and performance. *Journal of Humanistic Education and Development, 24*(4), 159-171.

Brand, Stewart (1999). The Clock of the Long Now. New York. Basic Books 176pp

Bruno, J. E. (1995). Doing time/killing time at school. *The Urban Review, 27*(2).

Bruno, J. E., (1997). *It's about time: leading school reform in an era of time scarcity.* Thousand Oaks: Corwin Press

Burr, Elizabeth, Hayward, Gerald C., Fuller, Bruce, and Michael Kirst. (2000) Crucial Issues in California Education 2000: Are the Reform Pieces Fitting Together, Policy Analysis for California Education PACE, UC Press, Berkeley, CA

Burt, Noel Ferman. The Relationship Between Myers Briggs and Individual Preferences for Dealing with Organizational Change. Georgia State University, USA UMI Order Number AAM9716677 Diddertation Abstracts Inetrnational Section B: The Sciences and Engineering, 1997 June 57 (12-B) p 7763

Colarusso, Calvin(1994), Fulfillment in Adulthood: Paths to the Pinacle of Life, Plenum Press, New York, NY

Cutler, A. B. (1993). Buying time for teachers professional development. *Educational Leadership*, March, 34-37.

Fullan, M., & Miles, M. (1992, June). Getting reform right: What works and what doesn't work. *Phi Delta Kappan, 73*(10), 744-753.

Fullan, Michael G. (1993). Why Teachers Must Become Change Agents. Educational Leadership. March 1993, Vol. 50 No. 4, pp. 12-17

Hannaway, J., & Carnoy, M. (1993). *Decentralization and school improvement: Can we fulfill the promise.* San Francisco: Jossey-Bass.

Hargraves, A. (1992). Time and teachers' work: An analysis of the intensification thesis. *Teachers College Record, 94*(1), 87-108.

Hill, P., & Bonan, J. (1991). *Decentralization and accountability in public education.* Santa Monica, CA: RAND Corporation.

Hussey, D.E.. (1995). How to Manage Organizational Change. Kopgan Page Limited. London, England.

Huyvaert, S.H. (1998). Time is of the Essence: Learning in Schools. Boston, MA Allyn and Bacon.

Iannaccone, Laurence R; Miles, Carrie A. Dealing with Social Change: The Mormon Church's Response to Change in Women's Roles. Social Forces, 1990 (June 68(4) pp 1231-1250

Johansen, J. J. (1992). Some characteristics associated with effectiveness of elementary school principals as demonstrated by role perceptions and the utilization of time. *Dissertation Abstracts International, 1984, Jan., 44*(7-A).

Judge, Timopthy A; Thorensen, Carl J; Pucik, Vladimir; Welbourne, Theresa M. Managerial Coping with Organizational Change: A Dispositional Perspective. Journal of Applied Psychology v 84, n. 1 (Feb 1999) :107

Lomranz, J., Shmotkin, D., Nitza, E., & Friedman, A. (1994). Expectations for changes in midlife men. *Social Behavior and Personality, 22* (2), 111-122.

Maccoby, Michael (1995), "Why Work: Motivating the New Workforce", Alexandria VA: Miles River Press 290 p

McDonnell, J. (1989). *School district restructuring in Santa Fe, New Mexico.* (ERIC Document Reproduction Service No. ED-315 902)

McGrath, J. E., & Rotchford N. L. (1981). Time and behavior in organizations. *Research in Organizational Behavior, 5,* 57-101.

Milstein, Mike (1990). Plateauing : A Growing Problem for Educational Organizations. Teaching and Teacher Education. Vol. 6 No. 2 pp. 173-181

Peretz, B. & Bromme, R. (Eds.). (1990). The nature of time in schools. New York: Teachers College Press.

Prick, L.G.M. (1989). Satisfaction and Stress Among Teachers. International Journal of Educational Research: Research on Teachers' Professional Lives, 13(4), 363-377

Purnell, S., & Hill, P. (1992). *Time for reform* (RAND Report). Santa Monica, CA: RAND Corporation.

Ravitch, Diane (1999). Left Back: A Century of Failed School Reforms. Simon and Schuster, New York.

Raywid, M. A. (1993, September). Finding time for collaboration. *Educational Leadership, 51*(1), 30-34.

Robertson, P. J., & Kwong, S. (1994). Decision-making in school. Based management leadership councils. *Urban Review, 26(*1), 41-51.

Schwartz, Tony (October 1988). Acceleration Syndrome. Vanity Fair. Pp144-149, pp 181-188.

Sheive, L. T., & Schoenheit, M. (1987). Vision and the work life of educational leaders. In L. Sheive & M. Schoenheit (Eds.), *Leadership: Examining the elusive. The 1987 yearbook of the association for supervision and curriculum* (pp. 93-104). Alexandria, VA: ASCD.

Shmotkin, D. (1991). The role of time orientation in life satisfaction across the life span. *Journal of Gerontology, 46* (5), 234-250.

Tye, K., & Tye, B. (1984). Teacher isolation and school reform. *Phi Delta Kappan, 65*(5), 319-322.

Watkins, P. (1993). Finding time: Temporal considerations in the creation of school communities. *British Journal of Sociology of Education, 14*(2), 131-146.

Watts, G. D., & Castle, S. (1993, December). The time dilemma in school restructuring. *Phi Delta Kappan, 75*(4), 306-310.

West, F. (1990). Educational collaboration and restructuring of schools. *Journal of Educational and Psychological Consultation, 1*(1), 23-40.

*Chapter 5*

# TUTORING ACTIVITY IN SCHOOL: PEDAGOGIC PRINCIPLES AND PARTICIPATION

## *Judith Ireson*
Institute of Education, University of London

## ABSTRACT

This chapter explores the structuring of pedagogic activity in dyadic and small group settings. It is argued that teachers' and learners' meanings and interpretations form an important aspect of teaching and learning contexts. A central part of the teacher's work is to organise and structure activity for children, so as to promote their learning. A dynamic model of teacher-child participation during the tutoring of reading is presented and considered in the light of observations of teaching in a small group context. Information from interviews, course documentation and video recordings of lessons is used in the analysis. It is argued that each programme establishes a particular cultural context for literacy teaching and learning, with its own set of principles underpinning lesson activities and the pedagogic relationship. The participation of an adult with a pupil in a dyadic interaction is influenced by a network of contextual factors, including teachers' beliefs and intentions. The structuring of activity influences the nature of children's participation and their opportunities for learning.

## INTRODUCTION

The aim of this chapter is to explore the structuring of pedagogic activity in dyadic and small group settings. It forms part of a series of studies of adult-child interaction during individual and small group teaching sessions and explores aspects of the pedagogical context that influence the structuring of activity. It is argued that teachers' and learners' meanings and interpretations form an important aspect of teaching and learning contexts. A dynamic model of teacher-child participation in pedagogic activity is presented and considered in the light of observations of teaching in a small group context.

Much of the research on the interactions between adults and children performing tasks outside school has drawn on Vygotskian and neo-Vygotskian theory, including the ideas of a 'zone of proximal development' (Vygotsky, 1978), 'scaffolding' (Bruner, 1983; Wood, Bruner, & Ross, 1976) and 'guided participation' (Rogoff, 1990). This research demonstrates that adults generally adjust their support to assist children, simplifying the task where necessary and taking over the more difficult parts. This form of assistance is found in many different cultures, although the variations in cultural norms and goals for development influence the nature of involvement of adults and children (Rogoff et al, 1993). It is likely that variations in norms among people within a particular culture also influence involvement.

The majority of more detailed, controlled investigations of adult-child interaction have studied the completion of well-defined tasks with clear endpoints. In these experimental situations, the dyads are typically presented with a task set by the experimenter (e.g. Gonzalez, 1996; Rogoff et. al, 1993; Nilholm & Saljo, 1996). Most of these tasks have been easy for the adults to perform and to break into simpler components for children to complete. Rather little consideration has been given to more complex learning or to situations in which children are unwilling or unable to complete the tasks. Likewise, there has been little analysis of the context of the activity, even though the quality of the interaction is likely to be influenced by the adults' perceptions of the nature of their role and of the task (Paradise, 1996; Wertsch, Minick, & Arns, 1984).

The context in which an activity takes place may be considered at a number of levels. Aspects of context may be considered as variables influencing task performance (e.g. Ceci & Bronfenbrenner, 1985; Nilholm & Saljo, 1996). Alternatively, contextual information, in the form of descriptions of cultural conventions and practices, may be used as a means of assisting in the interpretation of interactions between adults and children (Greenfield, 1984; Rogoff, 1990). This work indicates that adults' perceptions of their part in helping children to learn influences the quality of interactions (Levin & Korat, 1997; Rogoff, 1990; Rogoff et al, 1993; Wertsch, Minick & Arns, 1984). The performance of most activities offers a variety of potential meanings and interpretations, and the process of interaction involves a negotiation of shared context (Goodnow, 1990; Nilholm & Saljo, 1996; Wertsch et al, 1984).

In educational contexts, an important aspect of the teacher's work is to organise and structure activity for children so as to promote their learning. Teachers are faced with a complex task of structuring the learning situation for pupils. Structuring begins with setting up a curriculum and planning the teaching activities and continues as those activities unfold. It may be particularly challenging when pupils encounter difficulties in learning or when competing theories suggest very different teaching methods.

The teaching of literacy presents particular challenges and has been the subject of intense debate for many years. Competing theories suggest radically different teaching methods. Some theories of reading development are based on a view that there is a logical progression, starting with the individual letters and letter sounds, then moving to simple, phonically regular words before combining words into sentences and then into longer texts. Psycholinguistic theories, on the other hand, have encouraged a 'top down' approach, in which reading as seen as essentially a search for meaning, and individual letter sounds and words are learned in the context of reading longer texts, right from the start. The different epistemologies tend to be associated with different theories of learning, the bottom up approach being more behavioural and the top down approach being more constructivist (see Stanovich, 1994 for a discussion).

In line with these different epistemologies, there are a variety of approaches to the teaching of reading in the classroom. Children who do not make satisfactory progress may be offered individual tuition. The type of support offered during individual tuition is also quite varied. Some teachers offer very structured, phonic teaching, while others offer a mixture of phonics and text reading. Literacy teaching for pupils requiring additional support in secondary school also reflects these differences.

The contrasting pedagogical contexts offer an opportunity to explore the teachers' structuring of the teaching context and how it relates to the activities offered to the children. Two empirical studies will be reported. The first is an investigation of individual tuition, which has already been reported in some detail and will therefore only be outlined here. The analysis led to the construction of a model of participation, which will be presented to enable comparison with the second study, which is an investigation of literacy teaching in a small group. The aim of the comparison is to explore the participation of the teachers and pupils in the small group and dyadic situations.

## INDIVIDUAL LITERACY TUITION

The first study investigated the structuring of activity by teachers providing individual tuition to children experiencing difficulty learning to read. By comparing teachers engaged in different programmes, links between the programmes, the teachers' perceptions of the programme goals and the activities were drawn out. The interested reader is refered to Ireson (1997, 2000) for more detailed accounts of this research, which will be outlined here. A distinctive feature of the research is that information on teachers' views and perspectives, mainly from interviews, is utilised alongside observation of teaching. This provides a rich data set allowing connections to be made between teachers' interpretations and meanings, the activities and methods they use and the participation of children in those activities.

### Method

Five teachers providing individual tutoring for primary school children participated in the study. They were selected to represent a variety of methods for teaching early literacy. All five were experienced teachers specialised in literacy teaching, but the training they had undertaken was diverse, ranging from structured phonic programmes to Reading Recovery, a programme that emphasises working with text.

Each teacher was asked to select children aged 6-7 years old to form the focus of the research. Initial interviews were held with each teacher. They were asked to explain the procedures leading up to the children's referral for help with reading and the initial assessments of the children. The teachers were then asked to describe the way they generally worked with the children and this lead to a discussion about one or two children who would form the focus of the subsequent research. These interviews were tape-recorded. A time was arranged for the researcher to observe the teacher working with the children. During these sessions, the researcher made field notes covering the activity structure of the sessions and the emphasis of the teaching. The teacher was asked to provide copies of the records of each child's programme. Finally, the teachers were asked if they would be willing to have one teaching session with each child video recorded.

## Analysis

The interviews were transcribed and coded into broad categories encompassing the main topics, which were the assessment of the children and planning and structuring teaching. Observation notes of teaching sessions were written up and the video recordings were transcribed. As the teaching activities were the focus of the analysis, the video recordings were transcribed in sufficient detail to give information about the activities and discourse, but without intonation or detail of non-verbal communication.

The analysis of the interviews revealed two types of structuring that underpinned teaching, an activity structure and a curriculum structure. Activity structures represent particular sequences or combinations of lesson activities and were identified from the teachers' descriptions of how they worked with the children. Some lessons were reported to contain a specific sequence of activities, for example, reading a familiar text, work on letter-sound correspondence, writing, reading a new text. Other lessons contained a combination of activities that were not ordered, such as sequencing, sounds, spelling and a game. In two programmes, teachers based their lessons around particular combinations of activities. Children therefore experienced different combinations of activities in the programmes.

Curriculum structures differed according to the programmes being followed. One programme followed a sequence of teaching points and teachers worked through this sequence in order. It was described as a basic list of phonics, ordered in a sequence of teaching points of increasing difficulty. Another also started with phonic work, but then moved on to word and text reading. The third framework was more fluid than the first two in that no firm curriculum or lesson structure was stated. Instead, a variety of literacy work was mentioned, which when grouped, fell into five categories. These were work on letter sounds, work on letter patterns, syllables, word endings and beginnings, developing a sight vocabulary, dictation, and work on listening to and reading from text.

These curriculum and activity structures formed part of the particular literacy training programmes, which placed differential emphasis on curriculum sequencing and the types and sequences of activities. Although the term 'structure' has been used in relation to both curriculum and activities, it was clear that there were differences in the degree and type of structure. Some were highly determined while others were much more fluid. Where the curriculum was strongly predetermined, it mediated the steps in teaching, through the sequence of teaching points.

The analysis of the observations and video recordings confirmed the teachers' accounts of their teaching activities, with each teacher including the type of activities they reported in the interviews. This provided some validation of the interview data. Further evidence of the validity of the teachers' accounts was provided from the observation that teachers spent little time explaining the activities to the children. They all moved briskly from one activity to the next, which indicated that the activities were already familiar to the children and formed part of the normal teaching routine.

The children's experiences of activities during the sessions varied according to the programme being followed, particularly in relation to the amount of phonic work and text reading activities. Their participation in learning was also influenced by the nature of the activities. For example all the programmes required the children to memorise, but some also encouraged them to use strategies in the context of text, for example, self-correcting or reading back to help work out a word. In this programme the role of the child was not only to memorise but also to use a range of strategies.

In an attempt to capture the dynamic nature of the relations between the pedagogic context and activity, a tentative model of the dynamic and fluid influences on dyadic interactions in an educational context was proposed (Ireson, 2000). The interaction between the child and the adult is at the heart of the model, which is displayed in Figure 1.

A network of beliefs and intentions influences adult participation. One part of this network, drawn on the left of the diagram, represents the teachers' role in supporting learning through adjusting motivational support and encouraging independence. The second part, drawn to the lower right, represents a set of relations between the teacher's perceptions of the principles underlying the teaching programme, an activity structure and a curriculum structure, or content teaching sequence. These are all aspects of structuring the curriculum content through learning activities. The separation of the activity structure and the content teaching sequence derives from the analysis of the interviews and observations with the literacy teachers, some of whom articulated clear activity structures for lessons while others described a content teaching sequence for the programme. In addition, teachers' goals for the programmes and more specific intentions for particular teaching sessions are related to the activities. The upper portion of the model represents the influences on the child's participation, although there is insufficient evidence from the research to do more than sketch these.

## Figure 1. Dynamic model of interaction in tutoring

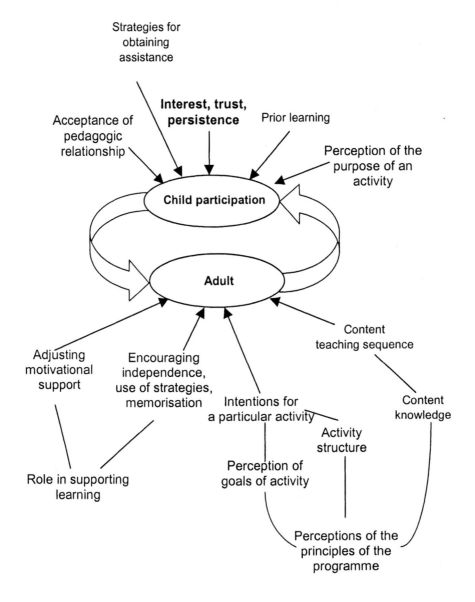

## SMALL GROUP TEACHING IN A SECONDARY SCHOOL

The aim of the second study was to explore the participation of the teachers and pupils in a small group setting and to consider the influence of the context on the interactions between the teacher and the pupils. A full account of the research is available in Marriott (1997).

The literacy programme was organised for pupils who entered the secondary school with low attainment in reading. Pupils with low reading attainment (two years below their chronological age) are likely to experience significant difficulties in secondary school (Clunies-Ross & Wimhurst, 1983). As learning becomes dependent on increasingly complex and efficient reading skills, many poorer readers find they cannot extract meaning from the texts used (Lunzer & Gardner, 1979, 1984). Poor literacy skills impact on pupils' learning across the curriculum and can have serious implications for pupils' subsequent academic success and employment opportunities. The teaching of reading skills and strategies by teachers in different subject areas at secondary level is very limited (Webster et al, 1996). Many secondary schools in England therefore run special programmes for pupils with difficulties in reading, withdrawing them from other lessons for small group instruction.

Literacy programmes in different schools are based on a variety of teaching approaches and resources. Pupils who enter secondary schools with poor literacy attainment frequently suffer from low self-concepts (Chapman et al, 1984). Teachers therefore need to offer sensitive support to these pupils. The particular programme forming the focus of this study was designed to provide an eclectic approach to the teaching of reading and to encourage pupils to become more independent as learners.

Although the pupils worked in a group, the design of the programme was such that each pupil had a programme of activities to work through individually. They were not working as a collaborative group. The teacher interacted with each child on an individual basis, offering help from time to time and marking completed work. In a sense the teacher was acting as a tutor to each pupil, sharing her time and attention between them. This provided an interesting extension of the research reported above. It raises a number of questions that have not been considered in previous work, concerning the nature of support needed for simultaneous tutoring and the participation of pupils in the group situation. As observed above, the teacher maintained strong control over the activity during one-to-one tutoring. Classroom research has also demonstrated that, in classes of lower ability, teachers tend to be directive and pupils are not encouraged to participate in discussion (Barr & Dreeben, 1991). We expected to find that the small group literacy instruction would be strongly teacher directed and that the pupils would not have much influence over the activity.

## Method

The research was undertaken in a mixed comprehensive school in a multi-racial, inner London borough. At the time, a major concern was the large number of pupils transferring to secondary school with poor literacy skills. The literacy programme was set up to provide help for these pupils. The participants in the study were two experienced teachers and eleven pupils, aged between 11 and 13 years. The pupils had been identified as needing additional help with literacy and were withdrawn from mainstream lessons each day.

The teacher with overall responsibility for the programme was interviewed to obtain information about the organisation of the programme, the special needs department's approach to teaching reading and the goals of the programme. Eight lessons were observed and recorded on videotape. Semi-structured interviews were conducted with the teachers after the first phase of data analysis, to obtain further information on their teaching goals.

Both teachers had over 20 years' teaching experience and extensive experience of working with pupils with special educational needs. They had worked together in the special needs department for 9 years. The pupils were all in Year 7, which meant that they were aged between 11 years 6 months and 12 years 6 months at the time of the observation, except for one pupil, U, who was 13. Most of these pupils had started the programme with reading ages below 7 years 6 months and five had statements of special educational need. One pupil had problems with attendance at school and another had received very little schooling before arriving in Britain two years previously. Five spoke English as an additional language. All the pupils had been following the reading programme for several months before the observations. They entered the programme in the autumn term and were observed the following May.

## Procedures

The aim of the initial interview with the teacher in charge of the programme was to obtain information about the reasons for choosing the programme, its objectives and organisation. The interview was semi-structured, allowing the researcher to follow up and ask for additional information where it was thought to be of interest

Eight lessons were observed and recorded, 4 for the entire 90 minutes of the lesson and 4 for part of the lesson. The camera was mounted on a tripod next to the table where the teacher was sitting for much of the time. As the focus of the observation was the verbal and non-verbal interactions between the teacher and the pupils, the camera focussed on the teacher when she moved around the classroom. An integral microphone enabled most of the verbal interactions to be recorded. Occasional field notes were taken to supplement the recordings, these included details of the worksheets or books pupils were working on and descriptions of the teaching room.

After the first stage of the data analysis had been completed, teachers were shown the summary of information compiled by the researcher from the initial interview and course documentation and were asked to indicate any inaccuracies or amendments. A short discussion, focussing on their teaching goals, was audio taped.

## ANALYSIS

### Initial Interviews

The interview with the special needs co-ordinator was transcribed and analysed in conjunction with the documentation about the literacy programme, produced by the department. The transcription was coded into broad categories corresponding to the main issues discussed. Statements relating to a particular issue were brought together and overlapping categories were collated and rephrased.

This analysis revealed that teaching goals were articulated for three main areas: language and literacy learning; organisational strategies; and developing motivation. The language and literacy goals included addressing pupils' individual needs in relation to reading, particularly reading for meaning; improving decoding skills; and developing spoken as well as written language. Organisational goals included developing independent learning, organisational skills, and regulating their own learning. Motivational goals included improving the pupils' self-confidence, self-esteem and motivation. It appeared that the affective goals were considered by the teacher to be facets of literacy teaching, which were integral to learning. For them, the teaching of reading involved addressing affective aspects of learning at the same time. They recognised that being a poor reader in secondary school could affect pupils' self-esteem. Both teachers' beliefs about teaching reading reflected a commitment to making reading and learning to read enjoyable. The overall aim of the programme was to "...create enjoyable and purposeful learning experiences; to help pupils become enthusiastic and effective readers..."

The programme was described as having an 'eclectic approach', based on each pupil's needs and incorporating several literacy goals. It included a mixture of phonics, whole word approaches, language experience, multi-sensory work, discussion, listening to taped stories, writing and using word processing and other computer based programmes. The teachers emphasised the interest level of the materials in the programme as a main reason for selection.

The organisation and structure of the programmes was designed to promote pupils' self-regulation of learning and the development of appropriate learning strategies. Pupils started at different stages in the programme, which depended on their performance in standardised reading tests. They were encouraged to develop organisational skills by keeping their work in order, collecting materials they needed and checking their own work, discussing it with a teacher and correcting it before going on to the next task. Teachers completed checklists recording the completion of activities but this was carried out in conjunction with the pupils so they knew what was expected of them and what they had achieved. During the post recording interviews, the three types of teaching goal (language and literacy, motivational and organisational) were presented to the teachers for comment. The teachers confirmed the three types of goal and their view of the learning and motivational goals as being integrated in their teaching.

## Lesson Observation and Recordings

The lesson recordings were first viewed in their entirety, at normal speed. During viewing, notes were taken on tape and sound quality; activities undertaken by each pupil and their locations; rough assessments of time on task; the spread of teacher attention and movement around the room. The recordings were viewed again, this time using the fast forward and rewind facilities. These initial runs revealed that the lessons consisted of three constituent segments, a beginning, middle and end. At the beginning of each lesson the pupils collected their folders and there were brief discussions about what they needed to do next. During the middle part of the lesson, some pupils moved away from the teacher to work independently, while others sat near her. This part of the lesson consisted mainly of dyadic interactions between the teacher and individual pupils. When this interaction had been completed, the pupils worked independently while the teacher interacted with other pupils. Occasionally the teacher walked around the room, visiting pupils to monitor their work or responding to requests for help. Certain pupils asked for help more frequently than others and the teacher monitored some pupils more actively than others. Those who sat nearest to the teacher were involved in more frequent interactions with her. The end of the lesson, which was often signalled by the school's 5 minute warning buzzer, consisted of pupils putting their work away, getting their merits from the teacher and some social chat as they waited for the final buzzer marking the end of the lesson.

Portions of the recordings were selected for transcription. Initially, this selection aimed to identify examples of support provided by the teacher. As the analysis unfolded, it became apparent that one of these extracts provided a good illustration of the way that individual differences between pupils affected the learning context and influenced their interactions with the teacher.

## Dyadic Interactions

Each pupil worked through the programme independently of the other pupils in the group. This way of working lead to a characteristic pattern of interaction during each session. For the most part, the teacher interacted with one child at a time, sometimes switching her attention between two pupils. An analysis of one extract, shown in Figure 2, illustrates this general pattern.

**Figure 2.** Sequence of interactions between the teacher, K, and three pupils (R, A and U), illustrating the dyadic nature of interaction.

R asks for help finding the next worksheets

K helps R

K checks that Andrew is clear about what he is to do

R asks for help with the worksheet

K helps R

K monitors A's work and corrects him, shows him how to proceed

K checks with U and updates her record of his work

A asks for help

K helps A

U brings his work to K for marking

K marks the work, points out errors, praises correct work

U returns to his seat to do the next piece of work

K goes over A's work with him, explains what he has to do next

R sits down next to K, asks for help

K finishes marking A's work

K helps R

K turns to A and helps him complete his worksheet

U approaches K, sits next to her and places his worksheet on the table between them

K marks his work

R asks for help

K asks her to wait, finishes updating her record of U's work

K helps R

K marks some work while listening to R

A asks for help with a spelling

K helps A

R asks for help

K helps R

A asks for help with a spelling

K helps

Karen was working with a group of four children, Rebecca, Elmas, Umit and Andrew. Elmas was in the reading corner, listening to a story on the tape recorder and following the story in the book. Umit was working alone on a table at the back of the room. Karen was sitting at a table with Andrew on her right. She had the folder with all the pupils' work records open in front of her. Rebecca was standing next to Karen.

From this extract we see that the session takes the form of a series of dyadic interactions between the teacher and each pupil in turn. The teacher provided individual help to each of the pupils as they worked through the programme. She monitored each pupil's work and responded to requests for help.

## Pupil Participation in the Activity

An important goal of this programme was for pupils to take responsibility for their learning and to organise their work. Teachers wanted to hand over responsibility to pupils and communicated this in a variety of ways, both verbally and non-verbally. They indicated their perception of the support as a joint activity, for example, frequently using the pronoun 'we' to establish the pupil's part in the activity and moving work-sheets into the space between themselves and the pupil.

At the beginning of each lesson, the pupils sat around the table with the teacher, sorting out their work for that lesson. Some pupils needed help to get started, while others started by themselves. The teachers supported by helping to identify the next task and checking that the pupils understood what they had to do. Umit needed little support at this stage, rarely consulting the teacher about which activity to do next. Rebecca, on the other hand, was less inclined to get started.

K: (to R) What you could do is get the first four phonic worksheets in Level 5
R: (walks over to the folders) Miss, where is it?
K: In the purple folders
R: There's two
K: Yes . . . there are quite a lot . . . just take one folder and find out if number one is in there and if it is, take the first four sheets out of there
R: It says sheet twelve
K: Right, take the other folder then and take the first four out of there
   Leans over towards Andrew Are you alright . . . you know what you're doing there?

Karen initially expected Rebecca to be able to find the worksheets herself, but when Rebecca asked for more support, she provided additional directions to help her. This was characteristic of Rebecca, who frequently asked Karen for help and generally received support in response to her requests. Andrew was less inclined to ask for help. Karen monitored his progress during the lesson, intervening when she judged he needed help completing a task. Like Andrew, Umit took responsibility for organising his work and his requests for support were generally related to the content of the activity rather than the organisation of the programme.

Some pupils wanted more help than the teachers judged appropriate for their development and used a range of tactics to obtain this. In the extract above, Karen indicated that she thought Rebecca was capable of working more independently, although she signalled this indirectly, for example by turning her attention away. Elmas was particularly skilled in obtaining and directing the teacher's support. During a lesson in which she was making a cut out model relating to a book she had been reading Elmas employed a variety of tactics to obtain Karen's assistance. These included direct requests, specific questions about the task, expressions of despair, playing with her model when Karen left her to work independently, placing her model in Karen's line of vision, shifting in her seat and looking at her watch. It is not clear whether Elmas wanted a higher level of support because she found the activity difficult or for some other reason. Whatever the reason, she successfully engaged Karen in the task and obtained a high level of assistance in completing it.

The interaction was necessarily asymmetrical, given the cultural context in which it was situated. The teachers had the knowledge about reading and how to support the pupils in their learning. Crucially though, the pupils had knowledge about their own needs in relation to completing each task and the teacher needed this information to enable them to offer effective support.

## Structuring the Learning Context

During the process of analysis, it became clear that the joint problem solving events that were a prominent feature of the lessons could not be understood in isolation from the cultural setting in which they took place. The structuring of this setting was an active, on-going process.

A framework for this structuring had been put in place during the selection and establishment of the teaching programme. The particular scheme chosen for use in the school was consonant with the teachers' stated aim of making the learning process enjoyable and helping pupils to become enthusiastic and effective readers. In addition, during the implementation of the programme in the classroom, further structuring was evident in the design of the teaching room, the ways of organising progress through the programme and through the pedagogic relationship.

The teaching room was designed to promote the goals of the programme. Learning materials were accessible and supported the pupils' independent organisation of their own learning. The lay-out of the room offered pupils a choice of literacy activities and the choice of working with others or independently, encouraging them to take an active part in structuring their own learning. In addition, wall displays of pupils' work affirmed the importance of the work they were doing and gave them an audience for their writing.

An important element structuring the teaching context was the way in which progress though the programme had been organised. The programme had been set up and resourced to enable the pupils to take on some responsibility for organising and monitoring their own learning. The programme enabled them to work out what they should be doing next, to see each task in the context of the whole programme and to monitor their progress. Pupils frequently made reference to the progress they had made through the programme and this appeared to be a key motivating factor. They appeared to have accepted the goals of the programme, including their own part in correcting their work and doing work with understanding. There was no evidence of copying or attempting to get others to do their work.

Underlying conceptions of motivation also influenced the teaching context. Merits for effort and good work were awarded at the end of each lesson and fun activities such as model making were included at the end of each section of work, although these seemed to be more important for some pupils than for others. Teachers had also designed other activities to enhance motivation, such as listening to tape recorded stories and computer-based activities. In addition, pupils were given some choice and control over the order in which they completed tasks. The degree of independence allowed by the teacher varied from child to child.

Another key element of the teaching context was the pedagogic relationship, which had been established at the beginning of the programme and was constantly reinforced and monitored during the observed teacher-pupil interactions. The framework for this relationship was strongly rooted in the ethos of the department and the school as stated in the school policy on Special Educational Needs and in the interview data. It encompassed both organisational aspects and also appropriate areas of negotiation, appropriate levels of task engagement, appropriate ways of communicating with each other and the availability of teacher support.

A high level of pupil acceptance of this pedagogic relationship was observed and the importance of this should not be underestimated. Many of the pupils had presented with challenging or off-task behaviour in the mainstream classrooms. In the literacy group there was evidence that the pupils had committed to the programme and believed that progress through the programme was positive for them.

## DISCUSSION

The aim of these two studies was to explore aspects of context that influence the structuring of activity between adults and children in educational settings. The strategy of including teachers and children from contrasting literacy training programmes has highlighted teachers' beliefs and intentions, activity structures and participants' interpretations of activities as potentially significant influences on interaction. In addition the group teaching highlights the structuring of the teaching context and the part played by the pupils in this process.

In the model presented above, the participation of an adult with a pupil in a dyadic interaction is seen as being influenced by a network of contextual factors, including the teachers' beliefs and intentions. One part of this network is a set of relations between the teaching activities and the principles underlying particular teaching programmes. The other part is a set of relations between the teacher's role in controlling the activity, including motivational aspects, and the pupil's role in learning. The findings will be discussed in relation to this model.

In both the individual and small group contexts there is a clear link between the activity structures and the principles underlying the programmes. In each case, the types of activity were based on the pedagogic principles incorporated in the respective programme and were articulated by the teachers in the course of the interviews. For individual tuition, these ranged from the principle of multi-sensory teaching to the principle that each teaching session should bring together five elements employed by children when reading. In the small group context, activities reflected the principles of fostering enjoyment and self-regulated learning. The mix of activities provided was explicitly designed to foster the enjoyment of reading. In addition, the small group context illustrates a link between the principles and the teacher's role in supporting learning, with the element of choice and pupil responsibility flowing from the principle of developing pupil self regulation.

Certain functions were distributed to the resources of particular programmes, which may be seen as offering supports to the pedagogic relationship, as suggested by Cole & Engstrom (1993). They discuss the idea of distributed cognition in relation to reading acquisition and argue that 'the requisite cognitive processes are distributed among teacher, pupil, other students, and the cultural artifacts which they co-ordinate in the activity called teaching/learning to read' (1993, p.23). The cultural artifacts include resources used as mediational means in teaching and the division of work between the teacher and the student. This distribution is most clearly seen in the group situation and is best illustrated by comparing the individual and group teaching activities. When teaching individually, the teachers presented each activity to the pupils directly and gave a great deal of thought to the choice of activities, even when they were working through a structured programme. In the group context, much of this work was distributed through the structuring of the programme and the resources such as worksheets, computer based activities and books, and through the responsibility given to the pupils for the organisation of their work. This distribution draws attention to the part played by the programme, which in this case carried the content knowledge and activity structure. The developers of the programme had done much of the work of transforming the principles of the programme into a content sequence and a set of activities. It is clear from our analysis that these do not exist in a capsule of activity but are connected with the wider set of cultural beliefs about appropriate methods and contexts for literacy teaching.

Each of the literacy programmes may be viewed as establishing a particular cultural context for learning to read. Each had a set of principles guiding and organising the pedagogical context and a set of practices which teachers and pupils were expected to follow. Two of the individual programmes required teachers to undergo a period of intensive training, with frequent observation of their work. They were inducted into a set of practices, the cultural tools of the programme were passed on to them through the training programmes together with mediational means in the form of assessments, resources and activities for teaching and learning. In the secondary school the teachers themselves were more involved in constructing the context, through selecting and setting up the programme and adapting it to meet the needs of their pupils. Although the aim of all the teachers was to help children become literate, their beliefs about the literacy curriculum and the nature of children's difficulties differed markedly and influenced the pedagogical context provided.

Although there are clear advantages in using a commercial scheme, there are also some potential drawbacks. In particular, if teachers are not informed about the theoretical basis and the principles underlying such schemes, their role may become technical or administrative. The secondary teachers in our study were highly experienced in literacy teaching, and were in a strong position to adapt the programme to meet the needs of their pupils. It is possible to envisage a situation in which teachers relinquish the content knowledge and the transformational work of developing the learning activities. This is more likely to occur when pressures mount to demonstrate effective performance. It could lead to teachers increasingly becoming technicians, following ready made solutions, rather than architects, designing and building their own teaching to meet the needs of their pupils. There is a delicate balance to maintain in the distribution of knowledge between the teachers and the established resources and materials.

The present findings revealed a tension between two elements of the teachers' role in supporting learning, namely encouraging independence and adjusting motivational support. In general, pupils appeared motivated to start work but some were reluctant to take responsibility for organising their learning. For some pupils, feeling comfortable was a prerequisite for starting working at all and this created a tension with the teachers' goal that they should take responsibility for their work. What emerged was a subtle combination of physical, cognitive and emotional support. The teachers clearly thought that some pupils were capable of greater independence, and at times they resisted the pupils' requests for help. They were also aware that some children were not inclined to ask for help, even when needed, and so they checked that certain pupils were not working on the wrong tasks, or started an activity without understanding the requirements. Providing support was not simply a matter of adjusting the cognitive demands of the task, it was also a matter of judging the emotional and motivational aspects of learning. The analysis highlighted the sensitive nature of support for each of the pupils as they worked through the programme.

Learners play an active role in structuring activities, particularly when tasks are open-ended (Elbers, 1996; Ireson & Blay, 1999) or when learners approach tutors for assistance (Fox, 1993). Individual literacy teaching was highly teacher directed and pupils had limited opportunity to influence the course of activities. The directive nature of the teaching may reflect beliefs about appropriate pedagogies for low attaining pupils, which tend to be more structured (Barr & Dreeben, 1991). Some pupils in the literacy group, however, appeared to want more support and reassurance and they used a variety of strategies to obtain assistance from the teacher. Others worked quite independently. It is not clear whether this was because the tasks were cognitively demanding, or whether more scaffolding of the regulative aspects of the work was needed. The teachers did not appear to give much explicit instruction to help pupils improve their self-regulation and organisation, but this may have formed part of the earlier stages of the programme.

In educational settings, an important aspect of teachers' work is to structure activity for children so as to promote their learning. This structuring takes places within a cultural setting, which acts as an influence on teachers' views of appropriate activities and teaching goals. The structuring of activity also influences the nature of children's participation and their opportunities for learning. It is a more complex process in naturalistic teaching contexts than in experimental settings and this complexity calls for further examination. The model presented here offers a tool for this exploration.

## ACKNOWLEDGEMENTS

The research was supported by a grant from the Institute of Education Research Fund. The author would like to acknowledge the contribution of Jane Marriott, who collected and analysed the data for the second study as part of her MA dissertation. The author would also like to thank all the teachers and pupils for their participation in the project.

## REFERENCES

Barr, R. & Dreeben, R. (1991). Grouping students for reading instruction. In Barr, R., Kamil, M., Mosenthal, P. & Pearson, PD (Eds.) *Handbook of Reading Research* Vol. 2, pp. 885-910. New York: Longman.

Bruner, J. S. (1983). *Child's Talk: Learning to Use Language.* New York: Norton.

Ceci, S.J. & Bronfenbrenner, U. (1985). Don't forget to take the cupcakes out of the oven: strategic time-monitoring, prospective memory and context. *Child development, 56,*175-190.

Chapman, J., Silva, P. A. & Williams, S. M. (1984). Academic self concept: some developmental and emotional correlates in nine-year old children *British journal of educational psychology,* 54, 284-92.

Clunies-Ross, L. & Wimhurst, S. (1983). *The Right Balance: Provision for Slow Learners in Secondary Schools.* London: NFER Nelson.

Cole, M. & Engstrom, Y. (1993). A cultural-historical approach to distributed cognition, In Salomon, G. (Ed) *Distributed Cognitions.* Cambridge: Cambridge University Press.

Elbers, E. (1996) Cooperation and social context in adult-child interaction *Learning and Instruction, 6(4),* 281-286.

Fox, B. (1993). *The Human Tutorial Dialogue Project: Issues in the Design of Instructional Systems* London: Lawrence Erlbaum Associates.

Gonzalez, M.-M. (1996). Tasks and activities: a parent-child interaction analysis. *Learning and Instruction, 6(4),* 287-306.

Goodnow, J. J. (1990). The socialization of cognition: what's involved? In Stigler, J., Schweder, R. & Herdt, G. (eds) *Cultural Psychology* (pp. 259-286) Chicago: University of Chicago Press.

Greenfield, P. (1984). A theory of the teacher in the learning activities of everyday life. In B. Rogoff & J. Lave (Eds.), *Everyday Cognition* (pp.117-138) London: Harvard University Press.

Ireson, J. (1997). Cultural contexts for learning to read: a case of conflicting pedagogies? *Paper presented at an international symposium Integrating research and practice in literacy,* Institute of Education, University of London, December 1997.

Ireson, J. & Blay, J. (1999). Constructing activity: participation by adults and children, *Learning and Instruction, 9,* 19-36.

Ireson, J. (2000) Activity and interaction in pedagogical contexts: towards a model of tutoring. In Cowie, H., van der Aalsvoort, G. & Mercer, N. (Eds.) *Advances in Learning and Instruction. Social Interaction in Learning and Instruction.* London: Elsevier Science.

Levin, I & Korat, O. (1997). Social effects on maternal role in child's literacy: maternal beliefs and interaction with her child *Paper presented at an international symposium 'Integrating research and practice in literacy',* Institute of Education, University of London, December 1997.

Lunzer, E. A. & Gardner, K. (Eds.) (1979). *The Effective Use of Reading.* London: Heinemann Educational.

Lunzer, E. A. & Gardner, K. (1984). *Learning from the Written Word.* Edinburgh: Oliver & Boyd

Nilholm, C. & Saljo, R. (1996). Co-action, situation definition and socio-cultural experience: an empirical study of problem solving in mother-child interaction. *Learning and Instruction, 6(4),* 325-344.

Marriott, J. (1997) An investigation of small group literacy teaching in year 7. Unpublished Masters dissertation, Institute of Education, University of London.

Paradise, R. (1996). Passivity or tacit collaboration: Mazahua interaction in cultural context *Learning and Instruction, 6, 4,* 379-390.

Rogoff, B. (1990). *Apprenticeship in Thinking.* Oxford: Oxford University Press.

Rogoff, B., Mistry, J., Goncu, A., & Mosier, C. (1993). Guided participation in cultural activity by toddlers and caregivers. *Monographs of the Society for Research in Child Development, 58(8).*

Stanovich, K. (1994). Constructivism in reading education *The journal of special education, 28, 3,* 259-274.

Vygotsky, L. (1978). *Mind in Society* Cambridge: Harvard University Press.

Webster, A., Beveridge, M. & Reed, M. (1996) *Managing the Literacy Curriculum.* London: Routledge.

Wertsch, J. V., Minick, N., & Arns, F. J. (1984). The Creation of Context in Joint Problem Solving. In B. Rogoff & J. Lave (Eds.) *Everyday Cognition: Its Development in Social Context (pp. 151- 171).* London: Harvard University Press.

Wood, D., Bruner, J. S., & Ross, G. (1976). The role of tutoring in problem solving. *Journal of Child Psychology and Psychiatry, 17,* 98-100.

# Chapter 6

# THE ROLE OF LITERACY AND KNOWLEDGE IN THE PURSUIT OF POPULAR EMPOWERMENT[*]

## *Thomas Sticht*
Consultant on Adult Education

## *Carolyn Huie Hofstetter*
Graduate School of Education
University of California, Berkeley

## *C. Richard Hofstetter*
Department of Political Science
San Diego State University

## ABSTRACT

The importance of content knowledge and reading practices to the achievement of power was studied with adults. Relationships were examined among general, "mainstream" society knowledge, domain specific political knowledge, the amount of reading engaged in and three indicators of power, occupation, income and political activity. Care was taken to ensure that extraneous cognitive processing variance did not influence the results by using simple checklists of declarative knowledge that required listeners, on the telephone, to simply say "yes" if they thought they recognized a given factual stimulus. The results of two studies indicated that there were positive relationships among amount

[*] A related, but much shorter, study was published by the authors in Communication Research, Vol. 26, no. 1, (February, 1999), pp. 55-80.. Support for this research was provided in part by the Williain and Flora Hewlett Foundation; the Lila Wallace Reader's Digest fund, the Department of Political Science, San Diego State University; and the Spencer Foundation. The opinions expressed are solely those of the authors, and no official endorsement by their institutional affiliations should be inferred.

of content knowledge, reading and power, even when age, education and ethnicity were held constant. The latter is important because it indicates that regardless of one's cultural background, possession of large "banks" of declarative knowledge about the "mainstream" culture of the United States is associated with achieving and manifesting power.

In democratic nations that subscribe to meritocratic principles, it is generally assumed that "knowledge is power," and that, to a large extent, knowledge is based on literacy (Lerner, 1958). The traditional view has been that, as a general rule, the more literate a person is, the more knowledgeable the person will be and the more likely he or she is to gain access to socially privileged positions or to gain a status that carries with it the capacity for influencing the thoughts and behaviors of others in direct or indirect ways, that is, power (Lipset, 1960; Verba & Nie, 1972; Wolfinger & Rosenstone, 1980).

Galtung (1964) stratified citizens on a center-periphery dimension according to socially prescribed values that included enlightenment. Those closer to the center of society were more literate, and enjoyed all the benefits of society including political power, to a much greater extent that those on the periphery.

In his studies of the manner in which dominant classes maintain their power, Freire (1970) acknowledged the role of knowledge in establishing and maintaining these power relationships. He argued against the "banking" concept of education in which the culture of the dominant classes is transmitted to the oppressed by requiring the latter to learn the facts, concepts, famous personalities, etc. of the dominant classes.

More recent discussions of knowledge, literacy and power, have carried on the tradition of Freire (1970) and Foucault (1980) and provided critical analyses of how some members of a society enjoy socially privileged positions that carry with it the capacity for influencing the thoughts and behaviors of others. In these analyses, knowledge and power have been discussed in terms of how language, that is, knowledge expressible in spoken or written words, may be used to contribute to the formation of unequal relations of power amongst social groups, to the point of permitting some groups to dominate or oppress others (Fairclough, 1989; Gee, 1996; Street, 1995).

Hirsch (1987; 1996), too, has underscored the importance of knowledge in the achievement of power in the United States. He acknowledges the importance of language and literacy in creating unequal power relations. But whereas the critical analysts aim to bring about social justice through the reformation of the social order, including the reform of education to broaden the concept of what is considered "mainstream" and to more broadly represent the cultural knowledge of the oppressed, Hirsch aims to maintain the social order by bringing more of the oppressed into the existing "mainstream" culture. He argues that one way to overcome the inequalities that language use produces is for the schools to teach all children a large body of declarative knowledge facts, names, concepts, and so forth, that will help them become broadly knowledgeable, linguistically facile, literate and productive adults who can continue to learn independently by reading.

**Knowledge and Reading**

Whether meritocratic capitalists or egalitarian socialists, all of the researchers and analysts mentioned above acknowledge the importance of literacy, especially reading, as a means of acquiring knowledge. Indeed, the fact that they all chose to write books indicates that they expected others to learn what they think by reading.

Significantly, the field of reading research has also revealed the importance of knowledge in acquiring reading ability. Bruer (1993, pp. 173-213) indicates the importance of acquiring an extensive and richly interwoven knowledge "bank" of various cognitive and metacognitive strategies for improving reading and learning from text, of vocabulary knowledge, background knowledge about the world around us, knowledge about topics for creating "gists," domain-specific knowledge for understanding texts in special areas of content, and knowledge of literary forms and genres to aid in understanding special forms of texts.

Since Bruer's review, the role of knowledge in reading comprehension and learning from text has been extensively examined in a special issue of the Educational Psychologist. In her introduction to the special issue, Alexander (1996) notes that "One of the most powerful and consistent findings to emerge from the research in cognitive psychology over the past several decades is the realization that what knowledge learners possess is a powerful force in what information they attend to..., how that information is perceived..., what learners judge to be relevant or important..., and what they understand and remember.... Truly, one's knowledge base is a scaffold that supports the construction of all future learning...." (p. 89).

## HOW DO PEOPLE BECOME HIGHLY LITERATE?

Several lines of research have converged to suggest that people become highly knowledgeable and highly literate largely by engaging in numerous literacy practices, such as reading books, magazines, newspapers, and so forth (Krashen, 1993; Reder, 1994; Kaplan & Venezky, 1994). A review of the major assessments of adult literacy in the United States revealed that, since 1937 it has repeatedly been found that for adults, as years of education increases there are corresponding increases in both the number of literacy practices in which adults engage and the amount of knowledge and skill displayed in the assessments (Sticht & Armstrong, 1994; Smith, 1996, p. 196).

Apparently, one of the major things that education does is lead children to read more and more in a greater diversity of materials over the school years, both in and out of school. This has the effect of developing both more knowledge and more skill (e.g., automaticity of word recognition), and with more knowledge and skill people may feel more comfortable in reading in different types of materials over their lives. This means that, among other things, education, engagement in reading practices and skill development form a sort of "triple helix" of cognitive activity that generates a growing body of knowledge and greater ability in reading.

Stanovich (1993) and associates have conducted research to explore how engagement in literacy practices by children and adults contributes to their declarative knowledge base. In this research, Stanovich and associates developed an innovative method for assessing declarative knowledge with checklists that reduce task demands to a simple "yes" or "no" judgment on the part of the reader. Performance on these checklists correlates significantly with a variety of literacy activities and cognitive assessments (Stanovich, 1993; Stanovich & Cunningham, 1993; Allen, Cipielewski, & Stanovich, 1992; West, Stanovich, & Mitchell, 1993).

From a causal perspective, the argument by Stanovich and associates is that those who read a lot acquire a large knowledge base containing the names of authors, magazines, and persons known for their contributions to film, theatre, music and other cultural activities, and a large vocabulary of words that are typically not encountered with high frequency in day-to-day oral communication nor on television or radio. The declarative knowledge base made-up of authors, magazines, famous people and vocabulary is an indicator of both the amount of reading in which individuals have engaged and of the cognitive outcomes of that reading in terms of the growth in the individual's declarative knowledge base.

The importance of the development of knowledge as both an outcome of and contributor to adult literacy was expressed in the definition of literacy that was adopted by the advisory panel of experts for the 1993 National Adult Literacy Survey (Kirsch, Jungeblut, Jenkins & Kolstad, 1993). The definition of literacy agreed to was "Using printed and written information to function in society, to achieve one's goals, and to develop one's knowledge and potential (italics added)."

This definition notes the important role that literacy plays in helping people develop their store of knowledge. In contrast, the role that one's prior store of knowledge plays in helping people use their literacy skills was also acknowledged by the advisory panel for the National Adult Literacy Survey in its acceptance of the definitions of the three different literacy scales that were developed. These included prose literacy, the knowledge and skills needed to understand and use information from texts, document literacy, the knowledge and skills required to locate and use information contained in materials, and quantitative literacy, the knowledge and skills required to apply arithmetic operations embedded in printed materials (Kirsch, Jungeblut, Jenkins & Kolstad, 1993).

It should be recognized that "skills" are, themselves, forms of procedural knowledge. Skills may be regarded as procedural knowledge that is acquired along with declarative knowledge. From these definitions, it is clear that the advisory panel for the National Adult Literacy Survey understood that the use of printed and written information to accomplish tasks requires, as a prerequisite, prior knowledge and skills to make such use possible. In this sense, knowledge is both a prerequisite for and an outcome of the use of literacy.

## Knowledge and Power

Despite the acknowledged importance of declarative knowledge as a component of all literacy practices, a review of every large-scale assessment of adult literacy since 1917, both military and civilian, revealed that there has never been an attempt to determine the validity of the maxim, "knowledge is power" by identifying the contribution to power of the declarative knowledge component of literacy, separate from the many other demands of more or less complex cognitive tasks that introduce unknown process variance in the study of relationships among literacy and power (Sticht & Armstrong, 1994; Messick, 1989). The research reported here aimed at determining empirically the value of "banking" declarative knowledge of the "dominant" or "mainstream" society in the United States of the mid-1990's as a contributor to achieving power.

In the present study we view "power" as indicated by the ability to acquire socially valued ends. More specifically, in American society, this includes achievement of a higher status occupation and/or the ability to earn an average or higher level of income. These achievements empower the person in the mainstream society (Galtung, 1964). For instance, a person who has acquired the higher levels of knowledge needed to achieve the relatively high status occupation of university professor in a school of education can exercise power over undergraduate and graduate students as their teacher, and additional power can be exercised over peers by serving as a reviewer of manuscripts for professional journals such as this one.

Additionally, we explore the hypothesis that the more knowledgeable person is more likely to exercise the rights (power) of citizenship and to engage in political activities, such as voting, to advance his or her causes (Neuman, Just, & Crigler, 1992; Zaller, 1992).

Previous studies have confirmed relationships among literacy and the indicators of power outlined above, occupation, income and political activity, including voting (Kirsch, Jungeblut, Jenkins & Kolstad, 1993; Sticht & Armstrong, 1994; Kaplan & Venezky, 1994). However, in these studies of literacy, declarative knowledge (i.e., factual or content knowledge available to people for use through language) is confounded with information processing skills of a largely unknown admixture. For instance, the prose, document and quantitative literacy tasks of the National Adult Literacy Survey incorporated a number of "search and locate" and other cognitive skills that placed heavy demands on working memory. It is well established that working memory becomes increasingly less efficient with advanced age (Bernstein, Roy, Srull, & Wickens, 1988; Meyer, Marsiske, & Willis, 1993) so it is possible that the load on working memory contributed to the decline in performance observed for adults over the age of fifty (Kirsch, Jungeblut, Jenkins & Kolstad, 1993, p. 31). Because of this commingling of declarative knowledge and skills, it is not possible to use such studies to evaluate the role of content knowledge in empowering people.

## Theoretical Basis for the Present Research

The present research used telephone survey and checklist methodologies to study relationships of declarative knowledge to power. The general approach is based on a model of the human cognitive system that has been examined and validated as a heuristic model for thinking about human information processing in over thirty years of research (see the review by Healy & McNamara, 1996, p. 143). This model conceives of a human cognitive system that includes both a knowledge base in long term memory consisting largely, though not exclusively, of language-based declarative and procedural knowledge, and a working memory in which active information processing takes place using the knowledge from long term memory and information picked-up from the external world through a perceptual system. Generally speaking, highly literate individuals possess large bodies of knowledge and information processing capacity and efficiency in working memory to process information in complex graphic documents (Kyllonen & Christal, 1990).

In the present research, two studies were conducted that examined how declarative knowledge relates to power, while minimizing the effects of information processing efficiency and working memory. Both studies used the checklist methodology developed by Stanovich and associates to obtain information about adults' declarative knowledge (Stanovich, 1993; Stanovich & Cunningham, 1993; Allen, Cipielewski, & Stanovich, 1992; West, Stanovich, & Mitchell, 1993). Lists containing discrete items, such as names or single vocabulary words, that require only a yes/no decision for each item are particularly suitable for presentation by telephone because they do not overload working memory and introduce unknown task variance (Messick, 1989).

Study 1 looks at relationships among various demographic variables, engagement in reading and electronic media usage, general, "mainstream," or "dominant" cultural declarative knowledge, and two indicators of power, occupational status and income. Study 2 focuses on domain specific political knowledge and looks at relationships among demographic variables, newspaper reading and electronic media usage, political knowledge and three power indicators, household income, voting, and engagement in political activities.

## STUDY 1: GENERAL DECLARATIVE KNOWLEDGE AND POWER

In Study 1, subjects' declarative knowledge was assessed using shortened versions of the Stanovich checklists for declarative knowledge of famous authors, magazine titles, famous people, and vocabulary words (West, Stanovich, & Mitchell, 1993). It provided information about respondent's general declarative knowledge taken from samples of the knowledge of the "mainstream" or "dominant" society. Study 1 examines for the first time the relationships of declarative knowledge to two indicators of power, occupational status and income, when information processing demands, age, education, and ethnicity are held constant.

# METHOD

## Subjects

Data for this study were derived from telephone interviews with 538 adults residing in households that could be reached by listed or unlisted telephone in San Diego county, California. This included approximately 96 percent of all households. Sampling was conducted by using a random-digit-dialing procedure designed to reach households without numbers listed in the telephone directory, due to unlisted numbers or newly listed numbers not yet printed, as well as households listed (Dillman, 1978, pp. 232-281; Frey, 1989, pp. 79-116). Respondents who agreed to participate further and were willing to provide their name and address were mailed a written questionnaire as an alternative modality follow-up.

In the telephone interview, the subjects' mean length of residence in San Diego was 20.6 years (SD=15.5), mean educational level was 14.5 years (SD=2.6), mean age was 41.0 years (SD=16.0), mean total household income was $34, 340 (SD=$12,240).

The survey procedures yielded a sample that matched the 1990 U.S. Census data closely, with some notable exceptions. Table 1 shows statistics for the telephone and U. S. Census population for San Diego county. The telephone sample's gender, age, and income were similar to census distributions. Minorities were somewhat underrepresented and the telephone data were skewed upward in educational attainment, underrepresenting the lowest level of educational attainment and overrepresenting the highest level, in comparison to census data. However, as pointed out in the discussion section, while these deviations from the census data place limitations on the generalizations to be drawn from the study, they do not pose a serious threat to the validity of the findings. Moreover, no significant differences in findings emerged when analyses were weighted by education, ethnicity, and income to correct for discrepancies.

## Interview Procedures

Interviewing was conducted by university students trained for telephone interviewing for the project during the late spring and early summer, 1994. The training included methods for rapport building that set respondents at ease, enhanced interviewer sensitivity to language and cultural backgrounds when the speech patterns of respondents suggested such factors to the interviewers, and stimulated interviewer patience and encouragement in conducting the interview with respondents who spoke hesitantly (Warnick & Lininger, 1975184-202; Dillman, 197811-19). Interviewers included whites, African-Americans, Hispanics, and Asians, but as is true in nearly all survey research using random-digit-dial sampling of total populations, it was not possible to match the ethnicity of the interviewers with that of the respondents. Previous research has indicated that biases due to ethnicity in face-to-face interviews are greatly reduced in telephone interviews (Frey, 198964-65; Dillman, 197862-63).

Subjects were called between 430 p.m. and 930 p.m. weekdays and between 900 a.m. and 930 p.m. on weekends. Interviewers introduced the survey to the person who answered the telephone, gained informed consent, and asked to speak to the adult (18 years of age or older) who had "the most recent birthday" as a random method of selection among adults in the household (Frey, 1989 79-116). No substitutions were allowed so interviewers frequently were required to call the household back in order to complete an interview with the appropriate respondent. Up to four callbacks were made to households and a response rate of approximately 50 percent was attained. Due to resource constraints, interviews were conducted only in English, a procedure that eliminated no more than five percent of households but restricts our findings to English-speakers only.

The telephone interviews provided an oral presentation of information requiring the respondents to listen and respond from what they heard. Interviewers followed a protocol containing 63 questions, some with multiple items. About half of the questions concerned the assessment of knowledge. These questions were interspersed among other questions that were part of another on-going research project concerned with personal health and community issues. The interviews required a mean of 27.7 (SD= 7.6) minutes to complete.

## Instrumentation

To save time, four abbreviated versions of the checklists used by West, Stanovich and Mitchell (1993) were used in the telephone survey. The appendix presents the items used in the Author Recognition Test, the Magazine Recognition Test, the Cultural Knowledge Test and the Vocabulary Knowledge Test. Generally, items were chosen to represent mainstream cultural knowledge (some items came from the work of Hirsch (1987), though some names were chosen to reflect multicultural knowledge within the United States (e.g., Steve Biko, Rosa Parks). Five of the vocabulary items included words typically known by students in the 8th through 12th grades, and the rest are typically familiar to adults with some college education. The four declarative knowledge checklists used in the telephone survey are given in Appendix A, along with the interview question number, the question asked, the means, standard deviations, and numbers of adults responding to the particular item, and the percentage of adults in each of five knowledge levels that knew the item. In the actual interview, the foils were mixed randomly among the genuine items.

For each checklist, an adjusted percent correct score was calculated. The adjusted percent correct score for an individual was the proportion of correctly identified real names or words minus the proportion of foils incorrectly identified as real names or words. For instance, if a person said "yes" to 10 of the 17 names of famous people on the Cultural Knowledge Test and to 2 of the 6 foils, the person's score for the Cultural Knowledge Test was 25.5 (10/17 minus 2/6, or 58.8 minus 33.3). The correction for guessing prevented the subjects from simply responding "yes" to all items. This procedure followed the signal detection rationale given in West, Stanovich & Mitchell (1993, p. 38).

**Table 1. Comparison of the San Diego telephone samples in Studies 1 and 2 with the 1990 U. S. Census figures for San Diego County.**

| Variables a | Study 1 | Study 2 | Census | |
|---|---|---|---|---|
| | | | | |
| Household Income | | (482)b | (530) | |
| Under $10,000 | | 8.9 | 9.1 | 6.8 |
| $10,000-49,999 | 59.8 | 59.8 | 56.5 | |
| Over $50,000 | | 31.3 | 31.1 | 36.7 |
| | | | | |
| Age | | (519) | (623) | |
| 18-24 | | 15.4 | 15.2 | 17.8 |
| 25-64 | | 72.4 | 70.1 | 67.6 |
| 65+ | | 12.1 | 14.6 | 14.4 |
| | | | | |
| Gender | (530) | (632) | | |
| Male | | 48.1 | 49.7 | 50.9 |
| Female | 51.9 | 50.3 | 49.1 | |
| | | | | |
| Education | | (524) | (632) | |
| 0-12 | | 25.6 | 28.5 | 40.9 |
| 13-16 | | 53.6 | 55.5 | 50.3 |
| 17+ | | 20.8 | 16.0 | 8.8 |
| | | | | |
| Ethnicity c | | (527) | (621) | |
| White | | 72.5 | 76.3 | 65.6 |
| Latino | | 13.9 | 9.7 | 20.0 |
| Black | | 4.9 | 6.8 | 6.0 |
| Asian | | 5.3 | 5.2 | 7.5 |
| Other | | 3.4 | 2.1 | 0.0 |

a Numbers are percentages with the characteristics listed.

b Numbers in brackets are total numbers in samples with data for a given characteristic. N's vary due to missing data (non-response or refused to answer).

c Respondents were classified as "other" when responses did not permit clear classification into a major racial-ethnic category. All persons of "Latino, Mexican, or Spanish descent" were classified as "Latino" regardless of race.

Split-half, internal consistency (Spearman-Brown) reliabilities of the checklists ranged from .80 (Magazine Recognition Test) to .88 (Cultural Knowledge Test). To increase the reliability of the checklists as measures of the knowledge component of literacy, a Total Knowledge score was calculated from percentages based on all 50 actual and 24 foil names and words. The internal consistency reliability for Total Knowledge was .91. For a sub-set of 140 respondents who completed the checklists by telephone and then later by reading and responding to mailed-out copies of the same checklists, test-retest ("alternate modality" or stability) reliabilities were obtained as Total Knowledge score ($r=.80$), Author Recognition Test ($r=.71$), Magazine Recognition Test ($r=.67$), Cultural Knowledge Test ($r=.73$), and Vocabulary Knowledge Test ($r=.63$). Thus, strong evidence of reliability ($p<.05$), both in terms of internal consistency and test-retest, was present for each of the four scales and the Total Knowledge scale.

Engagement in media practices. Subjects were asked the number of times in an average week they engaged in various media practices such as reading for pleasure newspapers, books, and newsmagazines or reading job-related materials for work, watching television, listening to the radio, etc. Table A-5 in the Appendix shows the questions used to explore engagement in literacy and other media practices. For each respondent, a total literacy practices score was obtained as the average of questions 25a-k in Table A-5. The literacy practice variable is a composite indicator of "print exposure" used to relate average frequency of weekly reading of different materials for various purposes to demographic variables and the knowledge checklists.

Defining knowledge levels. To determine the relationships among variables in this study the primary method of data analysis consisted of determining the correlations among variables. However, while such analyses show the overall proportion of variance shared among different variables, they fail to reveal what sorts of variations may be occurring within smaller parts of the distributions of scores. To overcome these limitations in the present study, the results of knowledge checklists used in the telephone survey were divided into five levels of declarative knowledge using Total Knowledge scores.

To obtain the five levels of knowledge, the Total Knowledge score was used to divide the sample into five groups or levels using the mean (45 adjusted percent correct) and the standard deviation (SD, 25 adjusted percent correct) for the total sample. Knowledge levels were defined in adjusted percent correct scores from low to high proficiency asLevel 1= scores at -1.0 SD below the mean or lower (0-20 adjusted percent correct), Level 2 = scores between -.5 to -.1.0 SD (21-32 adjusted percent correct), Level 3 = scores between - .5 SD (35-58 adjusted percent correct), Level 4 = scores between +.5 to +1.0 SD (59-70 adjusted percent correct), and Level 5 = scores from +1.0 SD and above (71-100 adjusted percent correct).

The five knowledge levels are used in presenting the findings for various demographic and media practice variables in two ways. First, the data are analyzed to find out what proportion of a given demographic or media practices sample is in each of the five levels. For instance, what percentage of all the males in the telephone interview sample are in level 1, what percentage are in level 2, and so on for levels 3, 4 and 5 on the Total Knowledge scale. In a second use of the five levels of Total Knowledge, the data are analyzed to find out what proportion of people in each level of knowledge are in a given demographic or media practices group. For instance, what percentage of people in knowledge level 1 are males, what percentage in knowledge level 2 are males, and so forth for each knowledge level.

The analyses by levels of Total Knowledge can be more revealing than the correlation coefficients because while low to moderate correlation coefficients may suggest only small relationships among variables in the total sample, the analyses by levels suggest what the probability would be that in samples similar to the one in the present study, a certain percentage of males would fall in each of the five levels of Total Knowledge, or what proportion of people in a given level would be males, and so forth for other demographic variables. These types of "odds" or "expectancy" analyses are useful for making decisions about the practical utility of relationships characterized by relatively small correlations among variables.

## RESULTS

Table 2 presents the correlations among key demographic variables, the four checklists, a "practice" variable (e.g., How often during an average week do you read a local or national newspaper?) computed as the average of questions 25a-k (see appendix), and two indicators of power, occupational status and income. The practice variable is a composite indicator of "print exposure" and relates average frequency of weekly reading of different materials for various purposes to education, age, and the knowledge checklists.

Table 2 shows positive correlations among demographic, knowledge, practice and power variables consistently found in adult literacy assessments for over 75 years (Sticht & Armstrong, 1994). Generally, better educated subjects scored higher than less well educated subjects, older adults scored better than younger, the majority group (whites) scored better than minorities (Hispanics, Blacks, Asians, others), managers and professionals performed better than clerical and sales persons, who, in turn, performed better than unskilled workers and laborers, those who earned more scored higher than those who earned less, and those who spent more time per week reading scored higher than those who read less.

Women in the sample tended to be somewhat less well educated, to engage in fewer literacy practices, to hold somewhat higher level jobs but to earn less than men.

**Table 2. Study 1 Correlations among knowledge and demographic variables.**

| Variables | 1 | 2 | 3 | 4 | 5 | 6 | 7 | 8 | 9 | 10 | 11 | 12 |
|---|---|---|---|---|---|---|---|---|---|---|---|---|
| 1. Education | 1.00 | .07* | .24 | .28 | .30 | .36 | .29 | .34 | .14 | -.10a | .38 | .31 |
| 2. Age | | 1.00 | .17 | .11 | .20 | .18 | .18 | .08* | .30 | .05* | .13 | .04* |
| 3. ART | | | 1.00 | .73 | .74 | .58 | .85 | .25 | .29 | .11* | .24 | .19 |
| 4. MRT | | | | 1.00 | .74 | .57 | .89 | .18 | .31 | .08* | .21 | .16 |
| 5. CKT | | | | | 1.00 | .62 | .89 | .23 | .34 | .05* | .20 | .12 |
| 6. VKT | | | | | | 1.00 | .73 | .24 | .30 | -.03* | .20 | .24 |
| 7. Total Knowledge | | | | | | | 1.00 | .18 | .32 | .07* | .20 | .15 |
| 8. Practice | | | | | | | | 1.00 | .09a | -.16 | .16 | .25 |
| 9. Ethnicity | | | | | | | | | 1.00 | .06* | .22 | .13 |
| 10. Gender | | | | | | | | | | 1.00 | .21 | -.16 |
| 11. Occupation | | | | | | | | | | | 1.00 | .17 |
| 12. Annual Income | | | | | | | | | | | | 1.00 |

ART=Author Recognition Test; MRT=Magazine Recognition Test
CKT= Cultural Knowledge Test; VKT=Vocabulary Knowledge Test
Total Knowledge= scores summed over the four checklists
Practice = mean scores on questions 25a through k (see appendix) for different reading practices.
*= Not significant, a= p < .05, all others significant beyond p < .01. Underlined r's are part-whole correlations.
Ethnicity= nonwhites (0) and whites (1); gender= males (1) and females (2). Weighting by income, education, race tended to increase the number and degree of significant findings

## Engagement in Literacy Practices and Print Exposure

Table A-5 in the appendix presents mean scores and SD's related to the respondent's estimates of the frequency they engaged in various literacy practices during a typical week. Overall, subjects reported reading a newspaper an average 4.4 times a week (SD=2.8) (Q's 7 & 25g). Reading for pleasure (Q25a) was the most frequent reading practice (Mean=4.68; SD=2.50) while listening to someone read aloud was the least frequently engaged in weekly literacy practice (Mean=0.52; SD=0.74).

Generally, the trends for practice follow those for Total Knowledge and are significant at p<.05. Except for age (NS), as educational attainment (r=.34), occupational status (r=.17), and income (r=.26) increase, the average frequency of weekly literacy practices increases. Whites were slightly more likely to engage in literacy practices than nonwhites (r=.09).

Questions 5A and 6 in Table A-5 of the appendix present the mean hours per day the subjects reported spending on either watching television or listening to the radio. There was a significant, negative (r=-.14, p<.001) relation between the number of hours of television watched and the average weekly literacy practice score. No relation between radio listening and literacy practices was found. Neither television viewing nor radio listening was related to any of the declarative knowledge checklist scores.

## Analyses by Knowledge Levels

As mentioned above, correlational analyses reveal the overall trends in relationships among the variables under investigation. But they do not reveal what goes on within the distributions of scores. For that reason analyses are presented here that show how different variables are distributed in the five different Total Knowledge categories defined above.

First, as given in Table 3, we take a demographically defined group of adults (excluding missing data), such as females, and show the percentage that fall into each of the five levels of knowledge. Looking at Table 3 it is clear that the less well educated, the younger, minorities, less occupationally skilled, and lower income respondents tend to fall with higher frequencies into the lower levels of Total Knowledge, confirming the correlation data of Table 2. However, it is also clear that in all of these groups, there is a wide range of knowledge. For instance, about one in five Blacks fell in the next to the highest category of knowledge, and about one in eight managers and professionals fell in the least knowledgeable category.

**Table 3. Study 1. Percentage of respondents in each demographic group falling into each of five levels of Total Knowledge. For instance, 9.2 percent of those with 17+ years of education were in Level 1 while 43.1 percent were in Level 5.**

| Variables | N | Total Knowledge Levels a | | | | |
| | | 1 | 2 | 3 | 4 | 5 |
|---|---|---|---|---|---|---|
| Total Sample | 538 | 19.2 | 14.1 | 31.4 | 16.7 | 18.6 |
| Normal Curve | | 16.0 | 15.0 | 38.0 | 15.0 | 16.0 |
| | | | | | | |
| Gender | | | | | | |
| Male | 250 | 21.2 | 19.2 | 22.0 | 18.8 | 18.8 |
| Female | 272 | 18.8 | 19.5 | 19.1 | 21.3 | 21.3 |
| | | | | | | |
| Education | | | | | | |
| 0-12 | 132 | 31.0 | 30.1 | 21.1 | 11.9 | 6.8 |
| 13-14 | 146 | 22.6 | 22.6 | 21.9 | 18.5 | 14.4 |
| 15-16 | 130 | 13.1 | 13.1 | 25.4 | 26.9 | 21.5 |
| 17* | 109 | 9.2 | 11.0 | 12.8 | 23.9 | 43.1 |
| | | | | | | |
| Age | | | | | | |
| 16-18 | 14 | 35.7 | 42.9 | 21.4 | 0.0 | 0.0 |
| 19-24 | 65 | 41.5 | 23.1 | 16.9 | 13.8 | 4.6 |
| 25-39 | 198 | 21.7 | 21.2 | 23.2 | 21.7 | 12.1 |
| 40-54 | 141 | 9.9 | 13.5 | 15.6 | 24.1 | 36.9 |
| 55-64 | 32 | 6.3 | 12.5 | 28.1 | 18.8 | 34.4 |
| 65+ | 62 | 17.7 | 19.4 | 22.6 | 21.0 | 19.4 |
| | | | | | | |
| Ethnicity | | | | | | |
| White | 379 | 11.9 | 17.4 | 22.4 | 23.2 | 25.1 |
| African-Amer. | 24 | 25.0 | 37.5 | 16.7 | 20.8 | |
| Hispanic | 71 | 45.1 | 19.7 | 18.3 | 8.5 | 8.5 |

| | | Total Knowledge Levels a | | | | |
|---|---|---|---|---|---|---|
| Variables | N | 1 | 2 | 3 | 4 | 5 |
| Asian | 28 | 42.9 | 21.4 | 14.3 | 14.3 | 7.1 |
| Other | 18 | 33.3 | 38.9 | 5.6 | 11.1 | 11.1 |
| | | | | | | |
| Occupation b | | | | | | |
| Labor/Operator | 50 | 42.0 | 26.0 | 14.0 | 12.0 | 6.0 |
| Semi/Skill | 103 | 21.4 | 22.3 | 25.2 | 20.4 | 10.7 |
| Clerk/Sales | 97 | 21.6 | 23.7 | 18.6 | 16.5 | 19.6 |
| Tech/Engr | 60 | 10.0 | 11.7 | 31.7 | 23.3 | 23.3 |
| Mn/Ex/Prf | 165 | 12.1 | 15.8 | 15.2 | 25.5 | 31.5 |
| | | | | | | |
| Hourly Pay | | | | | | |
| 0-$5.9956 | 26.8 | 26.8 | 17.9 | 10.7 | 17.9 | |
| $6-10.99 | 103 | 29.1 | 26.2 | 17.5 | 20.4 | 6.8 |
| $11-15.99 | 82 | 19.5 | 12.2 | 20.7 | 25.6 | 22.0 |
| $16-20.99 | 55 | 9.1 | 20.0 | 27.3 | 20.0 | 23.6 |
| $21+ | 82 | 13.4 | 12.2 | 22.0 | 24.4 | 28.0 |

A Data are percentages in each knowledge level. See text for definition of levels.
B Those not in labor force were excluded due to small N's.


The importance of Total Knowledge in relation to the power indicators of occupation and income is revealed again in Table 4 where each of the five Total Knowledge categories is analyzed to see how adults in a given category of knowledge are distributed across the demographic variables. As indicated, about one in five of the adults in the lowest knowledge category are managers/professionals, whereas over half of those in the highest category of knowledge are managers/professionals. Similarly, only one in six of those in knowledge category 1 earn over $50,000 a year while half of those in category 5 earn that much.

**Table 4. Study 1. Percentage of respondents in each level of Total Knowledge who are in each of the variable categories. For instance, 51 percent of those in Level 1 are males, 49 percent are females; in Level 5, 44.8 percent are males and 55.2 females.**

| Variable | Total Knowledge Levels | | | | | |
|---|---|---|---|---|---|---|
| | 1 | 2 | 3 | 4 | 5 | Total |
| Gender | | | | | | |
| Male | 51.0 | 47.5 | 51.4 | 44.8 | 44.8 | 47.9 |
| Female | 49.0 | 52.5 | 48.6 | 55.2 | 55.2 | 52.1 |
| | 100 | 100 | 100 | 100 | 100 | 100 |
| Education | | | | | | |
| 0-8 | 2.0 | 1.0 | 0.9 | 0.0 | 1.8 | 1.2 |
| 9-12 | 38.6 | 37.6 | 25.2 | 14.6 | 6.7 | 24.4 |
| 13-14 | 32.7 | 32.7 | 29.9 | 26.2 | 20.0 | 28.2 |
| 15-16 | 16.8 | 16.8 | 30.8 | 34.0 | 26.7 | 25.1 |
| 17+ | 9.9 | 11.9 | 13.1 | 25.2 | 44.8 | 21.1 |
| | 100 | 100 | 100 | 100 | 100 | 100 |
| Age | | | | | | |
| 16-18 | 4.9 | 6.1 | 2.8 | 0.0 | 0.0 | 2.7 |
| 19-24 | 26.5 | 15.3 | 10.5 | 8.6 | 2.9 | 12.7 |
| 25-39 | 42.2 | 42.9 | 43.8 | 41.0 | 23.5 | 38.7 |
| 40-54 | 13.6 | 19.4 | 21.0 | 32.4 | 51.0 | 27.5 |
| 55-64 | 2.0 | 4.1 | 8.6 | 5.6 | 10.8 | 06.3 |
| 65+ | 10.8 | 12.2 | 13.3 | 12.4 | 11.8 | 12.1 |
| | 100 | 100 | 100 | 100 | 100 | 100 |
| Ethnicity | | | | | | |
| Caucasian | 44.6 | 64.7 | 79.4 | 83.8 | 90.5 | 72.9 |
| African-Amer. | 5.9 | 8.8 | 3.9 | 4.8 | 0.0 | 4.6 |
| Hispanic | 31.7 | 13.7 | 12.1 | 5.7 | 5.7 | 13.7 |
| Asian | 11.9 | 5.9 | 3.7 | 3.8 | 1.9 | 5.3 |
| Other | 5.9 | 6.9 | 0.9 | 1.9 | 1.9 | 3.5 |
| | 100 | 100 | 100 | 100 | 100 | 100 |
| Occupation | | | | | | |
| Unemp./Student | 1.1 | 1.1 | 0.0 | 0.0 | 0.0 | 0.4 |
| Homemaker | 1.1 | 2.1 | 1.0 | 0.0 | 0.0 | 0.8 |
| Laborer/Operator2 2.5 | 13.7 | 8.2 | 6.1 | 3.0 | 10.6 | |

| Variable | Total Knowledge Levels | | | | | |
|---|---|---|---|---|---|---|
| | 1 | 2 | 3 | 4 | 5 | Total |
| Skilled/ | | | | | | |
| Semi-/skilled | 23.6 | 24.2 | 26.8 | 21.2 | 11.1 | 21.3 |
| Clerical/Sales | 23.7 | 24.2 | 18.6 | 16.2 | 19.2 | 20.3 |
| Technical/Engrs. | 6.5 | 7.3 | 19.6 | 14.1 | 14.2 | 12.4 |
| Mangrs./Profes. | 21.5 | 27.4 | 25.8 | 42.4 | 52.5 | 34.2 |
| | 100 | 100 | 100 | 100 | 100 | 100 |
| Hourly Pay | | | | | | |
| $0-5.99 | 19.5 | 20.5 | 12.8 | 7.6 | 14.1 | 14.8 |
| $6-10.99 | 39.0 | 37.0 | 23.1 | 26.6 | 09.8 | 27.2 |
| $11-15.99 | 20.7 | 13.7 | 21.8 | 26.6 | 25.4 | 21.7 |
| $16-20.99 | 6.5 | 15.1 | 19.2 | 13.9 | 18.3 | 14.6 |
| $21+ | 14.3 | 13.7 | 23.1 | 25.3 | 32.4 | 21.7 |
| | 100 | 100 | 100 | 100 | 100 | 100 |
| Household Income | | | | | | |
| <$10,000 | 15.6 | 9.7 | 8.2 | 8.0 | 3.3 | 9.0 |
| $10K-20,000 | 16.7 | 12.9 | 6.2 | 9.0 | 12.0 | 11.3 |
| $20K-30,000 | 30.2 | 21.5 | 20.6 | 19.0 | 10.9 | 20.5 |
| $30K-40,000 | 14.6 | 11.8 | 16.5 | 15.0 | 14.1 | 14.4 |
| $40K-50,000 | 7.3 | 10.8 | 18.6 | 20.0 | 9.8 | 13.4 |
| $>50,000 | 15.6 | 33.3 | 29.9 | 29.0 | 50.0 | 31.4 |
| | 100 | 100 | 100 | 100 | 100 | 100 |

## Analyses Holding Age, Education and Ethnicity Constant

Table 5 shows relationships among knowledge and literacy practices when knowledge scores were computed after having removed variation in knowledge due to the correlation of age, education, and ethnicity with Total Knowledge. Removing the variation due to these three variables reduced the numbers falling in the lowest and highest categories of knowledge and so the bottom two levels of knowledge and the top two categories of knowledge have been combined in Table 5. The data show a consistent, positive relationship between the number of literacy practices respondents reported engaging in and their scores on the knowledge checklists even when the latter are adjusted for age, education and ethnicity. All were in the predicted direction, with only "reading books or manuals" failing to attain statistical significance (p <.05).

Table 5. Study 1. Age, Education & Ethnicity held constant. Relationships of Knowledge Levels to various reading practices that respondents reported engaging in 6-7 times a week. For instance, 46.8 percent of those in Knowledge Levels (1+2) combined reported reading newspapers 6-7 times a week, while 61.4 percent of those in Knowledge Levels (4+5) combined reported reading newspapers that often.

|  |  | Knowledge Levels | | |
| --- | --- | --- | --- | --- |
| Variable |  | (1+2) | 3 | (4+5) |
| Read For Pleasure |  | 39.7 | 53.1 | 63.8 |
| Read For Job |  | 31.4 | 33.6 | 46.5 |
| Read Book for Pleasure | 31.7 | 39.8 | 43.0 |  |
| Read Books or Manuals | 17.5 | 24.8 | 25.7 |  |
| Read Newspapers |  | 46.8 | 56.8 | 61.4 |

a All relationships are statistically significant by Kendall's taub, P<.05, except reading books or manuals (p<.09).

The relationships of Total Knowledge to the power indicators of occupation and income, after having removed variation due to age, education, and ethnicity, are shown in Table 6. The proportion of those in the lower two knowledge categories who are laborers was twice that of those in the upper two categories of knowledge. About three out of ten of those in the lowest two categories of knowledge are managers/professionals, while four out of ten of those in the highest two categories of knowledge are in these manager/ professional jobs. Similar findings hold for income for those earning less than $10,000 and those earning $40,000 or more.

Together, Tables 5 and 6 indicate that more generally knowledgeable adults engage in greater amounts of reading, they hold higher status occupations and they earn higher levels of income, even when general knowledge scores are adjusted for differences in age, education and ethnicity.

Table 6. Study 1. Age, Education & Ethnicity held constant. Relationships among Knowledge Levels, Occupational Status, and Annual Income. Data are percentage of people in each Knowledge level who are in each of the demographic categories. For instance, 29.9 percent of those in Knowledge Levels (1+2) combined were Managers/Professionals, while 41.3 percent of those in Knowledge Levels (3+4) combined were in that occupational category.a

| | | Knowledge Levels | | |
|---|---|---|---|---|
| Variable | | (1+2) | 3 | (4+5) |
| Occupation | | | | |
| Laborer/Operator | | 13.0 | 13.5 | 5.8 |
| Skilled/Semi-skilled | | 23.4 | 20.9 | 20.0 |
| Clerical/Sales | | 13.0 | 12.2 | 14.2 |
| Technical/Engineers | | 20.8 | 20.9 | 18.7 |
| Managers/Professionals | 29.9 | 32.4 | 41.3 | |
| | | 100 | 100 | 100 |
| Annual Income | | | | |
| Under $10,000 | | 13.8 | 6.9 | 5.8 |
| $10-20,000 | | 15.1 | 7.5 | 11.6 |
| $20-30,000 | | 22.4 | 18.9 | 19.4 |
| $30-40,000 | | 13.8 | 13.8 | 16.1 |
| $40-50,000 | | 7.2 | 18.2 | 14.8 |
| $>50,000 | | 27.6 | 34.6 | 32.3 |
| | | 100 | 100 | 100 |

a Relationships are statistically significant, P<.01, by Kendall's taub.
Not in labor force categories (unemployed, student, homemaker) were removed from calculations due to very few cases (less than 2 in cells) from occupation cross tabulation.

## STUDY 2: DOMAIN SPECIFIC DECLARATIVE KNOWLEDGE AND POWER

In the preceding study, subject's general declarative knowledge was assessed using shortened versions of the Stanovich checklists for knowledge of famous authors, magazine titles, famous people, and vocabulary words (West, Stanovich, & Mitchell, 1993). It provided information about respondent's general declarative knowledge taken from samples of the knowledge of the "mainstream" or "dominant" society.

One critic of the Stanovich checklists has referred to them as being similar to the game of "trivial pursuit," and argued that there is essentially no "real world" value to showing that people possess such culturally "biased" knowledge (Taylor, 1994). However, the results presented above counter this argument by showing statistically reliable, positive, "real world" relationships among so-called "mainstream," "dominant" culture knowledge and the acquisition of power as reflected by social status.

While some may question the utility of cultural knowledge as defined in Study 1, there is no questioning the fact that citizens in a democracy need to possess considerable political knowledge to make informed choices among political candidates to represent them and to pursue their vital interests through political activities. Political knowledge is not "trivial." Therefore, to further examine the role of declarative knowledge in achieving and exercising power, Study 2 examines for the first time the relationships of domain specific, declarative, political knowledge to two indicators of power, income and political activities, when information processing efficiency, age, education, and ethnicity are held constant.

To establish concurrent validity of the declarative knowledge measures as indicators of political knowledge, conventional measures of political knowledge used by political scientists in earlier studies of political activity were administered (Delli Carpini & Keeter, 1993; Neuman, Just, & Crigler, 1992). If positive correlations of the checklist and traditional measures of political knowledge are obtained, this supports the validity of the checklist knowledge measures (Messick, 1989, p. 5). Checklist measures of declarative knowledge were also related to a four-item rating scale that attempted to directly gauge subject's sense of power. If positive correlations are obtained between the checklist measures of declarative political knowledge and perceived power, this provides additional evidence for the validity of the knowledge checklists and the relationship of knowledge to power.

## METHOD

### Subjects

Study 2 was conducted one year after Study 1 and it used the same general random-digit-dialing telephone survey procedures as used in Study 1. Analysis is based on 632 structured telephone interviews completed with English speaking persons selected to represent a cross-section of the population 18 or older who could be reached by residential telephone in San Diego county, California during late spring and early summer, 1995. Up to four call-backs were made resulting in an overall completion rate of 50 percent, a rate comparable to or surpassing that for the better survey research firms in the area. Fewer than five percent of respondents contacted were eliminated due to inability of the subject to respond to the protocol in English.

Respondents were generally well educated and affluent, reporting 14.5 (SD=3.2) years of formal schooling completed and mean household income of $34,380 (SD=$12,244). Mean age was 41.8 (SD=17.2). As indicated in Table 1, the sample generally corresponded to the sample of Study 1 and the 1990 U. S. Census data for San Diego, although minorities and less well educated were slightly underrepresented (see the comments on sampling issues in the Discussion section). As with Study 1, analyses were replicated successfully when data were weighted by education, race, and income to correct for discrepancies between sample and Census data.

## Instrumentation

For Study 2, a series of political knowledge checklists with foils was developed drawing on traditional bodies of political knowledge domains used by political scientists in studying political activism and voting (Delli Carpini & Keeter, 1993; Neuman, Just & Crigler, 1992). The measures of political knowledge were designed to tap those aspects of politics that are relevant for meaningful personal political action. For the present study, five political domains were identified including (1) Political Leaders, that is, actors or activists engaged in political processes, (2) Political Policies, policies produced by various political systems, (3) Political Groups, i.e., groups such as the National Organization for Women who are active in political movements, (4) Government Organizations, i.e., domestic or foreign government organizations such as the Bureau of Indian Affairs, and (5) Political Events such as the Three Mile Island or Exxon Valdez incidents.

In the study, subjects were presented with a series of declarative, political knowledge stimuli. The Appendix, Tables A6-A10, shows the five domains of political knowledge, the questions asked to elicit responses from subjects, mean percent correct and standard deviations for each item, and the percentage of subjects for each item falling into each of five levels of total political knowledge (see below).

Reliability data for each of the subscales and the Total Political Knowledge scale were computed using Cronbach's Alpha. The reliability coefficient for the Political Leaders scale was .73; for Political Policies, .63, Political Groups, .61, Government Groups, .58, and Political Events, .62. For the Total Political Knowledge scale the reliability coefficient was .88.

## Defining Political Knowledge Levels

As in Study 1, the Total Political Knowledge checklist scores of subjects were used to define five levels of Total Political Knowledge. Scores for each subscale and for the Total Political Knowledge scale (all items from all subscales) were computed by subtracting the percentage of foils misidentified as real from the percentage of real items correctly identified as real. These computations were designed to adjust for guessing (West, Stanovich, & Mitchell, 1993). Political Knowledge levels were defined in adjusted percent correct scores from low to high proficiency asLevel 1= scores at -1.0 SD (21.97) below the mean (53.36) or lower, Level 2 = scores between -.5 to -.1.0 SD, Level 3 = scores between ± .5 SD, Level 4 = scores between +.5 to +1.0 SD, and Level 5 = scores from +1.0 SD and above. Political knowledge scores were also adjusted for age, education, and ethnicity by computing residuals and grouped into those categories for analysis as in Study 1.

Conventional measures of political knowledge. To validate the political knowledge checklists as measures of political knowledge, political knowledge was also measured using a series of questions from political science studies (Delli Carpini & Keeter, 1993; Neuman, Just & Crigler, 1992). Subjects were asked which of the two parties "...is usually regarded as the most conservative" (Republican), "...currently has a majority in the U.S. House of Representatives" (Republican), "...had a majority ... before the last election" (Democratic), and "...currently has a majority in the U.S. Senate" (Republican). They were also asked the name of the first ten amendments to the Constitution (Bill of Rights), the number of times a person can be elected President (2), and the length of terms for the U. S. President (4 years), a U.S. Senator (6 years), and a U.S. Representative (2 years). For this nine item scale, called Conventional Political Knowledge, the Alpha reliability was .60.

Reading and media practices. To determine the role of media in developing political knowledge subjects were asked to indicate how many days a week they read a newspaper, how many hours a day they listened to the radio, and how many hours a day they watched television. They were asked to indicate about how many national network news programs, such as CBS, NBC, or ABC news they saw in an average week, how many local news programs they watched in a week, how many network news magazines such as 60 Minutes, 20/20, Frontline, Dateline, or Eye to Eye they watched during a week, and how many Public Broadcasting news programs such as the McNeil Lehrer News Hour, Washington Week in Review, or National Business Review they watched in an average week.

Political interests and activities. To determine relationships of political knowledge to political interests, subjects were asked to rate on a four point scale how interested they were in politics and public affairs. They were also asked to rate on a four point scale the amount of attention (high to low) they paid to politics or political issues when they watch television or read the newspaper.

Two questions were asked to determine the frequency on a four point scale (very often to never) with which subjects voted in local or national elections (combined into one voting score, Alpha reliability = .91), and 13 additional questions were asked about various activities (encouraged others to vote for one of the parties or candidates, worked for one of the campaigns, talked about politics with family members, etc.) using the same four point scale. The mean score for the 13 questions was used to form a political activities score for each subject that could be related to political knowledge (Alpha reliability = .83).

Measures of perceived power. To assess subject's sense of power directly, a scale of "powerlessness" taken from Kohn (1976) was used. Two items asked for respondents to state whether they 1-agree strongly, 2-agree, 3-disagree, 4-disagree strongly or 9-don't know. Scores of 9 were excluded from analyses. One of these items said, "I generally have confidence that when I make plans I will be able to carry them out." The second said,

"There are things I can do that might influence national policy." A third item asked, "Do you feel that most of the things that happen to you are the result of your own decisions or of things over which you have no control?" and were scored 1, meaning that things happened due to their own control, or 2, meaning things happen due to decisions over which they had no control. The fourth and final item asked, "How often do you feel powerless to get what you want out of life?" It was scored 4-very often, 3-often, 2-sometimes, 1-rarely/never. Summed over the four items, low scores indicate a feeling of power, high scores feelings of powerlessness. For the present analyses, signs of correlations were reversed to show that increments in knowledge correlate positively with increments in perceived power. Cronbach's alpha for the power scale was 39, a low but usable degree of reliability given that this is only a four item scale.

## RESULTS

Validity indicators. Convergent evidence for the validity of the Total Political Knowledge checklist method as a measure of political knowledge was obtained by the finding of a significant, positive correlation of Total Political Knowledge with the Total Conventional Political Knowledge scale (nine items) ($r=.47$ ; $p<.001$). Convergent evidence that the Total Political Knowledge checklist scale is an indicator of perceived power was obtained by the significant positive correlation between the total perceived power scale (four items) and Total Political Knowledge checklist scores ($r= .22; p<.001$).

Knowledge checklists. Tables A6-A10 in the appendix show each of the items in each of the political knowledge checklists along with the mean percentage correct and standard deviations for each item as well as the average correct and standard deviations for the sum of each checklist. These tables show that the Political Leaders checklist had the highest average correct scores (74 percent) and the Political Policies checklist had the lowest scores (31 percent). The remaining scales were about equal in average difficulty.

Tables A6-A-10 also show the percentage of subjects in each of the five Total Political Knowledge levels that got each item correct. For Political Leaders in Table A6, 25 percent of those in Level 1 knew of John Major, the Prime Minister of Great Britain, while almost 90 percent of those in Level 5 knew of him.

**Table 7. Study 2 Correlations among demographic variables, knowledge, literacy practice and power indicators.**

| Variables | 1 | 2 | 3 | 4 | 5 | 6 | 7 | 8 | 9 | 10 | 11 | 12 | 13 | 14 |
|---|---|---|---|---|---|---|---|---|---|---|---|---|---|---|
| 1. Education | 1.00 | .07* | .27 | .16 | .22 | .22 | .13 | .27 | .11 | .17 | -.06* | .16 | .24 | .16 |
| 2. Age | | 1.00 | .16 | .20 | .15 | .28 | .08 | .24 | .31 | .25 | .10 | .12 | .43 | .18 |
| 3. Leaders | | | 1.00 | .41 | .52 | .48 | .37 | .73 | .19 | .24 | -.07* | .19 | .25 | .06* |
| 4. Policies | | | | 1.00 | .45 | .45 | .34 | .72 | .19 | .15 | -.07* | .16 | .25 | .09 |
| 5. Groups | | | | | 1.00 | .50 | .39 | .80 | .13 | .27 | -.15 | .19 | .20 | .05* |
| 6. Organizations | | | | | | 1.00 | .39 | .78 | .18 | .20 | -.05* | .19 | .33 | .20 |
| 7. Events | | | | | | | 1.00 | .66 | .08 | .12 | -.09 | .07* | .09 | .05* |
| 8. Total Political Knowledge | | | | | | | | 1.00 | .20 | .27 | -.12 | .22 | .30 | .12 |
| 9. Literacy Practice a | | | | | | | | | 1.00 | .11 | -.11 | .18 | .23 | .15 |
| 10. Ethnicity | | | | | | | | | | 1.00 | .08 | .17 | .27 | .04* |
| 11. Gender | | | | | | | | | | | 1.00 | -.02* | .09 | .06* |
| 12. Annual Household Income | | | | | | | | | | | | 1.00 | .20 | .08 |
| 13. Voting | | | | | | | | | | | | | 1.00 | .36 |
| 14. Political Activism | | | | | | | | | | | | | | 1.00 |

*Not significant at p<.05 or lower; all others statistically significant. a Literacy Practice is frequency of reading newspaper in a week. Weighting by income, education, race tended to increase the number and degree of significant findings.

Correlational analyses. There were significant positive relationships of Total Political Knowledge checklist scores to political interest ($r=.28$, $p<.001$) and to the amount of attention adults said they paid to politics or political issues when they watch television or read the newspaper ($r=.11$, $p<.002$). Generally consistent with other research (Newman, Just & Crigler, 1992), there were no significant relationships of Total Political Knowledge to the frequency of listening to the radio or watching television, nor to the types of news programs watched on television, with one exception. The number of Public Broadcasting news programs watched during an average week was significantly correlated with the Total Political Knowledge checklist scores ($r=.14$, $p<.001$).

Interrelationships of demographic variables, political knowledge checklist scores, literacy practice and power indicators (household income, voting and political activism) are given in Table 7. These data show significant, positive correlations among the political knowledge scores and the indicators of power.

To sum up these correlational data, better educated, older, Caucasian adults who read newspapers and watch Public Broadcasting news programs more frequently, tend to have greater interests in politics, they are more knowledgeable about politics, they have higher household incomes, they vote more and they are more politically active.

## Analyses by Knowledge Levels

Following the method of presenting of results in Study 1, analyses are presented here that show how different variables are distributed in the five different Total Political Knowledge categories defined above. Occupation was not measured in this study.

Table 8. Study 2. Percentage of respondents in each demographic group falling into each of five levels of Total Political Knowledge. For instance, 6.9 percent of those with 17+ years of education were in Level 1 while 21.8 percent were in Level 5.

| Variables | N | Total Political Knowledge Levels a | | | | |
|---|---|---|---|---|---|---|
| | | 1 | 2 | 3 | 4 | 5 |
| Total Sample | 644 | 16.1 | 12.6 | 35.9 | 19.7 | 15.7 |
| Normal Curve | | 16.0 | 15.0 | 38.0 | 15.0 | 16.0 |
| Education | | | | | | |
| 0-12 | 180 | 31.1 | 11.7 | 38.3 | 14.4 | 4.4 |
| 13-14 | 127 | 25.2 | 15.7 | 36.2 | 15.0 | 7.9 |
| 15-16 | 224 | 9.4 | 12.9 | 38.8 | 25.0 | 13.8 |
| 17+ | 101 | 6.9 | 7.9 | 39.6 | 23.8 | 21.8 |
| Age | | | | | | |

| Variables | N | Total Political Knowledge Levels a | | | | |
|---|---|---|---|---|---|---|
| | | 1 | 2 | 3 | 4 | 5 |
| Total Sample | 644 | 16.1 | 12.6 | 35.9 | 19.7 | 15.7 |
| Normal Curve | | 16.0 | 15.0 | 38.0 | 15.0 | 16.0 |
| 16-18 | 16 | 56.3 | 18.8 | 25.0 | 0.0 | 0.0 |
| 19-24 | 79 | 38.0 | 15.2 | 34.2 | 7.6 | 5.1 |
| 25-39 | 246 | 17.1 | 15.0 | 41.5 | 16.3 | 10.2 |
| 40-54 | 130 | 7.7 | 5.4 | 36.9 | 33.1 | 16.9 |
| 55-64 | 61 | 14.8 | 11.5 | 42.6 | 18.0 | 13.1 |
| 65+ | 91 | 12.1 | 13.2 | 35.2 | 26.4 | 13.2 |
| | | | | | | |
| Ethnicity | | | | | | |
| Caucasian | 474 | 13.3 | 12.0 | 39.2 | 22.8 | 12.7 |
| African-Amer. | 42 | 35.7 | 9.5 | 33.3 | 11.9 | 9.5 |
| Hispanic | 60 | 31.7 | 18.3 | 35.0 | 8.3 | 6.7 |
| Asian | 32 | 40.6 | 12.5 | 40.6 | 3.1 | 3.1 |
| Other | 13 | 23.1 | 15.4 | 38.5 | 7.7 | 15.4 |
| | | | | | | |
| Household Income | | | | | | |
| <$10,000 | 48 | 25.0 | 20.8 | 31.3 | 12.5 | 10.4 |
| $10K-19,999 | 78 | 32.1 | 16.2 | 23.1 | 16.7 | 9.0 |
| $20K-29,999 | 90 | 20.0 | 15.6 | 40.0 | 17.8 | 6.7 |
| $30K-39,999 | 91 | 13.2 | 13.2 | 44.0 | 17.6 | 12.1 |
| $40K-49,999 | 104 | 14.4 | 8.7 | 40.4 | 27.9 | 8.7 |
| $50,000+ | 119 | 10.1 | 8.4 | 43.7 | 21.0 | 10.8 |
| | | | | | | |
| Voting Behavior b | | | | | | |
| Low | 147 | 32.7 | 18.4 | 36.1 | 10.9 | 2.0 |
| Medium | 199 | 13.6 | 12.6 | 42.2 | 20.1 | 11.6 |
| High | 278 | 13.3 | 9.4 | 36.7 | 24.8 | 15.8 |
| | | | | | | |
| Political Activismc | | | | | | |
| Low | 202 | 23.8 | 16.8 | 36.6 | 14.9 | 7.9 |
| Medium | 208 | 16.8 | 10.1 | 37.0 | 22.1 | 13.9 |
| High | 220 | 14.5 | 10.5 | 40.9 | 22.3 | 11.8 |

A Data are percentages in each knowledge level. See text for definition of levels.
N's vary due to the deletion of missing data.
B Voting FrequenciesLow=never/not very often; Medium=often; High=very often.
C Political ActivismLow=average mean frequency score for 13 activities of 1.43; Medium=1.78; High=4. Associations are statistically significant p<.001 by Kendall's taub or chi-square (ethnicity).

First, as given in Table 8, we take a demographically defined group of adults, such as age 16-18, and show the percentage that fall into each of the five levels of knowledge. Looking at Table 8 it is clear that the less well educated, the younger, minorities, lower household income adults who vote less and are less politically active tend to fall with higher frequencies into the lower levels of Total Political Knowledge, confirming the data of Table 7.

The importance of Total Political Knowledge in relation to the power indicators of household income, voting and political activism is revealed again in Table 9 where each of the five Total Political Knowledge levels is analyzed to see how adults in a given level of knowledge are distributed across the demographic variables.

Table 9. Study 2. Percentage of respondents in each level of Total Political Knowledge who are in each of the variable categories. For instance, 24.1 percent of those in Level 1 had 15 or more years of education, while 74.7 percent of those in Level 5 had that much education.

| Variable | Total Political Knowledge Levels | | | | | |
| | 1 | 2 | 3 | 4 | 5 | Total |
|---|---|---|---|---|---|---|
| Education | | | | | | |
| 0-12 | 48.3 | 26.9 | 28.5 | 26.8 | 11.3 | 28.5 |
| 13-14 | 27.6 | 25.6 | 19.0 | 15.2 | 14.1 | 20.1 |
| 15-16 | 18.1 | 37.2 | 36.0 | 44.8 | 43.7 | 35.4 |
| 17+ | 6.0 | 10.3 | 16.5 | 19.2 | 31.0 | 16.0 |
| | 100 | 100 | 100 | 100 | 100 | 100 |
| Age | | | | | | |
| 16-18 | 8.1 | 3.8 | 1.7 | 0.0 | 0.0 | 2.6 |
| 19-24 | 27.0 | 15.4 | 11.3 | 4.8 | 5.6 | 12.7 |
| 25-39 | 37.8 | 47.4 | 42.7 | 32.3 | 35.2 | 39.5 |
| 40-54 | 9.0 | 9.0 | 20.1 | 34.7 | 31.0 | 20.9 |
| 55-64 | 8.1 | 9.0 | 10.9 | 8.9 | 11.3 | 9.8 |
| 65+ | 9.9 | 15.4 | 13.4 | 19.4 | 16.9 | 14.6 |
| | 100 | 100 | 100 | 100 | 100 | 100 |
| Ethnicity | | | | | | |
| Caucasian | 55.8 | 73.1 | 77.8 | 90.0 | 84.5 | 76.3 |
| African-Amer.13.3 | 5.1 | 5.9 | 4.2 | 5.6 | 6.8 | |
| Hispanic | 16.8 | 14.1 | 8.8 | 4.2 | 5.6 | 9.7 |
| Asian | 11.5 | 5.1 | 5.4 | 0.8 | 1.4 | 5.2 |
| Other | 2.7 | 2.6 | 2.1 | 0.8 | 2.8 | 2.1 |
| | 100 | 100 | 100 | 100 | 100 | 100 |
| Household Income | | | | | | |
| <$10,000 | 12.8 | 14.3 | 7.4 | 5.7 | 8.6 | 9.1 |
| $10K-20,000 | 26.6 | 21.4 | 8.9 | 12.4 | 12.1 | 14.7 |
| $20K-30,000 | 19.1 | 20.0 | 17.7 | 15.2 | 10.3 | 17.0 |

| Variable | Total Political Knowledge Levels | | | | | |
|---|---|---|---|---|---|---|
| | 1 | 2 | 3 | 4 | 5 | Total |
| $30K-40,000 | 12.8 | 17.1 | 19.7 | 15.2 | 19.0 | 17.2 |
| $40K-50,000 | 16.0 | 12.9 | 20.7 | 27.6 | 15.5 | 19.6 |
| $>50,000 | 12.8 | 14.3 | 25.6 | 23.8 | 34.5 | 22.5 |
| | 100 | 100 | 100 | 100 | 100 | 100 |
| Voting Behaviora | | | | | | |
| Low | 42.9 | 34.6 | 22.2 | 12.8 | 4.3 | 23.6 |
| Medium | 4.1 | 32.1 | 35.1 | 32.0 | 32.9 | 31.9 |
| High | 33.0 | 33.3 | 42.7 | 55.2 | 62.9 | 44.6 |
| | 100 | 100 | 100 | 100 | 100 | 100 |
| Political Activismb | | | | | | |
| Low | 41.7 | 43.6 | 30.7 | 24.0 | 22.5 | 32.1 |
| Medium | 30.4 | 26.9 | 32.0 | 36.8 | 40.8 | 33.0 |
| High | 27.8 | 29.5 | 37.3 | 39.2 | 36.6 | 34.9 |
| | 100 | 100 | 100 | 100 | 100 | 100 |

a Voting Frequencies Low=never/not very often; Medium=often; High=very often.

b Political Activism Low=average mean frequency score for 13 activities of 1.43; Medium=1.78; High=4.

## Analyses Holding Age, Education and Ethnicity Constant

Analyses were conducted of relationships among Total Political Knowledge checklist scores and literacy practices (reading newspapers seven days a week) when knowledge scores were computed after having removed variation in political knowledge due to age, education, and ethnicity. As in Study 1, this procedure reduced the numbers falling in the lowest and highest categories of knowledge and so the bottom two levels of knowledge and the top two categories of knowledge were combined to form three categories of Total Political Knowledge. The analysis revealed that 35.1 percent of adults in the combined lowest two categories of political knowledge read newspapers seven days a week, 51.3 percent in the middle category and 47.9 percent of those in the highest two categories combined read newspapers seven days a week ($p<.007$). This indicates a positive relationship between the amount of political knowledge adults have and the number of literacy practices they reported engaging in, even when the effects of age, education and ethnicity on knowledge scores are held constant.

Table 10. Study 2. Age, Education & Ethnicity held constant. Relationships among Total Political Knowledge Levels on the checklists and three indicators of power. Data are percentage of people in each Total Political Knowledge level who are in each of the indicators of power categories. For instance, 19.4 percent of those adults in the two lowest combined levels of Total Political Knowledge reported household incomes over $50,000 while 37.6 percent of those in the two highest categories of Total Political Knowledge combined reported household incomes over $50,000.

| | Total Political Knowledge Levels | | |
| --- | --- | --- | --- |
| Variable | (1+2) | 3 | (4+5) |
| **Annual Household Income** | | | |
| Under $20,000 | 35.8 | 18.9 | 18.9 |
| $20,000-50,000 | 42.5 | 44.9 | 47.6 |
| $>50,000 | 19.4 | 43.0 | 37.6 |
| | 100 | 100 | 100 |
| **Voting Frequencya** | | | |
| Low | 31.4 | 24.9 | 16.2 |
| Medium | 29.7 | 32.2 | 32.9 |
| High | 39.0 | 42.9 | 50.9 |
| | 100 | 100 | 100 |
| **Political Activismb** | | | |
| Low | 37.4 | 33.2 | 26.7 |
| Medium | 29.3 | 32.3 | 36.9 |
| High | 33.3 | 34.3 | 36.4 |
| | 100 | 100 | 100 |

a Voting FrequenciesLow=never/not very often; Medium=often; High=very often.

Political ActivismLow=average mean frequency score for 13 activities of 1.43; Medium=1.78; High=4

All relationships are statistically significant, P<.05 by the Kendall's taub test.


The relationships of Total Political Knowledge to the power indicators of household income, voting and political activism are shown in Table 10. Altogether, the data indicate that more politically knowledgeable adults engage in greater amounts of reading, they have higher levels of household income, they vote more often and they are involved in more political activities than less knowledgeable adults, even when Total Political Knowledge scores are adjusted for differences in age, education and ethnicity.

# DISCUSSION

The research reported here explored the validity of the maxim, "knowledge is power." To determine the relationship of content knowledge to power in the contemporary United States, two studies were conducted. Together, they examined relationships among general, "mainstream" or "dominant" society knowledge, domain specific political knowledge and three indicators of power, occupational status, income and political activity. In both studies, care was taken to ensure that declarative knowledge was assessed, and that extraneous, complex cognitive processing variance did not influence the results. This was accomplished by using simple checklists of declarative knowledge that required listeners, on the telephone, to simply say "yes" if they thought they recognized a given factual stimulus. The task involved no reading, no drawing of inferences, no "critical thinking" and no complex "search and locate" processes that might tend to overload working memory.

The results indicated that there were low to moderate positive correlations among amount of content knowledge that adults possessed and the power indicators, even when the variance due to the combined effects of age, education and ethnicity were removed. The latter is important because it indicates that regardless of one's cultural or subcultural background, possession of large "banks" of declarative knowledge about the "mainstream" or "dominant" culture of the United States is associated with the possession and use of power in the "mainstream" society.

Through the use of expectancy tables formed by dividing Total Knowledge scores in each study into five levels, information beyond the correlation coefficients was obtained regarding the differences between the least and most knowledgeable adults. The tables suggested that the adults in higher knowledge were 1.4 times more likely to be managers and/or professionals than adults in lower levels. Following similar calculations, we found adults in higher levels were 1.2 times more likely to earn over $40,000 per year as were those in lower levels. In Study 2 (Table 10) adults in higher political knowledge were 1.9 times more likely to have households earning over $50,000, 1.3 times more likely to engage frequently in voting in local and national elections, and 1.1 times more likely to engage in various other political activities. Again, it should be recalled that these relationships were found with age, education and ethnicity held constant.

# VOCABULARY KNOWLEDGE AND POWER

Study 1 included a measure of vocabulary knowledge among the checklists of "mainstream" declarative knowledge and found statistically significant relationships among the vocabulary measures and the indicators of power (Table 2). These findings are consistent with research in which the vocabulary scores of the presidents of Fortune 500 companies were examined (Smith & Supanich, 1984). In a second study, the vocabulary scores of managers in Fortune 500 companies were examined (Gershon, 1990). The results showed that the company presidents scored higher than the managers and the latter scored higher than college graduates who routinely took the vocabulary tests as part of their career counseling. Thus, greater vocabulary knowledge was associated with higher levels of power (supervisory responsibility over larger numbers of others).

On the other hand, in the present studies, many of the adults in the lowest levels of knowledge were in the highest levels of occupation, income and political activity. Similarly, many of those in the highest levels of knowledge were in the lowest levels of the three power indicators. This indicates that knowledge as measured in these studies is neither necessary nor sufficient for guaranteeing access to power.

Still, those who scored higher on the various knowledge checklists had higher probabilities of being in the more powerful groups. In Galtung's (1964) terms, they were closer to the "center" of society and thereby enabled to enjoy its cherished values to a greater extent. This does not mean that the exact knowledge measured in these studies is what is important for gaining access to power. Instead, the various checklists of authors, magazines, famous people, vocabulary and political information represent samples from much larger knowledge bases that adults possess. The various checklists are probably best viewed as non-random samples of the knowledge in people's knowledge bases, as crude indicators of a vast amount of other knowledge not assessed in the checklists. The fact that in both Studies 1 and 2 better educated people knew more suggests that one way that education affects the human cognitive system is to contribute to the development of a large knowledge base. We have no way of knowing how to representatively sample all the knowledge that a person might possess, and so we can not say how representative the knowledge in the checklists are of knowledge bases in general.

## KNOWLEDGE AND READING

The correlational data of Tables 2 and 7 show positive relationships among the amount of reading practices that adults engage in and the levels of knowledge that they possess. Even when age, education and ethnicity are controlled, more knowledgeable adults reported more reading of books, newspapers, and so forth than the less knowledgeable adults (Table 5). Importantly, knowledge was not associated with amount of listening to the radio or to watching television news programs (except for those who watched the Public Broadcasting System news shows in Study 2).

More knowledgeable adults read more and there is reason to believe that as knowledge grows, one's literacy skills increase. As mentioned in the introduction, a review of every major adult literacy survey since 1931 indicates that as years of education increases, amount of reading increases and reading skill increases, representing a sort of "triple helix" of literacy development (Sticht & Armstrong, 1994). These adulthood findings are collaborated by research with children in the school grades where it has been found that children who read more during the school years develop larger bodies of knowledge and more skill in reading (Stanovich, 1993; Krashen). One study found that over the summer, when children are not in school and are less likely to read widely, those in the lower levels (25th percentile) of reading ability tended to lose skill, while those at the higher levels (75th percentile) actually gained in reading ability (Heyns, 1987).

The checklists of Study 1 were designed to sample knowledge that people might be expected to have acquired more from reading than from other information sources. The fact that scores on these checklists were positively related to amount of reading that people engage in suggests that the checklists did in fact sample information at least correlated with greater amounts of reading. The findings that as age increased the amount of engagement in reading increased and the amount of knowledge increased (Tables 2,3,and 4) further supports the design of the checklists as instruments especially sensitive to knowledge gained by reading.

The findings of this research are consistent with the practice-engagement theory of literacy development (Reder, 1994). This theory contends that by engaging in extensive practices involving reading of a wide-ranging nature literates build vast bodies of knowledge (both declarative and procedural) and automaticity of word recognition. This makes it possible to engage in and successfully complete a large number of literacy tasks. In turn this leads to greater knowledge and greater literacy skill.

The importance of reading as a major means of acquiring knowledge has not gone unrecognized by many business executives. In the studies of presidents and managers mentioned above, over half the presidents and managers said they had made deliberate efforts to increase their vocabulary knowledge since leaving school. Company presidents were asked what they did to increase their vocabularies and over a quarter said that just general reading was used and over half said that general reading plus some method like use of a dictionary, vocabulary books, and so forth were their main methods for developing their vocabulary knowledge.

## KNOWLEDGE AND ASSESSMENT PRACTICES

Several studies have demonstrated that high levels of "prior" or "background" knowledge in a specific domain can compensate for several "years" of "general" reading skill (Recht & Leslie, 1988; Sticht et al, 1986). The National Adult Literacy Survey (Kirsch, Jungeblut, Jenkins, & Kolstad, 1993) concluded that high levels of "prior" or "background" knowledge about what one reads is prerequisite for comprehending at a high level across the wide range of tasks in the battery. For these reasons, it is likely that assessments of knowledge would be useful in estimating adults' abilities to perform "real world" literacy tasks like those in the National Adult Literacy Survey.

The present results suggest that the assessment of knowledge (by checklists and/or other methods) may be a useful method for characterizing the knowledge associated with functioning in a technological society. The Department of Defense uses the Armed Services Vocational Aptitude Battery (ASVAB), consisting of ten tests of general and special vocabulary and conceptual knowledge (e.g., knowledge of geometry, electronics, automobiles, etc.) to select applicants for military service and to predict who will be most likely to succeed in different kinds of technical training and jobs (Sticht & Armstrong,

1994, pp. 31-39). This suggests that knowledge assessment can serve to identify those who can use printed and written materials to function in society, at least in the high-technology world of the military.

## LIMITATIONS OF THIS RESEARCH

There are two main types of limitations to this research that need to be taken into account in drawing inferences from these two studies about relationships among knowledge, literacy and power. One type of limitation is typical of all survey studies and concerns issues regarding the samples used in these studies. A second set of issues is concerned with the question of the causal relationships among knowledge and power given the correlational nature of the research.

Sampling issues. The less well educated and minority groups in San Diego county were underrepresented in our sample and this limits our ability to generalize to all segments of the population in the county. However, we do not believe these limitations undermine the main findings of the study for several reasons. First, all English-speaking groups were represented in the telephone survey, and we limit our findings and conclusions to just those groups. Second, though the representation of both the less well educated and minorities in our sample is below that of the U.S. Census for San Diego county, our major argument about knowledge and power is based on analyses in which variance due to age, education and ethnicity is removed, so for this research project we do not use weights to project our findings to lower educated or minority groups when these main effects are presented. It should be realized however that this would be possible if generalization to these underrepresented groups was desired. Third, we replicated several of the findings of Study 1 in Study 2, indicating some degree of reliability in the findings. Fourth, findings were replicated when analyses were repeated after weighting by education, income, and ethnicity to correct for discrepancies. Fifth, we do not know how many disenfranchised adults who regard themselves as "oppressed" by the "dominant" society were contacted during the telephone survey and chose not to participate.

However, we included in Study 2 a rating scale to directly assess adults' perceived power or lack thereof. This instrument indicated that at least some adults who felt less powerful were included in the sample and they were not so intimidated by the telephone approach that they refused to be interviewed. There were statistically significant, positive correlations among the knowledge and perceived power measures indicating that knowledge is associated with perceived power as well as the power indicators of occupation, income and political activity. Sixth, the thrust of our argument is based on correlational analyses. The kinds of sample biases present would be expected to reduce, not increase correlations among knowledge, occupational status, income and political activity.

Questions of causation. What comes first, knowledge or power? In Studies 1 and 2 it is not known whether the adults who possessed higher levels of knowledge achieved their positions of power because of their higher knowledge, or whether they were members of the "dominant" society in the first place, and through some form of "cultural bias" this may have given them access to positions of power. However, those with college degrees must have possessed the extensive knowledge required to successfully pass college entrance exams, and some had to pass graduate school exams, before they finally graduated and achieved their positions of power. To the extent that explicit gate-keeping tools exist that require adults to possess and exhibit large bodies of knowledge before they can enter into a position of power, then knowledge comes first.

## CONCLUSION

The two studies reported here have examined for the first time the relationships among amount of declarative knowledge, literacy practices and power, as indicated by occupational status, income, and political activities when the effects of age, education and ethnicity are held constant. The results suggest the conclusion that, while high levels of knowledge are not absolutely necessary for achieving power, they do seem to help. Therefore, in addition to helping students develop the processes of thinking and learning, educational practice should also emphasize the acquisition of broad bodies of content knowledge.

Further, literacy, that is reading, seems to be a much more frequent activity of the more knowledgeable adults and it appears to be a more important activity for the acquisition of knowledge than are listening to the radio or watching television. More research is needed to discover how other types of content knowledge, of both a generic and domain-specific nature, beyond that in the checklists used herein, relate to important outcomes in adult life. In general, though considerable research has been conducted on the relationships of knowledge to comprehension in reading, and in certain problem-solving situations.

(Alexander, 1996; Reynolds, Sinatra, & Jetton, 1996; de Jong & Ferguson-Hessler, 1996), there is surprisingly little research on how the quantity of ones declarative knowledge base grows over the school years or in adult education programs and how the extent of one's knowledge base relates to various out-of-school activities and achievements.

Additionally, research is needed in the K-12 school system and in adult literacy education programs to discover methods for encouraging students to do what many business managers and professionals reported doing, that is, developing self-management plans for guiding their engagement in reading and then spending a considerable amount of time in wide-ranging reading. Conceivably, sharing the results of studies like those reported here with students might serve to elucidate the importance of reading and knowledge acquisition to students and serve to motivate those having difficulty in reading to exert the extra effort needed for greater engagement in reading practices.

# REFERENCES

Alexander, P. A. (1996). The past, present, and future of knowledge research. A reexamination of the role of knowledge in learning and instruction. *Educational Psychologist*, 31, 89-92.

Allen, L., Cipielewski, J., & Stanovich, K. E. (1992). Multiple indicators of children's reading habits and attitudes construct validity and cognitive correlates. *Journal of Educational Psychology*, 84, 489-503.

Bernstein, D., Roy, E., Srull, T., Wickens, C. (1988). *Psychology*. Boston Houghton Mifflin.

Bruer, J. T. (1993). Schools for thought A science of learning in the classroom. Cambridge, MIT Press.

de Jong, T. & Ferguson-Hesler, M. G. M. (1996). Types and qualities of knowledge. *Educational Psychologist*, 31, 105-113.

Delli Carpini, M. X., & Keeter, S. (1993). Measuring Political Knowledge Putting First Things First. *American Journal of Political Science*, 37, pp.1179-1206.

Dillman, D. A. (1978). Mail and telephone surveys the total design method. New York John Wiley & Sons.

Faircough, N. (1989). Language and power. New York Longman.

Foucault, M. (1980). Power/knowledgeSelected interviews and other writings 1972-1977. New York Pantheon.

Freire, P. (1970). Pedagogy of the oppressed. New York Seabury Press.

Frey, J. H. (1989). Survey research by telephone. 2nd edition. Newbury Park Sage Publications.

Galtung, J. (1964). Foreign policy opinion as a function of social position. *Journal of Peace Research*, 1, 200-210.

Gee, J. P. (1996). Social linguistics and literacies. London Taylor & Francis.

Gershon, R. (1990, December). The vocabulary scores of managers. Chicago Johnson O'Connor Research Foundation, Inc.

Healy, A. F., & McNamara, D. S. (2996). Verbal learning and memory Does the modal model still work? Spence, J., Darley, J. & Foss, D. (eds.) *Annual review of psychology*, Vol. 47, Palo Alto, CA Annual Reviews, Inc., pp. 143-172.

Hirsch, Jr., E. D. (1987). Cultural literacy. What every American needs to know. Boston Houghton Mifflin Company.

Hirsch, Jr., E. D. (1996). The schools we need & why we don't have them. New York Doubleday.

Kaplan, D. & Venezky, R. (1994). Literacy and voting behaviora bivariate probit model with sample selection. *Social Science Research*, 23, 350-367.

Kirsch, I., Jungeblut, A., Jenkins, L., & Kolstad, A. (1993, September). Adult literacy in America. A first look at the results of the National Adult Literacy Survey. Washington, DCU. S. Government Printing Office.

Kohn, M. L. (1976). Occupational structure and alienation. *American Journal of Sociology*, 82, pp. 111-130.

Krashen, S. (1993). The power of reading. Insights from the research. Englewood, CO. Libraries Unlimited.

Kyllonen, P. C. & Christal, R. E. (1990). Reasoning ability is (little more than) working-memory capacity?!. *Intelligence*, 14, 389-433.

Lerner, D. (1958). The passing of traditional society. Glencoe The Free Press.

Lipset, S. M. (1960). Political man the social bases of politics. Garden City, NY Doubleday & Company.

Messick, S. (1989). Meaning and values in test validationthe science and ethics of assessment. *Educational Researcher*, 18, 5-11.

Meyer, B. J. F., Marsiske, M, & Willis, S. L. (1993). Text processing variables predict the readability of everyday documents read by older adults. *Reading Research Quarterly*, 28, 235-248.

Neuman, W. R. Just, M. R., & Crigler, A. N. (1992). Common knowledge news and the construction of political meaning. Chicago University of Chicago Press, 1992.

Recht, D. R. & Leslie, L. (1988). Effect of prior knowledge on good and poor reader's memory of text. *Journal of Educational Psychology*, 80, 16-20.

Reder, S. (1994). Practice-engagement theoryA sociocultural approach to literacy across languages and cultures. InB. M. Ferdman, R-M. Weber, & A. G. Ramirez (Eds.), Literacy across languages and cultures (pp. 33-74). New York State University of New York Press.

Reynolds, R. E., Sinatra, G. M., & Jetton, T. L. (1996). Views of knowledge acquisition and representation: A continuum from experience centered to mind centered. *Educational Psychologist*, 31, 93-104.

Smith, M. C. (1996, April/May/June). Differences in adults' reading practices and literacy proficiencies. *Reading Research Quarterly*, 31, pp.. 196-219.

Smith, R. & Supanich, G. (1984, August). The vocabulary scores of company presidents. Chicago: Johnson O'Connor Research Foundation, Inc.

Stanovich, K. E. (1993). Does reading make you smarter? Literacy and the development of verbal intelligence. In H. Reese (Ed.), *Advances in child development and behavior*, vol. 24. New York Academic Press.

Stanovich, K. E. & Cunningham, A. E. (1993). Where does knowledge come from? Specific associations between print exposure and information acquisition. *Journal of Educational Psychology*, 85, 211-229.

Sticht, T. G.& Armstrong, W. B. (1994, February). Adult Literacy in the United StatesA compendium of quantitative data and interpretive comments. Washington, DC. National Institute for Literacy.

Sticht, T. G., Armijo, L. A., Koffman, N., Roberson, K., Weitzman, R., Chang, F., & Moracco, J. (1986). Teachers, books, computers, and peers. Integrated communications technologies for adult literacy development. Monterey, CAU. S. Naval Postgraduate School.

Street, B. V. (1995). Social literaciesCritical approaches to literacy in development, ethnography and education. New York Longman.

Taylor, D. (1994). The trivial pursuit of reading psychology in the "real world:" A response to West, Stanovich, and Mitchell. *Reading Research Quarterly*, 29, 277-288.

Verba, S. & Nie, N. (1972). Participation in America political democracy and social equality. New York Harper & Row

Warwick, D.P. & Lininger, C.A. (1975). The sample surveytheory and practice. New York McGraw-Hill.

West, R. F., Stanovich, K. E. & Mitchell, H. R. (1993, January/February). Reading in the real world and its correlates. *Reading Research Quarterly*, 28, 35-50.

Wolfinger, R. E. & Rosenstone, S. J. (1980). Who votes? New Haven Yale University Press.

Zaller, J. R. (1992). The nature and origins of mass opinion. Cambridge University Press.

*Chapter 7*

# Shortcut: High School Grades as a Signal of Human Capital

## Shazia Rafiullah Miller

Consortium on Chicago School Research
University of Chicago

## ABSTRACT

Research shows that employers are dissatisfied with their ability to hire good workers out of high school (Barton, 1990; Cappelli and Rogovsky, 1993). This paper considers whether employers could benefit from using high school grades to identify workers who they will value more in the long-run. Using the High School and Beyond data on the sophomore cohort this paper examines the effects of high school grades on long-term productivity as measured by earnings. It finds that high school grades do have a strong and significant effect on earnings nine years after high school for both men and women, those with and without a bachelor's degree, and controlling for race/ethnicity, SES, region of the country, and whether the school is public or private. Using a fixed effect model it also demonstrates that these findings are robust even after controlling for school level differences. The paper further confirms other researchers' findings of no or negative short-term effects of high school grades on earnings. It argues that this connection between grades and long run productivity suggests that employers could use high school graduates' grades to identify workers they will value.

Common sense suggests that employers want good workers. Human capital theory explains it more precisely: At a given wage employers will try to hire workers with as high a level of human capital as possible, and employers will pay more productive workers more money in order to keep them (Ehrenberg and Smith, 1994. pp. 42-43). Yet it is difficult for employers to identify who will be highly productive workers. It is therefore difficult for employers to hire the most productive employees or immediately pay new hires what they are worth. Employers have an especially difficult time making such determinations about young workers who have little work history and few employer references.

While teachers try to motivate students by claiming that their school efforts will be rewarded, work-bound students say that high school efforts are irrelevant to their future jobs. Unfortunately for teachers, these students are correct. Research repeatedly finds that high school grades have no effect on students' early earnings (Gamoran, 1994; Rosenbaum and Kariya, 1991; Kang and Bishop, 1984; Althauser and Kalleberg, 1981). However, existing research has generally focused on earnings in the first few years after graduation. This study examines the effects of high school grades on later earnings.

This paper uses the High School and Beyond data set (HSB) to study the relationship between high school grades and long-term labor market earnings and finds evidence to suggest that high school grades are more strongly correlated with earnings in the long-run than they have been shown to be in the short-run, and therefore they provide a possible signaling device for the productivity of high school graduates.

## LITERATURE REVIEW

While human capital theory suggests that individuals will be paid wages that match their productivity, it is difficult for an employer to immediately identify a worker's level of productivity. Hence, employers are often initially unable to reward workers with higher productivity. Over time, however, one would expect employers accumulate more information on workers performances and be able pay them commensurate wages. As a result, wages should be linked to productivity in the long run.

Several scholars have examined this aspect of human capital theory and found that over the long-term people are indeed paid wages according to their productivity. Altonji and Pierret (1995) found that the wage effects of unobservable productive capacities rise with time in the labor market. Murnane, Willett, and Levy (1994) found increases in returns to cognitive skills using test scores six years after high school graduation, at age 24, but not 2 years after graduation. In a related study, Neal and Johnson (1994) used the Air Force Qualifying Test (AFQT) to measure human capital and found that with the AFQT as a control, all of the wage differences between black and white women evaporate, and three-quarters of the differences between black and white men disappear, and they suggest that human capital as measured by the AFQT predicts long-term productivity as measured by wages.

The evidence suggests that employers benefit from academically prepared employees in the long-run. However, this does not solve employers' problem when they are making hiring decisions. Can they identify early the people they will later value? The evidence is clear that employers do not reward employees for having stronger academic skills in the short-run. Studies find that employers of high school graduates rarely look at measures of high school achievement, including grades, so individuals who learn more in high school reap little or no immediate benefit in the labor market (EQW, 1994; Crohn, 1983). Employers do not reward high school graduates' academic skills, as measured by test scores, in terms of hiring, better jobs, or better pay in the short run (Altonji and Pierret, 1995; Gamoran, 1994;[1] Rosenbaum and Kariya, 1991; Kang and Bishop, 1985; Gardner, 1983.  Kang and Bishop (1984) find no effect of grades or test scores on wages for jobs obtained immediately after high school using HSB and neither do Hotchkiss, Bishop, and Gardner (1982).  Murnane, Willett and Levy find the effects of test-measured cognitive skills on earnings do not show up after two years, and Gardner (1982) and Meyer (1982) find only very small effects of test-measured cognitive skills on wages in that time period.

Do employers initially fail to pay new high school graduates more for the skills they later value because these skills are not valuable in the short run?  Or are these skills that do increase productivity from the outset, but which employers have difficulty identifying?  Studies suggest that the latter answer is correct, that high school learning is relevant to immediate productivity in the workplace, but employers do not know how to identify it.

Bishop (1987, 1989a) found that achievement in math, science, and English, as measured by test scores, has large effects on job performance in clerical, technical, service, and blue collar jobs as measured by supervisory ratings of job performance and by work samples.  Similarly, Hunter, Crosson and Friedman (1985) and Bishop (1988) show that scientific, technical, and mathematical reasoning competencies have large effects on both paper and pencil measures of job knowledge and hands-on measures of job performance.

The greater productivity from workers who learn more in high school gives employers good reason to want an easy-to-use measure of the human capital youth have acquired by graduation, but they do not seem to have discovered it.  Is there a viable measure for determining such human capital?  Altonji and Pierret (1995) suggest that AFQT could be such a measure because it adequately measures human capital and has been demonstrated to be unbiased.  Yet most high school students do not take the AFQT, and employers are generally reluctant to give tests, in part because they are costly and time consuming to administer (Miller and Rosenbaum, 1997).

As an alternative, employers could use high school grades to measure human capital. High school grades have the advantage of already existing for every high school graduate and of measuring overall mastery of the high school curriculum.  Of course, grades are significantly more subjective measures than well-developed tests like the AFQT; they are skewed from teacher idiosyncrasy, varying difficulty and relevance of course-work, and varying school standards.  Nonetheless the question remains:  Do these idiosyncrasies average out, leaving grade averages as a valuable signal of student value, or do they render grades a useless artifact with little predictive value in the work world?  This study examines this question:  Are grades, in spite of their inaccuracies, correlated with earnings in the long-run?

---

1 Gamoran reviews the literature and finds no positive connection between test scores and long-term work outcomes, even among persons with the same amount of schooling.

# METHODS

To determine whether grades can predict long-term earnings, a customary indicator of human capital, this paper uses the sophomore cohort of the High School and Beyond data set (HSB). The 14825 sophomores originally surveyed in 1980 came from a sample of 1015 high schools throughout the United States. Follow-up surveys were administered in 1982, 1984, 1986, and 1992. Because not all students answered all questions or completed the follow-up surveys, using listwise deletion of missing data, the total samples include 4262 men and 4160 women for the long-run samples, and 1582 men and 1594 women for the short-run samples.

For short-run earnings, this paper uses individuals' annual wages for their first job after high school, for all respondents who said they had a first job between graduation and February 1984. This allows the respondents to have had more than a full year to find work after graduation. The study also includes only those respondents who said they were not in college full-time during this period, because full-time college-goers are likely not to be in the best possible job, but rather a job that is convenient for also taking classes. Because all respondents graduated from the same high school class, they should all be roughly the same age, so there should be no differential maturity effects.

While hourly earnings might be considered a more accurate measure of productive value, HSB does not permit this to be calculated for the 1991 data used for long-run calculations - it asks only for annual earnings with no information about the number of hours worked, so annual earnings must be used for comparability between the two years. However, first job annual wages are calculated by using both pay rate and hours of work for greater accuracy. The sample also excludes those who said they made more than $60,000 per year for short-run earnings, because anything over that figure seemed likely to be faulty data, and even if it is not, such outliers might skew the analysis; this restriction removed less than one percent of the cases.

For the long run, this paper uses 1991 annual earnings, earnings nine years after high school. (1992 earnings are not used because they are based on only a partial year.) I use the natural log of both long and short-run earnings which reduces the distortions from extremely high wages. Furthermore, using the natural log means that the coefficients of the independent variables can be interpreted as the percentage change in the dependent variable resulting from a one unit change in the independent variable.[2]

Because men and women have different earnings trajectories, I ran separate, weighted least squares regressions for each. I also controlled for race/ethnicity, because blacks and Latinos tend to have lower earnings than whites (Cancio et al., 1997; Farkas and Vicnair, 1997), for private and Catholic schools, because HSB oversampled these types of schools compared to their prevalence in the general population of schools, and

---

[2] The analyses use weighted regressions using the HSB variable FU4WT. FU4WT is HSB's weight variable for the fourth follow-up wave of data created to adjust for non-response and permit analysis of prior survey data for these respondents. It ensures population totals are consistent with those of the base year survey. Running the regressions without weights does not substantially change the outcomes.

for region of the country, because Freeman (1982) suggests that there are regional differences in earnings. For a more expansive set of variable definitions and explanations of how variables were created, see Appendix A.  For descriptive statistics on the variables, see Appendix B and Appendix C.

Finally, to test the robustness of the findings I ran a fixed-effect model to see if the differences between individual school grading systems substantively changed the results. This model controls for the possibility of variations between schools rather than between students of different schools.

## FINDINGS

### Effects on Short-Term Income

In the short-run, we find some significant effects for region of the country and a negative SES effect for women but no significant relationship between earnings and grades for men or women; furthermore, the coefficients on grades are negative (Table 1). However, it is possible that there are only wage gains for people with especially good grades, or losses for those with really bad grades or some other permutation.  To test the possibility of a non-linear relationship, we use dummy variables, excluding the category of those who received mostly B's (Table 2).  Using dummy variables for grades rather than the seven-point scale, we still see no significant effects of grades on short-term earnings for men.  For women we find no significant effects for grades above B's, but find a positive significant effect at the .05 level for with mostly C's rather than mostly B's, and a strong positive effect of 131% for those with mostly D's rather than mostly B's.  In the category of those with mostly D's, there are only 28 cases in this category, so the finding might be spurious.  The positive effect for women with mostly C's is harder to understand, perhaps women with average (C) grades have traits that schools do not measure but do provide them with short term earnings benefits.  For example, women who received C's may be working in more service oriented jobs which reward sociability over cognitive skills, but more exploration of this anomalous finding would be worthwhile.[3]  That there is little or no consistent effect of grades on short-term earnings is not surprising as it confirms other researchers' findings of no impact of grades on short term earnings (EQW 1994; Gardner 1982; Meyer 1982).  It also confirms employers' reports that they rarely pay attention to grades or consider them important when hiring (EQW 1994; Crain 1984), making it unlikely that grades would affect what new workers are paid.

---

[3] Running the regressions not excluding those who were in college full-time makes the effects of grades slightly negative for men, and there are no significant effects for women.

## Effects on Long-Term Income: Basic Model

If employers are not paying workers who received higher grades higher wages in the short-run, do they do so in the long run as it becomes more clear who productive workers are? Nine years later the story about grades' effects on earnings does indeed prove to be quite different; gains in earnings for higher grades are significant and substantial.[4] For men nine years out of high school, a one unit higher grade is associated with 8.4% higher earnings (Table 3). Since a unit on the grade scale is half a grade, a person with all the same characteristics who got mostly B's rather than mostly C's is predicted to have 16.8% higher earnings nine years after graduation. For women the effect is even stronger (Table 4). Women gain 11.7% in earnings for each higher grade unit, so the difference between a woman with mostly C's and mostly B's would be a huge 23.4%.[5]

The control variables also show strong effects by gender. Most notably, while being a black man predicts a 13.0% lower earnings and being a black women predicts 22% higher earnings, while being Latino has no significant effect for either gender. SES has a much stronger positive effect for women (20.8% versus 7.5% for men). Attending a private or Catholic school also has a slightly stronger effect for women, at 10.9% for men and 13.2% for women. Of the regional effects, only living in the northeast is positive and significant (6.6% for men and 25.7% for women), and living in the West has a negative effect for men only (7.2%).

## Effects on Long-Term Income: Dummy Variables for Grades

Again, to test for the possibility of non-linear effects by grades we use dummy variables. Using dummies we find the same general pattern of better grades improving long-term earnings (Table 5). The pattern is generally linear for men with a roughly 8% increment per grade unit. For example, men with Mostly A's have 20.7% higher predicted earnings than those with mostly B's, and men having mostly C's have 17.7% lower predicted earnings than those receiving mostly B's. At the lowest grades this relationship is weaker, and the coefficient for getting mostly D's in non-significant.

For women the story is similar, but not quite as smoothly linear. There is roughly a 10% difference for each grade increment. More specifically, the difference between mostly A's and mostly B's is 18.4%, and between mostly B's and mostly C's is 20.5%. However, the difference for women who get grades lower than C's becomes stronger for women with mostly C's and D's rather than B's who receive almost double the expected linear drop in pay, and again an even more enormous drop for women getting mostly D's (Table 5). This mirrors Grubb's (1993) findings on the class of 1972, that grades effects

---

[4] Primarily because the short-run sample excluded respondents who were in college full-time after high school, it is substantially smaller than the long-run sample. Running the regression on long-term earning using the short run sample still shows strong and significant effects, albeit somewhat smaller effects that those for the whole group. See Table 10.

[5] Running the regressions unweighted does not substantially change the outcomes.

differ at the low end of the distribution, but this study finds this true only for women, not for men.[6] Because using dummies explains only a little more of the variance for either men or women and makes for less clear analysis, I will use the linear scale for the rest of the models.

## Long-Term Income: Path Analysis with Years of Education

It is possible that grades' effect on long-term earnings occurs because people with higher grades are more likely to acquire more years of education; the effect of grades could simply be masking a well documented effect of years of education on wages (see, for example, Katz and Murphy, 1992; Blackburn, Bloom, and Freeman, 1990; Bishop, 1987; Grubb, 1993.) It is quite plausible that people with higher grades finish more years of education, and it is the extra years of education which are the causal agent in predicting higher wages.

Using a path analysis to test this possibility, we find that while higher grades in high school have a strong and significant effect on years of education, additional years of education explain only about one-third of the long-term earnings returns to grades for both men and women. (Tables 3 and 4.) Approximately one-third of the effect of grades, 1.7% of the effect grades on men's earnings nine years after high school is through the additional years of education men with higher grades are likely to get. The other 6.7% comes directly through grades. For women the story is quite similar. 3.4% of the effect comes through the additional years of education, while the other 8.3% comes directly through the higher grades. This suggests that the human capital developed in high school is important both with and without additional schooling.[7]

To further test the relevance of additional education we check the effect of grades when controlling for levels of education achieved by using dummy variables for level of education and found very similar results, with an 8.2% expected increase for women and 6.2% expected increase for men with only a high school degree. (High school diploma only is the excluded category.) This model shows a substantial "sheepskin effect" of benefits for credentials, especially the BA with an 11.8% expected increase in long-term earnings for men and 26.7% for women, but the importance of high school grades remains. (Table 6.) Interestingly, while associates' degrees and certificates pay off for women they have only a negligible effect for men.

---

[6] While Grubb was the first to present these findings using NLS72 data, his focus was not on the effect of high school grades on long-term earnings, but the effect of post-secondary schooling. As such, he did not discuss his findings on grades. Grubb's findings are also from a cohort ten years earlier, and suggest a less linear pattern to the relationship between grades and long-term earnings than this paper finds.

[7] Running the regressions unweighted does not substantially change the results, although the effects of the control variables become stronger. This is to be expected, because HSB deliberately oversampled for blacks, Latinos, and private schools, and therefore by weighting variables we take this into account.

Because the possibility that high school grades can predict on-the job productivity would be most relevant for people with only a high school degree and the employers who hire them (because other employers could look at grades from more later schooling) we checked to see if the effect held up when using a sample of only those who did not go immediately on to college. Using the same sample as the one we used to test grades' effect on short run earnings still found sizable effects, especially for women. Women can expect an 11.4% higher income for each increase in grade unit, and men can expect a 5.9% increase. Even those who do not go on to additional schooling can expect long-term gains from better performance in high school. (Table 7.)

## Including School Averages

Of course grades do not just vary by student, they vary by the difficulty of the school itself. To test to what extent school-level differences mitigate the extent to which employers could rely on grades in predicting performance we control for school (rather than individual) effects by using a fixed-effect model. (Table 8.)

Fixed-effect models address the issue of possible omitted, group-specific variables that might impact the outcome of interest (long-term earnings) by allowing for correlations between unmeasured, school-specific characteristics and other variables. This is done by expressing all of the variables as deviations from the mean scores for schools. In this case, the fixed-effect model controls for the possibility that the schools have different grading systems (or other school based differences) which negate the effect that grades have on individuals' long-term earnings.

Using the fixed effect model we find that the effect of grades on long term earnings continues to be strong, significant and robust. For men there is a 8.7% increase in earnings for each grade unit higher, so a man who received mostly B's rather than mostly C's would be expected to earn 17.4% more nine years after high school, even after the controls for between school variation. Similarly, women are expected to earn 13.3% more per grade unit, so a woman who received mostly B's rather than mostly C's would be expected to earn 26.6% more nine years after high school, even after the control for between school variation in grades.

# TABLES

## Table 1: First Earnings After High School, Non-College Goers

| VARIABLE | Men | | Women | |
|---|---|---|---|---|
| | B | SE B | B | SE B |
| HS GRADES | -.020 | .019 | -.027 | .017 |
| BLACK | -.013 | .077 | .017 | .077 |
| SES | .019 | .033 | -.080** | .030 |
| LATINO | .004 | .066 | -.071 | .069 |
| PRIVATE SCHOOL | -.127 | .079 | -.013 | .066 |
| NORTHEAST | .153* | .063 | .138* | .057 |
| SOUTH | .134* | .058 | .211** | .051 |
| WEST | -.001 | .066 | .108 | .063 |
| (Constant) | 7.979** | .088 | 7.788** | .085 |
| $R^2$ | .009 | | .020 | |
| Adj. $R^2$ | .004 | | .015 | |
| N | 1582 | | 1594 | |

**Note: For all tables, * = significant at the .05 level, ** = significant at the .01 level, N = number of respondents.**

## Table 2: Dummies for Grades on Short-Run Earnings

| | Men | | Women | |
|---|---|---|---|---|
| VARIABLE | B | SE B | B | SE B |
| BLACK | -.015 | .078 | .025 | .077 |
| SES | .024 | .034 | -.084** | .030 |
| LATINO | .011 | .066 | -.063 | .069 |
| PRIVATE | -.123 | .079 | -.004 | .066 |
| NORTHEAST | .143* | .064 | .130* | .057 |
| SOUTH | .130* | .058 | .215** | .051 |
| WEST | -.012 | .066 | .104 | .063 |
| MOSTLY A'S | -.133 | .139 | -.013 | .105 |
| MOSTLY A'S AND B'S | -.138 | .092 | .032 | .064 |
| MOSTLY B'S AND C'S | .069 | .064 | .065 | .053 |
| MOSTLY C'S | .015 | .066 | .117* | .059 |
| MOSTLY C'S AND D'S | -.071 | .091 | -.151 | .111 |
| MOSTLY D'S | .342 | .361 | 1.313** | .323 |
| (Constant) | 7.897** | .062 | 7.62** | .051 |
| $R^2$ | .014 | | .033 | |
| Adj. $R^2$ | .006 | | .025 | |
| N | 1582 | | 1594 | |

## Table 3: Path Analysis for Men on Long-Term Earnings

| VARIABLE | Ln 91 Income B | SE B | Ln 91 Income B | SE B | Yrsed B | SE B |
|---|---|---|---|---|---|---|
| HS GRADES | .084** | .008 | .067** | .009 | .654** | .022 |
| YRSED | | | .026** | .006 | | |
| BLACK | -.130** | .035 | -.133** | .035 | .131 | .092 |
| SES | .075** | .015 | .057** | .015 | .711** | .039 |
| LATINO | -.045 | .030 | -.042 | .030 | -.095 | .080 |
| PRIVATE | .109** | .035 | .090** | .035 | .719** | .092 |
| NORTHEAST | .066* | .027 | .055* | .027 | .407** | .072 |
| SOUTH | -.013 | .025 | -.009 | .025 | -.127 | .067 |
| WEST | -.072* | .031 | -.059 | .031 | -.497** | .082 |
| (Constant) | 9.654 | .038 | 9.37** | .073 | 10.739** | .101 |
| $R^2$ | .058 | | .062 | | .312 | |
| Adj. $R^2$ | .056 | | .060 | | .310 | |
| N | 4262 | | 4262 | | 4262 | |

## Table 4: Path Analysis for Women on Long-Term Earnings

| VARIABLE | Ln 91 Income B | SE B | Ln 91 Income B | SE B | Yrsed B | SE B |
|---|---|---|---|---|---|---|
| HS GRADES | .117** | .010 | .083** | .011 | .582** | .021 |
| YRSED | | | .060** | .008 | | |
| BLACK | .221** | .042 | .211** | .042 | .163 | .086 |
| SES | .208** | .019 | .157** | .020 | .860** | .038 |
| LATINO | -.020 | .042 | -.024 | .042 | .077 | .086 |
| PRIVATE | .132** | .040 | .105** | .040 | .461** | .082 |
| NORTHEAST | .257** | .034 | .232** | .034 | .411** | .070 |
| SOUTH | -.012 | .033 | -.006 | .032 | -.125 | .066 |
| WEST | -.011 | .040 | .005 | .039 | -.261** | .080 |
| (Constant) | 9.028 | .053 | 8.380** | .098 | 10.880** | .108 |
| $R^2$ | .098 | | .111 | | .318 | |
| Adj. $R^2$ | .096 | | .110 | | .317 | |
| N | 4160 | | 4160 | | 4160 | |

## Table 5: Dummies for Grades on Long Term Earnings

| VARIABLE | Men | | Women | |
|---|---|---|---|---|
| | B | SE B | B | SE B |
| BLACK | -.135** | .035 | .226** | .042 |
| SES | .075** | .015 | .209** | .019 |
| LATINO | -.046 | .030 | -.011 | .042 |
| PRIVATE SCHOOL | .108** | .035 | .130** | .040 |
| NORTHEAST | .064* | .027 | .261** | .034 |
| SOUTH | -.012 | .025 | -.016 | .033 |
| WEST | -.072* | .031 | -.016 | .040 |
| MOSTLY A'S | .208** | .059 | .184** | .055 |
| MOSTLY A'S AND B'S | .082* | .037 | .118** | .038 |
| MOSTLY B'S AND C'S | -.087** | .027 | -.110** | .034 |
| MOSTLY C'S | -.177** | .029 | -.205** | .039 |
| MOSTLY C'S AND D'S | -.251** | .040 | -.477** | .071 |
| MOSTLY D'S | -.092 | .110 | -1.155** | .250 |
| (Constant) | 10.074** | .026 | 9.617** | .031 |
| $R^2$ | .059 | | .101 | |
| Adj. $R^2$ | .056 | | .098 | |
| N | 4262 | | 4160 | |

## Table 6: Long-Term Effect with Dummies for Educational Level

|  | Men | | Women | |
| --- | --- | --- | --- | --- |
| VARIABLE | B | SE B | B | SE B |
| HS GRADES | .062** | .009 | .083** | .011 |
| DROPOUT | -.319** | .066 | -.432** | .140 |
| CERTIFICATE or AA | .008 | .028 | .134** | .032 |
| BA | .118** | .027 | .267** | .035 |
| ADVANCED DEGREE | .111* | .052 | .248** | .065 |
| BLACK | -.126** | .035 | .210** | .042 |
| SES | .056** | .015 | .159** | .020 |
| LATINO | -.040 | .030 | -.022 | .042 |
| PRIVATE SCHOOL | .088* | .035 | .106** | .040 |
| NORTHEAST | .053* | .027 | .232** | .034 |
| SOUTH | -.014 | .025 | -.011 | .032 |
| WEST | -.058 | .031 | .000 | .039 |
| (Constant) | 9.719** | .040 | 9.089** | .055 |
| $R^2$ | .068 | | .114 | |
| Adjusted $R^2$ | .065 | | .111 | |
| N | 4262 | | 4160 | |

## Table 7: Long-Term Effect for Those Who Do Not Attend College

|  | Men | | Women | |
| --- | --- | --- | --- | --- |
| VARIABLE | B | SE B | B | SE B |
| HS GRADES | .059** | .014 | .114** | .019 |
| BLACK | -.190** | .056 | .362** | .086 |
| SES | .131** | .024 | .147** | .035 |
| LATINO | -.000 | .048 | .106 | .079 |
| PRIVATE SCHOOL | .024 | .057 | .180* | .074 |
| NORTHEAST | .034 | .042 | .229** | .065 |
| SOUTH | -.043 | .042 | -.099 | .058 |
| WEST | -.094* | .047 | -.102 | .072 |
| (Constant) | 9.915** | .064 | 9.076** | .098 |
| $R^2$ | .063 | | .078 | |
| Adjusted $R^2$ | .058 | | .072 | |
| N | 1465 | | 1304 | |

## Table 8: School Level Differences -- Fixed Effect Model

|            |          | Men     |          | Women   |
|------------|----------|---------|----------|---------|
| VARIABLE   | B        | SE B    | B        | SE B    |
| HS GRADES  | .087**   | .009    | .133**   | .012    |
| BLACK      | -.102*   | .043    | .039     | .056    |
| SES        | .036*    | .018    | .132**   | .023    |
| LATINO     | -.038    | .033    | -.051    | .044    |
| PRIVATE SCHOOL | (dropped) |    | (dropped) |      |
| NORTHEAST  | (dropped) |        | (dropped) |        |
| SOUTH      | (dropped) |        | (dropped) |        |
| WEST       | (dropped) |        | (dropped) |        |
| (Constant) | 9.671**  | .042    | 9.102**  | .058    |
| $R^2$      | .034     |         | .062     |         |
| N          | 4276     |         | 4166     |         |

## CONCLUSION

Overall, this evidence suggests that high school grades do predict higher earnings, and therefore predict higher productivity over the long-term, for both men and women, even after controlling for SES, race/ethnicity, region of the country, and type of school and including only those with a high school degree. This finding also proves robust under a fixed effect model which looks at the possible mitigating factor of differences between individual schools. Furthermore, the majority of this effect comes independent of additional education.

One might question whether employers are really benefiting from higher grades or from the greater aptitude which is reflected in higher grades. Bishop (1994) and Jencks and Phillips (1996) both offer evidence suggesting that it is the actual learning, not aptitude that matters in predicting long-term productivity. Furthermore, the evidence presented here suggests that some part of the productivity gains might be coming from the soft skills that employers say that want and grades appear to contain. These soft skills of regular attendance, preparation, hard work, and lack of disciplinary problems that employers say they value are also valued by schools and reflected in grades.

Yet if grades are so successful in predicting long-term productivity, why have employers failed to identify and use them? There are at least four possible answers to this question? First, employers may have not considered this option. All ideas are new and infrequently used at some point; using grades in hiring might be a possibility that simply needs more exposure. Yet high school grades have been available for over half-a-century; the idea to use grades for hiring has had plenty of time to become established. Of course, the kinds of skills measured by schools may have only recently begun affecting productivity as work places have become more demanding in terms of higher level skills (Murnane, Willett, and Levy, 1994). If this is the case, grades might eventually be used.

Second, while grades might have been technically available for a long time, employers may find them too difficult to obtain in spite of the Buckley amendment which requires schools to make transcripts available. Bishop (1989b) cites a telling example of the Nationwide Insurance company which received only 93 responses from its over 1200 signed requests to schools for transcripts. Schools, while quite comfortable sending transcripts to colleges, may not be accustomed to sending them to employers and therefore may too frequently fail to do so. Furthermore, if schools respond, but too slowly, transcript information may come too late to be of use to employers who often make hiring decisions quickly. The idea to use grades would probably spread more readily if they were easier to obtain, and the costs expediting this process should be relatively small.

Third, employers might already be satisfied with the tools they use to make hiring decisions and may not need another predictive measure. Yet employers have repeatedly complained about the quality of their workforce which suggests that they are not able to make as good hiring decisions as they wish (Barton, 1990; Cappelli and Rogovsky, 1993).

Fourth, employers may not use grades because they do not trust them (Miller and Rosenbaum, 1997). Employers do not believe grades are useful because individual teachers grade on idiosyncratic factors or on those that are not relevant to the workplace. Yet while employers may believe this, the evidence in this study suggests that while individual grades may be subject to individual teachers' idiosyncrasies, overall grades have a predictable effect on at least long-run productivity and reflect just those attributes that employers say they value.

So while there are many possible explanations for employers' failure to use grades in hiring, this evidence suggests that grades do actually measure something that employers value, and they might benefit by using grades when making hiring decisions. While other means of identifying good workers might be better, for example the use of the less subjective AFQT proposed by Neal and Johnson, using grades would be easier, because all students already have grades, and most students do not take the AFQT. Grades offer a potential shortcut for employers seeking productive workers in the long run.

## REFERENCES

Altonji, J. G. (1995). The Effects of High School Curriculum on Education and Labor Market Outcome. *Journal of Human Resources*. 409-438.

Altonji, J. G. and Pierret, C. (1995). *Employer Learning and Statistical Discrimination*. Presented at the Labor Seminar, Northwestern University.

Ashenfelter and Rouse. (1995). Schooling, Intelligence and Income in America: Cracks in the Bell Curve. Paper presented at the Meritocracy and Inequality Conference at the University of Wisconsin at Madison.

Barton, P. E. (1990). Skills Employers Need - Time to Measure Them? *Policy Information Proposal*. Policy Information Center, Educational Testing Center.

Bills, D. (1992). "A Survey of Employer Surveys: What We Know About Labor Markets from Talking with Bosses. *Research in Social Stratification and Mobility*. 11, 3-31.

Bishop, J. (1987) Information Externalities and the Social Payoff to Academic Achievement. *Working Paper 87-06*. Center for Advanced Human Resource Studies, School of Industrial and Labor Relations, Cornell University.

Bishop, John. (1988). The Productivity Consequences of What is Learned in High School. Center for Advanced Human Resource Studies *Working Paper #87-06*, Cornell University.

Bishop, J. (1989a) Incentives for Learning: Why American High School Students Compare So Poorly to Their Counterparts Overseas. *Working Paper #89-09*. Center for Advanced Human Resource Studies, School of Industrial and Labor Relations, Cornell University.

Bishop, J. (1989b) Why the Apathy in American High Schools? *Educational Researcher*. 6-10.

Blackburn, M. L., D. E. Bloom, and R. B. Freeman. (1990). The Declining Economic Position of Less Skilled American Men. In Gary Burtless (ed.) *A Future of Lousy Jobs?* Washington, D.C.: The Brookings Institution, 1990.

Borman, K. M. (1991). *The First Real Job.* Albany: SUNY.

Byrne, S.M, A. Constant, and G. Moore. (1992). Making Transitions from School to Work. *Educational Leadership.* 49(6), 23-26.

Cancio, A. Silvia, T. David Evans, and David J. Maume, Jr. (1997). "Reconsidering the Declining Significance of Race," American Sociological Review, Vol. 61: 4, pp. 541-556.

Cappelli, P. and Rogovsky, N. (1993). Skill Demands, Changing Work Organization and Performance. *Working Paper.* National Center for Educational Quality in the Workforce, University of Pennsylvania, 1993.

Crain, R. L. (1984). *The Quality of American High School Graduates: What Personnel Officers Say and Do.* Center for the Study of Schools, John Hopkins University.

Crohn, R. L. (1983). *Technological Literacy in the Workplace.* Portland, Oregon: Northwest Regional Educational Laboratory.

Educational Quality in the Workplace. (1994). *Issues Number 10.* Washington D.C.: Bureau of the Census.

Ehrenberg, R. G., and R. Smith. (1994). *Modern Labor Economics.* New York: HarperCollins.

Farkas, George, and Vicknair, Kevin. (1997). "Appropriate Tests of Racial Wage Discrimination Require Controls for Cognitive Skill: Comment on Cancio, Evans and Maume," American Sociological Review, Vol. 61: 4, pp. 557-560.

Freeman, R. B. (1982). Economic Determinants of Geographic and Individual Variation in the Labor Market Position of Young Persons, in *The Youth Labor Market Problem,* ed. Richard B. Freeman and David A. Wise. Chicago: University of Chicago Press.

Gamoran, A. (1994). *The Impact of Academic Course Work on Labor Market Outcomes for Youth Who Do Not Attend College: A Research Review.* Prepared for the *National Assessment of Vocational Education,* (draft version).

Gardner, J. A. (1983). *Influence of High School Curriculum on Determinants of Labor Market Experience.* Columbus, Ohio: The National Center for Research in Vocational Education, The Ohio State University.

Granovetter, M. (1995) Getting a Job. Chicago: *University of Chicago Press,* (second edition).

Griffin, J.L. et al. (1981). Determinants of Early Labor Market Entry and Attainment: A Study of Labor Market Segmentation. *Sociology of Education.* 54, 206-221.

Grubb, W. N. (1993). "The Varied Economic Returns to Postsecondary Education: New Evidence from the Class of 1972," Journal of Human Resources, Vol. 28:2, pp. 365-382.

Hotchkiss, L., J. Bishop, and J. Gardner. 1982. "Effects of Individual and School Characteristics on Part-Time Work of High School Seniors." Columbus, OH: The Ohio State University, The National Center for Research in Vocational Education.

Hunter, John E. Crosson James J., and Freidman, David H. (1985). The Validity of the Armed Services Vocational Aptitude Battery (ASVAB) For Civilian and Military Job Performance. Department of Defense, Washington, D.C., August, 1985.

Imel, S. (1991) School-to-Work Transition: It's role in achieving universal literacy (Digest No. 1-6). Columbus: ERIC Clearinghouse on Adult, Career and Vocational Education.

Jencks, C., and Phillips, M. (1996). Does Learning Pay Off in the Job Market. Presented at the Meritocracy and Equality seminar at the University of Chicago.

Kang, Suk and Bishop, John. (1986). The Effect of Curriculum on Labor Market Success. *Journal of Industrial Teacher Education.* Spring, pp. 133-48.

Katz, L. F. and Murphy, K. M. (1992) Changes in Relative Wages, 1963-1987: Supply and Demand Factors. *Quarterly Journal of Economics.* 107, 35-78.

Meyer, R. (1982) Job Training in the Schools. In *Job Training for Youth*, edited by R. Taylor, H. Rosen, and F. Pratzner. Columbus, Ohio: The National Center for Research in Vocational Education, The Ohio State University.

Murnane, R. J., J. B. Willett, and F. Levy. (1994) The Growing Importance of Cognitive Skills in Wage Determination. *Review of Economics and Statistics.*

Neal, D. A. and Johnson, W. R. (1994). The Role of Pre-Market Factors in Black-White Wage Differences. *Journal of Political Economy.* 104:31, 869-895.

Rosenbaum, J. E. (1989) What If Good Grades Meant Good Jobs? *American Educator.*

Rosenbaum, J. E. and Kariya, T. (1991) Do School Achievements Affect the Early Jobs of High School Graduates in the U.S. and Japan? *Sociology of Education* 64, 78-95.

Stone, J.R. (1992). School-to-Work Transition: Definitions and Directions. Paper presented at the annual meeting of the American Educational Research Association, San Francisco.

# APPENDIX A: VARIABLE DEFINITIONS

| VARIABLE | COMPOSITION |
|---|---|
| LNINC91 | Log of total, self-reported earnings for 1991 -- long-term earnings. Chose 1991 rather than 1992, because there is a full-year rather than half a year of data. Included all earnings over zero. From HSB variable 4301B9 |
| LNFSTJOB | Log of total, self-reported earnings for the first job after high school including anything over zero. I excluded those who reported any earning more than $60,000 per year under the assumption that such high earnings in the year after high school were probably mis-reported. Dropping these participants reduced the sample by less than 1%, and does not significantly change the outcomes of the regressions. Also included only those who were not in school in 1983 (from HSB variable SY18). From HSB variables SY46GA, and SY46GB.[8]) |
| HS GRADES | High school grades from transcripts, sorted into a 7 point scale, (mostly A's, mostly A's and B's, mostly B's, mostly B's and C's, mostly C's, mostly C's and D's, mostly D's and F's). From HSB variable HSGRADES, transposed so that 7 = A. Dummies used the same variable split into six separate variables with Mostly B's as the residual category. |
| YRSED | Created using data about highest degree completed (12=high school, 13=certificate, 14=associates, 16=bachelors, 18=masters, professional, or Ph.D.), and completed high school from HSB variables Y4205 and HSDIPLOM. Used Y4205 as base and assigned missing values as 11 for dropouts and 12 for high school graduates from HSDIPLOM. |
| PRIVATE | School-type dummy -- either Catholic or other private school. (other = public school) From HSB variable PHSTYPE. |
| SOUTH | School region dummy -- school located in the southern U.S. (other = midwest) From HSB variable HSREG. |
| WEST | School region dummy -- school located in the western U.S. (other = midwest) From HSB variable HSREG. |
| NORTHEAST | School region dummy -- school located in the north eastern U.S. (other = midwest) From HSB variable HSREG. |
| BLACK | Black racial dummy -- Black (other = white) From HSB variable RACE. |
| LATINO | Latino ethnicity dummy -- Latino (other = white). From HSB variable RACE. |
| SES | Sophomore year socio-economic status -- a composite of father's occupation, father's education, mother's education, family income, and material possessions in the household. From HSB variable BYSES. |
| FEMALE | Dummy for gender. From HSB variable SEX. |
| VOCTRAC | Dummy for in vocational track, from BB002, (other = academic track). |
| GENTRAC | Dummy for in general track, from BB002 (other = academic track). |

---

[8] I adjusted for a clear error in HSB. Records for participants who reported hourly earnings which was clearly off by two decimal points. To fix the error I divided the earnings of this group by 100 before calculating annual earnings.

## APPENDIX B: LONG-TERM EARNINGS DESCRIPTIVE STATISTICS

| VARIABLE | MEAN | STD DEV | MINIMUM | MAXIMUM | N |
|---|---|---|---|---|---|
| | | | | | |
| 91 EARNINGS | 9.87 | .75 | 4.61 | 14.22 | 8424 |
| HS GRADES | 4.40 | 1.29 | 1.00 | 7.00 | 8424 |
| MALE | .51 | .50 | .00 | 1.00 | 8424 |
| BLACK | .11 | .32 | .00 | 1.00 | 8424 |
| LATINO | .21 | .40 | .00 | 1.00 | 8424 |
| SES | .01 | .75 | -2.574 | 1.858 | 8424 |
| PRIVATE SCHOOL | .24 | .43 | .00 | 1.00 | 8424 |
| NORTHEAST | .25 | .43 | .00 | 1.00 | 8424 |
| SOUTH | .29 | .45 | .00 | 1.00 | 8424 |
| WEST | .18 | .39 | .00 | 1.00 | 8424 |
| A'S | .05 | .23 | .00 | 1.00 | 8424 |
| A'S & B'S | .15 | .36 | .00 | 1.00 | 8424 |
| B'S & C'S | .29 | .45 | .00 | 1.00 | 8424 |
| C'S | .19 | .40 | .00 | 1.00 | 8424 |
| C'S & D'S | .06 | .23 | .00 | 1.00 | 8424 |
| D'S | .00 | .07 | .00 | 1.00 | 8424 |
| YEARS OF ED | 13.76 | 2.09 | 11.00 | 20.00 | 8424 |
| VOCATIONAL | .15 | .35 | .00 | 1.00 | 8424 |
| GENERAL | .38 | .49 | .00 | 1.00 | 8424 |

## APPENDIX C: SHORT-TERM EARNINGS DESCRIPTIVE STATISTICS

| VARIABLE | MEAN | STD DEV | MINIMUM | MAXIMUM | N |
|---|---|---|---|---|---|
| 1ST EARNINGS | 7.88 | .83 | 4.32 | 10.94 | 3547 |
| GRADES | 4.22 | 1.25 | 1.00 | 7.00 | 3547 |
| MALE | .51 | .50 | .00 | 1.00 | 3547 |
| BLACK | .11 | .31 | .00 | 1.00 | 3547 |
| LATINO | .21 | .41 | .00 | 1.00 | 3547 |
| SES | -.07 | .71 | -2.27 | 1.83 | 3547 |
| PRIVATE | .21 | .41 | .00 | 1.00 | 3547 |
| NORTHEAST | .24 | .43 | .00 | 1.00 | 3547 |
| SOUTH | .31 | .46 | .00 | 1.00 | 3547 |
| WEST | .20 | .40 | .00 | 1.00 | 3547 |
| A'S | .04 | .20 | .00 | 1.00 | 3547 |
| A'S & B'S | .12 | .33 | .00 | 1.00 | 3547 |
| B'S & C'S | .31 | .46 | .00 | 1.00 | 3547 |
| C'S | .23 | .42 | .00 | 1.00 | 3547 |
| C'S & D'S | .06 | .25 | .00 | 1.00 | 3547 |
| D'S | .00 | .06 | .00 | 1.00 | 3547 |
| IN COLLEGE | .44 | .50 | .00 | 1.00 | 3547 |

# Chapter 8

# TOWARDS A MULTICULTURAL PSYCHOLOGY OF HUMAN DEVELOPMENT: IMPLICATIONS FOR EDUCATION

## *Norman Giesbrecht*
Department of Psychology
University of British Columbia

Recent political, economic, and technological changes around the globe have prompted an unprecedented degree of international exchange of people and information across previously separated cultural blocks (Kashima, 2000). These changes have heightened societal awareness of cultural difference and placed us at a crossroads between the resurgence of ethnic intolerance and the creation of a multicultural society based on mutually enriching cross-cultural dialogue. Cross-cultural understanding has emerged as a critical social issue for our school populations and an important component of our mandate to prepare students to become responsible participants within a larger society and global community. Since learning is a social interaction mediated by shared symbols and concepts (Vygotsky, 1978), the self-other-world conceptions embedded in culture have important implications for our students' cognitive, affective, and motivational engagement with the educational process (Markus & Kitayama, 1991). These issues are particularly critical for students from ethnic minority groups, since research indicates they are particularly at risk in traditional North American educational contexts (e.g., Ogbu, 1990; Sternberg, 1997). This chapter contributes to the emerging interdisciplinary dialogue on culture and psychology with a theoretical perspective that integrates current cross-cultural research and existing developmental theory, and highlights the implications of this perspective for our understanding of human psychosocial development and our educational theory and practice.

# Defining "Culture"

Although everyday language usage associates the term "culture" with distinctive actions, attitudes, rituals, and traditions, these concrete observable characteristics are behavioral manifestations of culture and not culture per se. Race and ethnicity are also typically used as cultural markers, but they tend to degenerate to stereotypes associated with blatant physical features and ignore the fact that culture is the social reality that gives race and ethnicity its meaning (Whiting, 1976). Culture is more accurately conceptualized as a "domain of shared meanings" (Kashima, 2000) that provide a sense of identity and continuity for a community of people across generations. Geertz's (1973) definition of culture as an "historically transmitted pattern of meanings embodied in symbols, a system of inherited conceptions expressed in symbolic form by means of which men [and women] communicate, perpetuate and develop their knowledge and attitudes towards life" (p. 89) provides a useful perspective that continues to inform current discussions in cross-cultural psychology (e.g., Shweder & Sullivan, 1993). The shared pattern of meanings that constitute culture function as a psychosocial lifeblood whereby communities transmit information from one generation to the next, and supply the "material and symbolic (a special kind of material) tools by which humans adapt to their ecological and social environment and construct their own images of their world and themselves" (Kashima, 2000, p. 20). Race and ethnicity interact with culture in that race provides a biological vehicle for the transmission of important genetic information relevant to community survival, and ethnicity maintains the adaptive social organization of a people within a specific geographical, historical, political, and economic context.

Although meaning-laden conceptions of the world provide the foundation for cultural organization, cultures are not simply incarnations of static abstract perspectives but rather dynamic and changing systems in which individuals contribute to and reinforce (or change) culture, and cultures change as they encounter other cultures and people groups. However, for the purpose of comparing cultures, "it is necessary to treat them *as if* they are stable systems" (Kashima, 2000, p. 22). Such an approach is justifiable if we recognize that certain elements of culture are more fundamental to cultural identity (both individual and communal). Specifically, the underlying conceptions of oneself, others and the surrounding world, and the meanings associated with these perspectives, are relatively stable and enduring whereas social norms and behavioral manifestations tend to adapt themselves to (or assimilate elements of) the surrounding socio-cultural milieu. When these core self-other-world understanding are threatened, as the histories of First Nations people groups and African Americans bear evidence, a community of people may struggle with loss of identity or negative identity. Problems in psychosocial development and academic performance also result when minority students are educated and evaluated in terms of developmental theories and standardized criteria based on the cultural values and experiences of students within a contrasting dominant culture (e.g., Ogbu, 1990). Kashima (2000) argues that such problems are the product of an Enlightenment empiricist tradition in which psychological phenomenon are abstracted from their socio-cultural context, universal causal laws are formulated, and then the resulting logico-mathematical inferences are experimentally tested with various populations. In contrast, cultural psychologists propose that "humans' experiences and actions should be interpreted and understood within the sociocultural-historical context of their enactment" (Kashima, 2000, p. 17). In this interpretivist approach, researchers and educators come to understand a cultural community on the basis of insiders' meanings and perspectives, seeking to discover rather than impose definitions, and formulate theories and evaluative criteria consistent with the values and standards of that cultural community. Although this perspective resonates with current post-modern constructivist sensibilities, we must also guard against the danger of adopting a cultural-psychological relativism that implicitly assumes there are no *human* commonalities or characteristics. Such relativism provides no common ground for communicating and connecting across cultures and limits us to simply observing and accepting (without truly understanding) diverse "ethnopsychologies" (White & Kirkpatrick, 1985).

Researchers and educators are thus faced with the challenges of recognizing the interplay between individual psychological and cultural sociological processes (Phinney, 1993), balancing cultural relativism (or particularism) and human universalism, and understanding a culture's self-other-world conceptions (from an insider's perspective) and their implications on important domains of human development and learning such as cognition, affect, motivation, and socio-moral reflection. In an attempt to address these concerns, this chapter proposes a multicultural psychology based on the following theses, namely that:

- Cultures place varying emphasis on the intra-personal, inter-personal, and existential dimensions of human existence, that result in Autonomy, Community, or Divinity cultural worldviews with distinct self-other-world conceptions.
- Cultures define normative tasks and psychosocial competencies, and provide supportive social institutions, that direct the psychosocial development of persons.
- Individual psychosocial maturation entails increasingly complex and integrative reflection upon the ideals embedded in cultural worldviews.
- The self-other-world conception of cultural worldviews impact multiple domains of human experience, including cognition, emotion, motivation, and moral reflection.

## CULTURAL WORLDVIEWS

Culture provides a domain of shared meanings embedded in symbols whereby a community develops, perpetuates, and communicates their identity and self-other-world conceptions across generations. At the social level, these self-other-world understandings have implications for the normative tasks, psychosocial competencies, and behavioral and attitudinal norms expected of group members, and the social structures and institutions that will enable individuals to develop these characteristics. At the individual level, these self-other-world understandings provide a repertoire of symbolic conceptions that people use to perceive, interpret, and respond to one another's behavior. Shweder (1991), a cultural anthropologist, proposed three cultural worldviews or self-other-world representations that underlie a diversity of racial, ethnic, and national expressions: an Autonomy worldview, a Community worldview, and a Divinity worldview. The Autonomy and Community worldviews reflect an individualism-collectivism dimension that research indicates is one of the most effective measures of cultural variability (Matsumoto, 2000). In an Autonomy worldview, the person is conceptualized as a separate, more or less integrated whole constituted by internal attributes such as ability, intelligence, personality traits, goals, or preferences. In most Western societies, a consumer-oriented free market system reinforces the cultural emphasis on inner self-knowledge (e.g., preferences, desires) and personal choice. Since societal structures and social interactions consider individual liberty and self-determination to be of paramount importance, social decision-making is a function of democratic discourse and majority rule. The normative psychosocial task is to maintain independence and persons are socialized to be unique, express themselves, and actualize their "inner" self.

In a Community worldview, the fundamental connectedness and interdependence of human beings is of primary importance and the person is conceptualized in terms of their roles and relationships with the larger community. Societal structures and social interaction reflect a communal tradition in which roles and their attendant duties and responsibilities are clearly defined, and social decision making is a function of consensus building and the interests and well-being of the larger group. The normative psychosocial task is to fit in and maintain interdependence and persons are socialized to adjust themselves to the attendant relationship or group to which they belong, read one another's minds, be sympathetic to the feelings and needs of others, and fulfill their assigned roles and responsibilities. A communal orientation does not mean that the needs of the self are forgotten, but rather that relationships are built on the expectation that "while [one is] promoting the goals of others, one's own goals will be attended to by the person with whom one is interdependent" (Markus & Kitayama, 1991, p. 229). Cooperative and mutually beneficial social interaction requires that there be reasonable assurance of the good intentions of others (i.e., commitment to reciprocal support), so persons will passively monitor the reciprocal contributions of others while actively promoting the goals of others.

In a Divinity worldview, the person is conceptualized as "a spiritual entity connected to some sacred or natural order of things and as a responsible bearer of a legacy that is elevated and divine" (Shweder, Much, Mahapatra, & Park, 1997, p. 138). Societal structures and social interaction are based on principles and values outlined in divine revelation, and the insights of spiritual exemplars and interpreters of divine texts (e.g., yogi, master, priest, rabbi) guide social decision-making. The normative psychosocial task is the renunciation of the earthly or carnal aspects of human nature, commitment to transcendent values and character formation, and propagation of divine truth. Shweder's (1991) worldview categorizations provide a useful perspective for cultural analysis because they focus on dimensions of social identity, meaning, and self-other-world conceptualization that are relevant across multiple racial, ethnic, national, and geographic expressions of cultural community.

## CONFLICTING WORLDVIEWS

Inter-ethnic dialogue is most challenging when there are conflicts in the fundamental self-other-world conceptualizations or cultural worldviews of communities. Since cultural worldviews provide the cognitive schema whereby individuals interpret the behaviors and make attributions regarding the motives of others, there is greater potential for misunderstanding, anxiety, and outright conflict between divergent worldviews. Individuals and communities selectively attend to the virtues of their own cultural context and overlook its shortcomings, and often contrast the stereotypical qualities of alternate worldviews with an idealized conception their own cultural worldview. As a consequence, an Autonomy culture will highlight its commitment to individual achievement and expression and downplay the dangers of social fragmentation, a Community culture will pride itself on communal care and interdependence while minimizing concerns about the subjection of individual needs to group interests, and a Divinity culture will emphasize the expression of faith, altruism, and moral virtue but disregard the potential dangers of other-worldliness and moralistic legalism. Even sincere attempts at cross-cultural understanding may be unwittingly short-circuited if multiculturalism is defined in culturally bounded ways. A North American Autonomy culture, for example, emphasizes the primacy of individual self-determination, so it socially constructs "multiculturalism" as the tolerance of diverse (unique) individuals with self-determinative beliefs, opinion and values. However, this definition of multiculturalism often co-opts the integrity of other cultures by reframing core Community and Divinity values and characteristics as simply "alternate individual choices". As an illustration, spiritual connection with creation and community are an integral part of aboriginal identity but aboriginal persons, communities, and culture are devalued if reverence for creation is viewed as a personal religious belief or following the advice of tribal elders is interpreted as an individual decision-making strategy.

These challenges to cross-cultural understanding can be addressed if we recognize that the Autonomy, Community, and Divinity worldviews emphasize intra-personal, interpersonal, and existential concerns that are addressed (implicitly or explicitly) within all cultures. The challenges of individual identity, interpersonal relationship, and existential meaning-making in the face of mortality confront all persons and hence all cultures. However, the inherent tension among these dimensions (e.g., individual self-determination versus communal commitment) causes cultures (and individuals) to selectively attend to or hierarchically order these dimensions. Since both cultures and persons exist in a three-dimensional space of intra-personal, interpersonal, and existential concerns, the Autonomy, Community, and Divinity worldviews each emphasize a dimension that is neglected or underdeveloped in the sociological and psychological self-other-world understanding of alternate worldviews. Cultural differences (at the societal or individual level) thus provide potential opportunities for growth and development, and hold forth the promise of a multicultural synergism that extends beyond simple tolerance or cultural relativism. However, the cross-cultural engagement that can promote this mutual growth and multicultural synergism (whether at the societal or personal level) requires openness to paradigmatic shifts in the constructions of meaning and conceptions of oneself and others that constitute individual and social identity. These concerns are particularly relevant to psychologists and educators, since "we are not only influenced by the prevailing [cultural] conception of the person but also participate in the production and maintenance of the conception" (Kashima, 2000, p. 29).

## NORTH AMERICAN WORLDVIEW

A theoretical perspective that recognizes the presence of intra-personal, interpersonal, and existential themes within all cultures enables us to analyze how various cultures (and persons) address these concerns and how particular value configurations influence social organization and individual psychosocial development. For example, cross-cultural research consistently observes that white, middle-class Americans are more Autonomy-oriented and less Community-oriented than non-Westerners (Triandis, 1995). It is not without cause that a fundamental document of American political life is entitled the Declaration of Independence. Bellah et. al. (1985) observed that middle-class Americans speak a "first language" of individualism that encompasses both utilitarian individualism (i.e., fulfilling one's own interests) and expressive individualism (i.e., expressing one's emotions). However, Americans still retain the "second languages" of communal obligation (i.e., a republican tradition of communal and civic participation) and divinity (i.e., a biblical tradition emphasizing life infused with faith and moral purity) (Bellah et. al., 1985). The influence of this value ordering is evident in a social organization based on a democratic electoral system and a clear separation of church and state, and in the tensions that accompany communitarian movements or public school debates about creationism versus evolutionary theory. Sociologists have observed that much of the conflict over moral issues, such as abortion and homosexuality, in the current American "culture wars" is rooted in a tension between a primary progressivist (Autonomy) worldview and a secondary orthodox (Divinity) worldview (Hunter, 1991, 1994). Autonomy-oriented progressivists stress the importance of human agency in understanding and formulating socio-ethical precepts, drawing upon either the scientific empiricist approach of Enlightenment naturalism or the personal experience tradition of Enlightenment subjectivism. In contrast, Divinity-oriented orthodox persons hold that transcendent authority is prior to and more powerful than human experience and that religio-moral precepts are sufficient for all times and circumstances so individuals and societies should adapt themselves accordingly. The conflict in self-other-world understanding between these worldviews is usually so great that "it would seem that no matter how much reversibility of thought orthodox and progressivist adults engaged in, they would not be likely often to arrive at similar moral reasoning" (Jensen, 1997, p.

341). Any resolution of the progressivist versus orthodox "culture war" (Hunter, 1991) therefore requires that each group first acknowledge a neglected or underdeveloped dimension within its own worldview that is present (in some form) in the opposing perspective. This not only legitimates and facilitates mutual contribution to the discourse, it also provides the possibility for a psychological "common ground" as each party comes to understand and appreciate the socio-cultural ideals and psychological dynamics that give rise to the other's perspective.

## PSYCHOSOCIAL DEVELOPMENT

The development of moral perspective and personal identity is not a private but a group endeavor for each self is constructed, engaged, and affirmed through socio-cultural participation (Markus, Mullally, & Kitiyama, 1997). Every culture has normative tasks and psychosocial competencies that are expected of its members (Cantor & Kihlstron, 1987). To accomplish this, cultures formulate age-appropriate behavioral expectations and provide social institutions to support the development of these socio-cultural competencies and integrate the person into the meanings and practices of the cultural community. The biological and psychological maturation of group members facilitates their response-ability, and the interaction of societal expectation and personal maturation contributes to the advancement and well-being of both the individual and society (Erikson, 1968). Although cultural groups define culturally relevant social expectations and tasks, there are psychosocial challenges – rooted in biological and evolutionary imperatives, the necessities of social organization, and the existential reality of human mortality - that must be addressed within every socio-cultural community. Erikson (1982) proposed that all cultures must concern themselves with, and hence develop normative expectations and provide social support for, the psychosocial issues of infant-caregiver attachment, childhood socialization into relevant cultural competencies (e.g., autonomy, initiative, industry), consolidation of adolescent identity within the larger community, interpersonal intimacy, generative care for future generations, and formulating a vision of a meaningful and integral life. Although Erikson's proposed childhood competencies (i.e., autonomy, initiative, and industry) are relevant primarily within Autonomy oriented cultures, Erikson's theory does provide a useful perspective for understanding socialization and the development of culturally relevant psychosocial competencies that is supported by cross-cultural and anthropological research (Ferrante, 1992; Matsumoto, 2000). In particular, Erikson's thesis that psychosocial conflicts are not resolved in terms of either / or alternatives, but along a continuum, provides for a theoretical openness to individual and socio-cultural variations in the definition of what is a "successful" resolution.

Although these psychosocial issues confront persons across cultures, each culture frames the dilemma in particular ways, implicitly defining both the "ideal" or desirable outcome and providing the symbolic conceptual tools with which persons will grapple with the issue. Autonomy, Community, and Divinity culture worldviews vary in their structuring of the intra-personal, interpersonal, and existential dimensions, and these value configurations impact both the saliency and resolution of these psychosocial concerns. In an Autonomy culture (e.g., America), the emphasis on individual self-determination and self-realization places the psychosocial issue of personal identity at center stage in social and individual awareness and weaves it as a thread through psychosocial challenges across the life span. Separation and independence thus become important hallmarks of child-rearing practices and infant-caregiver attachment, competitiveness and achievement values guide childhood education and socialization practices, interpersonal intimacy concerns are subservient to concerns about individual uniqueness and self-determination, generativity is primarily realized through personal accomplishment and achievement, and a meaningful existence is interpreted as the realization of individual goals, preferences, and personality characteristics in light of one's potential. In contrast, a Community culture's concern with communal relationships and attentiveness to the "other" results in a particular emphasis on the psychosocial issues of interpersonal intimacy (in a friendship and kinship rather than romantic sense) and generative care (for both the young and elderly). As a result, child-rearing practices involve multiple caregiver-infant attachments, childhood education and socialization practices focus on group-oriented goals and practices, adolescent identity consolidation entails adoption of progressively more responsible roles that enable greater contribution to the well-being of the larger group, and a meaningful existence entails finding and fulfilling one's proper place within the family, community, and ancestral tradition. Although offspring reflect personal preference and choice in an Autonomy culture, they are essential to complete personhood in a Community culture since they connect persons to their future and fulfill the role of building the collective (Markus, Mullally, & Kitiyama, 1997). In a Divinity culture, transcendent values guide one into a life of meaning and integrity, so childhood education and socialization practices focus on inculcating understanding of and obedience to religio-moral values, adolescent identity consolidation is affirmed through ritualized acceptance into the community of faith, and generative concern is expressed in modeling and teaching transcendent values to subsequent generations. These cultural differences highlight the need for educators and researchers to adopt a culturally relevant frame of reference when evaluating and facilitating the psychosocial development of students. As an example, Cooper (1999) suggests that educators must recognize that the identity development concerns of Community-oriented students "challenge us to expand our definitions of adolescent maturity beyond individualistic qualities such as autonomy, self-reliance, and emancipation from parents to include enduring family responsibilities and norms of communication" (p. 38).

## GENDER ROLES AND PSYCHOSOCIAL DEVELOPMENT

Psychosocial development is also influenced by culturally embedded gender role ideologies and socialization practices (e.g., Josselson, 1987). The label of male or female "provides a structure around which behavioral expectancies, role prescriptions, and life opportunities are organized" (Worrel, 1981, p. 313). Distinctions between gender roles appear to be a function of the socio-cultural dimension of power distance or status differentiation, with gender role differences greatest among conservative hierarchical cultures (Williams & Best, 1990) and lowest among cultures that value harmony and egalitarianism (Matsumoto, 2000). Research indicates a consistency in gender role stereotypes across a multitude of cultures whereby men are endowed with qualities of virility, strength, and critical thought and psychological needs of dominance, autonomy, aggression, and achievement, and women are viewed as passive, nurturing, and adaptive with psychological needs of affiliation, nurturance, and deference (Williams & Best, 1990). These perceptions may be rooted in socio-historical divisions of labor associated with reproductive processes that were later reified in cultural self-other conceptions and social organization. The psychological characteristics attributed to each gender influence the social participation and psychosocial developmental pathways available to each gender, and differences in gender power and status typically relegate women's development to a secondary cultural dimension. Research in a North American Autonomy culture indicates that men's social communication style tends to be status defining and competitive whereas women's communication tends to be relationship enhancing (Smith-Lovin & Robinson, 1992). In a structural equation analysis of gender patterns of psychosocial development in a Divinity subculture with hierarchical gender roles, Giesbrecht (1998a) found that generative care for others was more salient to the personal identity of women than men and that this generative concern was prompted by empathic concern for others. Such findings are consistent with current theories of women's development (e.g., Gilligan, 1982) that suggest gender inequalities in American Autonomous culture enable men to develop an independent self-sufficient identity but restrict women's identity and psychosocial development to a subservient cultural theme of interdependence and care.

## CULTURAL IDEALS AND SELF DEVELOPMENT

Persons, both female and male, differ in the degree to which they adopt and engage in the predominant attitudes, values, beliefs, and behaviors of their culture. The concept of a self is thus an important component of the interactional interface between society and person, and necessary "to account fully for the process of 'internalization' as the means by which social norms are transformed into individualized goals, dispositions, and meanings" (Wells & Stryker, 1988, p. 203). A comprehensive multicultural psychology therefore needs to elucidate the process whereby a socio-cultural set of meanings and conceptions of the world are incorporated into individual constructions of a sense of self.

Since socialization results in both conscious and unconscious self-other-world assumptions and perceptions, a theory of self needs to focus on the unconscious "I" (i.e., self-as-subject) that conceptualizes, experiences emotion, and acts as well as the "me" (i.e., self-as-subject) that is accessible to conscious awareness and self-description. Loevinger's (1976, 1987) theory of ego development is useful in this regard since it focuses on the core aspect of personality – the ego – which establishes the unity of the self by constructing and synthesizing the meanings one gives to oneself, other people, and the surrounding world. The primary function of the ego is to formulate a framework of meaning that synthesizes experience and shapes perception and interpersonal interaction. Ego development entails qualitative changes in self-other-world understanding that encompass various strands of personality, including ways of perceiving oneself and others, interpersonal relational style, cognitive complexity, impulse control, and moral or character development. Ego maturity is associated with increased self-awareness and psychological mindedness, cognitive complexity, sense of agency and active mastery, and coherent integration of perception and cognition (Hauser, 1993; Noam, 1993). Ego ideals provide direction for this meaning-making process and influence the individual's perception and interaction with the surrounding social world.

The self-other-world understandings implicit in cultural worldviews provide idealized conceptions that serve as ego ideals in the individual's construction of a sense of self. These ego ideals direct cognitive (and affective) attention to the salient concerns that must be reflected upon and addressed in the development of a culturally relevant sense of self. The self is thus not simply a passive recipient of cultural values, but an active participant whose increasing capacity for reflection, evaluation, and self-integration is directed toward the values embedded in the cultural surround. This interaction between the symbolic meaning-laden conceptions of a cultural worldview and the self-integrative actions of the ego can produce diverse configurations of the self. For example, persons may uncritically incorporate stereotypical cultural ideals, recognize and reclaim essential principles that underlie socio-conventional norms and ideals, or consciously reject the dominant cultural values and construct an alternate or counter-cultural sense of self. The psychological complexity and desire for integration that characterize higher levels of ego development orient the individual to an increasingly conscious and radical (i.e., from *radix* or "return to the roots") reflection upon the principles and ideals that constitute the cultural surround. Culture and personality thus function as a mutually constituted system in which each creates, maintains, and revitalizes the other (Markus & Kitayama, 1998). Cultures provides ideals and principles that guide the self development of its members, and the ego maturity of persons within the social group enables them to direct their "loyalties and energies both to the conservation of that which continues to feel true and to the revolutionary correction of that which has lost its regenerative significance" (Erikson, 1968, p. 134).

Developmental theories, like self-constructions, reflect the presuppositions of their cultural surround. As result, Western psychological theories often appear to describe the emergence of truly higher orders of human functioning, while actually naturalizing and legitimizing a specific, preferred world view ... [based on] a critique of the conventions of other world views, rejecting them as less advanced than its own, [so that] socialization into the normative "autonomous" character structure gives the impression of a revolutionary, postconventional maturity and independence (Broughton & Zahaykevich, 1988, p. 195). This caution applies to Loevinger's theory of ego development, which provides a useful perspective for understanding the interplay between socio-cultural ideals and self-development, but also reflects an Autonomy-oriented bias. Specifically, Loevinger's (Hy & Loevinger, 1996) higher stages are described in both name and characteristic as "Individualistic" and "Autonomous", and the theorized but empirically rare endpoint is an "Integrated" stage that reflects Maslow's (1954) description of a self-actualizing person. If we accept that ego development entails reflection upon salient cultural ideals, we must ensure that both the theoretical conceptualization and empirical assessment of ego development incorporates culturally relevant referents. In a test of this hypothesis, a Delphi panel developed a Spiritual Reflection measure of ego development, similar to Loevinger's Sentence Completion Test of ego development, focused on issues and ideals salient to a Divinity worldview. Both measures were administered to a sample of 165 spiritual exemplars from four major religious traditions and the responses were scored using the criteria outlined in Hy and Loevinger (1996), such as complexity, breadth and depth of response. The results revealed that the participants obtained a significantly higher ego development score in response to Divinity-oriented concerns versus Autonomy-oriented concerns (Giesbrecht, 2000). Such findings are consistent with the thesis that culturally relevant ideals provide an important reference point for the ego's synthesizing, meaning-making, and self-construction activities.

## CONSEQUENCES OF SOCIO-CULTURALLY EMBEDDED SELF

The ego ideals and self-other-world conception embedded in a cultural worldview "shapes, bounds, and molds [a person's] sense of self so that the self-concept 'makes sense' within that cultural milieu" (Matsumoto, 2000, p. 55). As a result, when psychological processes such as cognition, emotion, or motivation explicitly or implicitly reference the self, the nature of these processes will vary depending on the conception and organization of the self (Markus & Kitayama, 1991). Within an Autonomy culture, the self is defined as a separate entity with unique inner attributes so the primary cognitive referent will be the personal self, emotions will focus on the realization or frustration of inner goals and desires, and a primary motivation will be the expression of inner self-defining attributes and the accomplishment of personal goals. Within a Community culture, the normative imperative of interdependence means the primary cognitive referent will be another and persons will be motivated to engage in behaviors and emotional expressions that enhance relationship. Within a Divinity culture, the focus on transcendence means that the primary cognitive referent will be the unseen sacred order and persons will be motivated to engage in behaviors and emotional expressions that encourage the realization of transcendent ideals in the natural human order.

## IMPLICATIONS FOR COGNITION

The self-other-world representations of cultural worldviews direct cognitive attention to the salient aspects of a situation and determine what other relevant information should be retrieved to supplement available sense data (Markus & Kitayama, 1991). In a social interaction, the cultural construal of the self provides the basis for cognitive elaboration of the self and others, interpretations of the behavior of others, and attributions about the motives underlying these behaviors. The concept of self in a Community culture derives its meaning through mental links to concepts of other people, whereas the concept of self in an Autonomy culture has an intrinsic or cognitively isolated characterization (Niedenthal & Beike, 1997). As a consequence, the representation of the self in an Autonomy culture is more elaborated and distinctive in memory than the representation of another (Greenwald & Pratkanis, 1984). Cognitive representation of others is based on the assumption that they have a set of relatively stable internal self-defining attributes (e.g., personality traits, attitudes, or abilities), and inferences about another's internal state or disposition are drawn from behavioral observations. This is reinforced by the cultural perception that inhibition or inconsistency in the expression of one's inner feelings or opinions reflects a characterological weakness (i.e., lack of courage) rather than social sensitivity. As a result, Autonomous persons are more prone to commit the fundamental attribution error (Ross, 1977) of attributing to personality or motive what may actually be a function of the situation or context. In contrast, the greater attention and sensitivity to others among Community-oriented persons prompts greater cognitive elaboration of the other or of the self-in-relation-to-other. Since the social relationship rather than the self is the basic cognitive unit of representation, knowledge of others is not abstracted and generalized across context but remains specific to the social context. Community persons recognize that what an individual does is contingent on and guided by the duties and responsibilities that accompany social roles, so they are more inclined to explain behavior in terms of situational forces impinging on the person rather than making global inferences about internal predispositions. Because the social situation is a primary referent, contextual sensitivity is also more important than verbal articulation in social interaction since "most of the information is either in the physical context or internalized in the person, while very little is in the coded, explicit, transmitted part of the message" (Hall, 1976, p. 79). In a Divinity culture, the salient referent is transcendent ideals and the natural human order is considered to be an incomplete material reflection of the unseen sacred order. Events in the physical and social realm are therefore connected to and influenced by a religious or moral causal ontology (Shweder, Much, Mahaptra, & Park, 1997). Empirical knowledge is bounded by the limitations inherent in all temporal perceptions and hence must be subservient to and interpreted in the context of broader existential concerns and ethical considerations. Human beings are regarded as temporal mortal beings but with a divine essence or a "soul", so social interactions and communication are guided by the religio-moral imperative to reflect and realize divine character attributes.

These cultural differences have important implications for our conceptualization and assessment of intelligence. Western educational psychologists have assumed that Piaget's theory provides a cultural-neutral model of cognitive development but other cultures "do not share the conviction that abstract, hypothetical thought processes are the ultimate or desired end point in the cognitive development process. ... [but] consider cognitive development to be more relational – involving the thinking skills and processes needed to engage successfully in interpersonal contexts" (Matsumoto, 2000, p. 196). Intelligence should therefore be conceptualized as the skills and abilities necessary to effectively accomplish cultural goals, and researchers and educators should be sensitive to multiple forms and processes of intelligence (e.g., Gardner & Hutch, 1989; Sternberg, 1986). Cultures influence the development of particular forms and processes of intelligence by providing a specific repertoire of concepts and symbols, and tools for intellectually processing these concepts (Vygotsky, 1978). Socio-cultural educational practices also reflect and hence communicate epistemological assumptions about the nature, source, acquisition, and validation of knowledge. For example, Autonomy-oriented American education reflects a rationalistic Enlightenment epistemological tradition that holds that knowledge is constructed through abstract hypothesizing and empirical testing, practical utility is the ultimate confirmation of theoretical validity, and that knowledge in all domains of life (including relationships and spirituality) can be subjected to empirical testing. In contrast, Divinity-oriented Islamic education reflects the epistemological perspective that all human knowledge and experience is subservient to religious understanding so the primary educational objective is not to train people in the scientific method but to transmit faith, general knowledge about life, and deep appreciation for poetry and literature (Matsumoto, 2000).

Research indicates the cognitive differences between Community and Autonomy cultures have important implications for educational assessment and pedagogical practice. Since the salient aspects of the self are determined by social context, Community-oriented students find it difficult or unnatural to state anything in abstract non-contextual terms (Chiu, 1972). Research indicates that American students tend to generate a greater number of abstract traits than Asian subjects, whereas Asian student identify more social categories, relationships, and groups to which they belong (Triandis, 1989). As a consequence, Asians students are at a disadvantage in an unstructured creativity task in which the goal is to generate as many ideas as possible (Liu, 1986). Bruner (1986) suggests that these differences arise from a paradigmatic versus a narrative mode of thought, where the paradigmatic goal is abstraction and analyzing common features and the narrative goal is connection or interdependence among elements. The social-narrative perspective of Community-oriented students focuses their attention on the perceived intention of the teacher and the accompanying social-contextual considerations of "What is being expected of me here? What is my proper place? What are the potential ramifications of answering one way or another in respect to my relationship with this person?" (Triandis, 1989). The approval or disapproval of the teacher will be considered a more important source of feedback than their own performance, and Community-oriented students will make inferences about their level of ability from cues in the social situation where the task is performed. These Community culture versus Autonomy culture differences are evident not only in students' academic performance, but also in the presuppositions that educators bring to the assessment process and the learning climate they create. Although standardized tests indicate the range of student ability is approximately the same across American and Japanese students, Japanese teachers rarely explain performance differences in terms of ability differences since they view intellectual achievement not as a fixed attribute but as the product of individual effort in a given social context (Kitiyama, Tagaki, & Matsumoto, 1995). Asian teachers therefore engage the entire group in the educational process, sharing responsibility for mistakes among members of the group and using incorrect answers as examples for class discussion on process. In contrast, the North American Autonomy-oriented educational system emphasizes innate differences in cognitive ability among students (e.g., "gifted"), generates special classes for unique groups of students, and individualizes the process of instruction. Autonomy-oriented teachers spend more time on individualized instruction than whole-group instruction and use praise to reward correct responses, thus reinforcing the cultural self-construal of uniqueness and individualism. As a result Autonomy-oriented students thus develop a habitual intentional orientation to positive self-relevant information (Damon, 1995) whereas Community-oriented students follow a script of self-improvement that attends to personal failings and strategies for future remediation (Kityama & Wakabayashi, 1996).

## IMPLICATIONS FOR EMOTION

The socio-cultural construal of a situation influences a person's experienced emotion, and affective responses instigate a person to certain actions that in turn allow a new construction of the situation to emerge (Markus & Kitayama, 1991). The emotional experiences that accompany a cultural interpretation of social situation also promote particular patterns of affect regulation since people are motivated to seek positive states (i.e., that confirm one's view of self) and avoid negative ones (i.e., that challenge this view). In an Autonomy worldview, the individual self (and its internal attributes) serve as the primary referent and promote the experience and expression of ego-focused or socially disengaged emotions (Kitayama, Markus, & Matsumoto, 1995). Feelings of pride and superiority result when one's goals or desires are accomplished and feelings of anger and frustration occur when own goals and desires are interfered with or blocked. Social expression of these emotions further reinforces a person's self-defining attributes so individuals become "experts" in the expression and experience of these emotions, and public emotional expression is regarded as an accurate indicator of a person's inner "authentic" self. In a Community culture, however, the public display of inner emotions can result in confrontation, conflict, or overt aggression that hinder the maintenance of cooperative interdependent interaction. Since the relationship is the primary referent, the expression of other-focused or socially engaged emotions highlights one's interdependence and promotes the reciprocal exchange of well-intended actions leading to further cooperative social behavior (and self-validation). Sympathetic, friendly, and respectful feelings encourage interpersonal bonding, and feelings of indebtedness, shame, or guilt motivate persons to restore harmony or fulfill an obligation or debt. Interpersonal harmony assumes priority so self-restraint is accorded a higher value and an individual's emotional expression is often regarded as a socially appropriate instrumental action rather than an expression of the inner self. In a Divinity culture, the sacred or divine order is the primary referent so emotional experience is guided by the evaluation of actions and situations in light of transcendent ideals. Feelings of fulfillment and peace accompany communion with the Divine and the realization of divine will whereas self-deprecation, guilt, and remorse occur when the sacred order is violated or one is polluted by baser desires. The social desirability of religio-moral purity and the tension between this ideal and the "natural" human condition can also foster a pseudo-spirituality which addresses inner conflicts and guilt through denial, repression, or projecting unacceptable desires and emotions onto others.

## IMPLICATIONS FOR MOTIVATION

The motivation to individuate, relate, or transcend one's natural state are salient and important features of the internal self that direct and energize overt behaviors. Actions consistent with shared socio-cultural ideals are more likely to result in positive outcomes and hence prompt self-attributions of agency and efficacy. In an Autonomy culture, the independent self-construal motivates a person to seek situations and engage in actions that allow them to verify and express important attributes and convey the sense that they are appropriately autonomous. Selves are assumed to function as incentives or guidelines for behavior by providing images of possible future selves and their accompanying desirable or undesirable end-states (Markus, Mullally, & Kitiyama, 1997). Agency is experienced when one is able to withstand social pressures towards conformity, control one's own actions, future destiny, and surrounding situation, and express one's internal needs, rights, and capacities. In a Community culture, the relational self-other construal motivates persons to seek situations and engage in actions that affirm they are succeeding in their interdependent relationships and social roles. Agency is experienced when one is able to be receptive to others, adjust to the needs and demands of others, and restrain one's inner needs or desires; i.e., through the secondary control of accommodating to existing realities rather than the primary control of pushing oneself ahead of others and actively seeking personal success (Weisz, Rothbaum, and Blackburn, 1984). Whereas an Autonomy culture views conformity as a personal weakness evidenced in the inability to resist social pressure and stick to one's own perceptions, attitudes, or beliefs (i.e., the defining features of the Autonomous self), a Community culture considers it a highly valued end-state that signifies a willingness to be responsive to others and adjust one's own demands and desires to maintain relationship. In a Divinity culture, the self-Divine construal motivates persons to seek situations and engage in actions that honor the Divine and further the realization of transcendent ideals in society. Since the visible natural world is intricately connected to the unseen sacred realm, agency is typically experienced in accepting the existing situation in submission to transcendent purposes rather than in the attempt to change circumstances or pursue ego-focused goals. Self-affacement and accommodation to the existing reality are thus regarded more positively in Community and Divinity cultures than in an Autonomy culture since the primary referent is not the self but the interdependent or divine "other" (e.g., Takata, 1987). Similarly, Community-oriented persons experience a generalized self-liking as an outcome of group-esteem (Tafarodi & Swann, 1996) and Divinity-oriented persons find self-worth as an outcome of divine acceptance and benevolence, whereas self-esteem among Autonomy-oriented persons is the result of competitive social comparisons and personal attributions of self-competence.

These cultural differences will also impact students' motivation for and participation in educational activities. The Autonomous conception of self and group as separate entities implies conflict and competition and promotes self-enhancing biases among Autonomy-oriented American students, whereas the Community value of knowing one's place in the social order generates negative reactions to such self-enhancement or self-promotion tendencies among Asian students (Yoshida, Kojo, & Kaku, 1982). Educators need to be sensitive to the impact of self-construal on student motivation and performance, such as when a particular assessment task requires performance that is considered immodest or arrogant in a Community culture but desirable in an Autonomy culture. North American educators typically assume that being considered as positively different from or superior to others enhances student self-esteem and motivation, but such attributions and communications will have a negative impact on motivation and performance for Community-oriented students. Culture worldview also impacts educator and student attributions of success and perceptions of potential academic performance. Mainstream American students believe internal attributes such as ability or competence are extremely important to their performance, particularly their successes, whereas Asian students attribute failure primarily to lack of effort and may attribute success to the ease of the task (e.g., Yan & Gaier, 1994). As a result, Asian parents believe that high personal investment, sacrifice, and effort will enable their children to succeed (Chao, 1996) so they structure their children's lives with more after-school and extra-curricular programs to complement formal school learning (Yao, 1985). In contrast, American parents believe that a child's performance is limited (as well as enabled) by innate characteristics such as ability or intelligence so they are more easily satisfied at lower levels of competence and academic performance (Matsumoto, 2000).

## IMPLICATIONS FOR MORAL DEVELOPMENT

The self-other-world conceptions of cultural worldviews prescribe the primary moral values, construction and interpretation of socio-moral dilemmas, and moral competencies required for effective moral reasoning and action. In an Autonomy culture, the primary moral value is individual freedom of choice constrained by concerns over impinging on the rights of others or inflicting harm on others. Moral dilemmas occur when there is a conflict over limited resources between parties with conflicting interests, and an effective moral resolution results in socio-political justice accomplished through democratic discourse or legal recourse. Since moral dilemmas are resolved primarily through discourse and negotiation, the requisite moral competencies are cognitive perspective-taking of another's position and rational reflection upon shared democratic principles (e.g., individual rights supersede conventional societal norms). In a Community culture, the primary moral value is the well-being and harmony of the social group and moral dilemmas occur when a person fails to fulfill their social role or places their individual interests and goals ahead of those of the family or community. Resolution of these dilemmas entails the restoration of harmony and interdependence through group consensus building or an appeal to tradition. Virtue is understood as the development of the individual into a "social man" (Yu, 1992), and the relevant moral competencies include a sense of duty and responsibility, commitment to the responsibilities associated with a particular social role, empathy and sensitivity to the needs and feelings of others, and a willingness to sacrifice one's own interests for the greater good. In a Divinity culture, the primary moral value is the subservience of the natural realm to the ordained spiritual order and moral dilemmas occur when instinctive human passions are given free reign. Resolution of these dilemmas entails renunciation of the unacceptable thought or behavior, ritualized absolution, and renewed commitment to transcendent values. The requisite moral competencies include awareness and understanding of divine ideals, obedience to the sacred text and submission to masters or interpreters of the tradition, and a willingness to follow the disciplines that promote spiritual character. Since moral values are a defining element of a Divinity cultural worldview, violation of the community's socio-cultural moral ideals can have profound consequences on a person's sense of identity and social participation (Giesbrecht & Sevcik, 2000).

The moral ethics implicated in cultural worldviews reflect ego ideals and cognitive, affective, and motivational orientations that are intricately "wrapped up with one's sense of self" (Wren, 1993, p. 83) so they create a "volitional necessity" (Frankfurt, 1993, p. 20) that moves persons beyond moral reasoning into moral action. Unfortunately, the field of moral psychology has tended to separate morality and culture and view morality as primarily a cognitive method or "'logic' for coordinating the viewpoints of subjects with conflicting interests" (Kohlberg, 1981, p. 200) – a perspective that reflects an individualistic rationalistic Enlightenment tradition. The higher principled stages in traditional moral cognitive-structuralist psychology reflect Autonomous Western liberal values that presuppose individual rights take precedence over social organization (versus a Community perspective) and that human reasoning is the primary foundation for socio-ethical norms and moral evaluation (versus a Divinity perspective). As a consequence, researchers and educators operating within this paradigm can mistakenly interpret the "principled conservatism" of Community and Divinity oriented students as indicative of a lower level of conventional or conformist moral reasoning in comparison with the normative individualistic socio-critical perspective of Autonomy-oriented students (Giesbrecht, 1998b). These concerns are particularly salient to socio-moral issues such as adolescent sexuality that are critical to students' identity and psychosocial development, impact multiple domains of the self (e.g., cognitive, affective, social, motivational), and are linked to culturally-embedded self-other-world understandings. Cultural worldviews influence not only the concepts and values that students use to interpret and respond to salient moral issues, but also the very questions that are raised and how these questions are constructed. Morris (1994) observed that American sexuality education has attempted to address cultural and other differences by demonstrating respect for a pluralism of values, but in the process has failed to distinguish subjectivity from subjectivism, integrity from validity, and pluralism from relativism. The challenge of multicultural cultural dialogue on these topics is to recognize cross-cultural difference without engaging in relativism and allow these differences to stimulate thoughtful reflection without implicitly endorsing mainstream hegemony. Morris (1994) suggests that a stance of value neutrality does not require a clarification of values "already there", but allows for mutual interaction that challenges the validity of different value positions while respecting the integrity of the valued participants. Such multicultural dialogue can prompt greater awareness and deeper reflection upon the multiple dimensions of social context (Community worldview), meaning and commitment (Divinity worldview), and personal responsibility (Autonomy worldview) that accompany students' negotiation of the psychosocial issues related to sexual intimacy.

To explore the influence of cultural worldview on issues of moral development, we analyzed the responses of 36 Divinity-oriented college students to three Thematic Apperception Test images depicting: an individual on the floor with their head bowed down, a woman clutching the shoulders of a man who appears to be trying to pull away, and a young man standing with downcast head standing in front of a partially-clothed woman lying on a bed (Giesbrecht & Walker, 2000). We expected that issues of identity consolidation and interpersonal intimacy would be relevant psychosocial challenges among these young adults (Erikson, 1968, 1982), and that the negotiation of these challenges would be influenced by Divinity-based ego ideals regarding moral purity (e.g., premarital sexual abstinence) and the renunciation of instinctual desires. Themes of sexual temptation and moral struggle were prominent in participants' responses, and a thematic analysis revealed increased intrinsic moral motivation, broader perception of ethical dilemmas, greater self-acceptance following moral failure, richer conceptualization of a moral self, and holistic integration of personal and moral identity as a function of participants' ego development stage. The responses suggested an ego-development related progression from projecting unacceptable urges upon others (self-protective stage), to formulating stereotypical solutions for sexual-moral challenges (conformist stage), to experiencing guilt as the primary consequence of and motivation for renewed submission to divine norms following sexual-moral transgression (self-aware stage), to recognizing morality as encompassing emphasizing thoughts and attitudes rather than simply isolated actions (conscientious stage), and to empathically accepting both oneself and others as complex human beings "in process of becoming" (individualistic / autonomous stages). Across all stages of ego development, the influence of cultural worldview on these students' moral reflection on sexual intimacy was evident in the cognitive (e.g., Divine revelation as a reference point for interpreting moral dilemmas), affective (e.g., guilt, shame, forgiveness, reconciliation), and motivational (e.g., desire to realize the religio-social ideal of sexual purity) dimensions of the Divinity-oriented students' moral reflection. These findings highlight the integral connection between the socio-cultural ideals and self-other-world conceptions of a cultural community and the construction, interpretation, and resolution of moral and psychosocial dilemmas.

## FORGING A MULTICULTURAL COMMUNITY OF LEARNERS

All human development occurs within a cultural context, and the consequence of this enculturation process is the ethnocentric tendency to view the world through one's own cultural filters. The self-other-world conceptions of one's cultural worldview provide a set of expectations and socio-conventional norms about the kinds of behavior that people should exhibit and guide how persons perceive others, interpret their behavior, and make interpretive judgments about those behaviors. These shared understandings provide a basis for initiating and interpreting behaviors within one's culture, but inter-cultural communication introduces unexpected behaviors that lend themselves to misinterpretation regarding both the intent of the actors and the meaning of the action. The primary roadblocks to effective intercultural communication include assumptions of similarity, language differences, nonverbal misinterpretations, anxiety or tension, and preconceptions about others (Barna, 1997). To deal with the cognitive dissonance and anxiety that occur when cultural self-other-world conceptions collide, persons develop generalized or stereotypical attitudes, beliefs, and opinions about people from other cultures. Matsumoto (2000) suggests that the formation of these generalized mental categories are motivated by psychological imperatives to selective attention (i.e., filter which stimuli to attend to), appraisal (i.e., evaluate the relevance of a stimuli), concept formation and categorization (i.e., form mental representations that organize the diversity of the world), and attribution (e.g., infer causes of our own and other's behavior). Although stereotypical categories are useful in giving people some basis for judging, evaluating, and interacting with people of other cultures, they become a basis for prejudice "when we consider these mental categories as endpoints in and of themselves, instead of gatekeepers to important socio-psychological – that is, cultural – differences and similarities" (Matsumoto, 2000, p. 34). The journey from stereotypical perception to multicultural understanding begins with the mutual "construction of reality as increasingly capable of accommodating cultural difference that constitute development" (Bennet, 1993, p. 4). This multicultural synergism is facilitated when we conceptualize culture as a domain of meaning and self-other-world conceptions that encompass intra-personal, interpersonal, and existential concerns that confront (and are explicitly or implicitly addressed by) all persons and all cultures. Since different cultures embody alternate social constructions of shared human dilemmas, inter-ethnic dialogue can provide new insights into the self as well as the other and hence promote mutual growth and development. A recognition of the role of cultural participation in personal psychosocial development (including the domains of cognition, affect, motivation, and moral reflection) also enables educators to adapt their pedagogical perspectives and practice to the needs of students from minority cultures. Educators can then bring students from diverse ethnicities together to form a community of shared learners – where both education and personal development is facilitated by the challenge and possibilities present in multiple cultural perspectives.

To accomplish this goal, teachers and students must develop cultural flexibility – a mental stance that entails: recognizing how our own cultural filter and distort reality, appreciating that others have different filters that generate alternate experiences of reality that are just as real to them as ours appear to be, learning to put the emotions and judgments associated with our own ethnocentrism "temporarily on hold", and recognizing that the most troublesome cross-cultural differences often reflect blind spots in our own cultural worldview and hence hold forth the greatest potential for mutual growth and development (Boucher, Landis, & Clark, 1987; Brislin, 1993). At a systemic level, cultural flexibility requires a collaborative approach that includes all stakeholders (e.g., students, parents, teachers, community leaders) in the development of educational policy, curriculum, and practice (Cooper, 1999). At the classroom level, it necessitates that teachers are mindful of the influence of cultural worldview on their own pedagogy and learning assessment and on students' sense of identity, motivation, social interaction, learning strategies, and academic performance (e.g., Oyserman, Gant, & Ager, 1995). To facilitate cultural flexibility in student-student interaction, teachers can model cross-cultural understanding and provide students with cognitive and social tools for effective cross-cultural communication and the resolution of cultural conflicts. Specifically, North American Autonomy-oriented students can be encouraged to approach Community-minded minority students with an attitude of social respectfulness, sensitivity to the importance of mindful observation, attentive listening skills, and a willingness to accept indirect problem-solving approaches (Ting-Toomey, 1997). Community-oriented students can be encouraged to approach Autonomy-oriented students with a willingness to express their feelings and opinions openly, engage in assertive conflict behavior, take individual responsibility for dealing with conflict, provide verbal feedback and use direct verbal messages, and commit themselves to working out problems directly with the other person. Educators also need to recognize that many students live in multiple cultural worlds of family, school, and peer relationships, and support these students in integrating their cross-cultural experiences into a coherent sense of self (Phelan, Davidson, & Yu, 1991). Educators can empower such students by affirming that successful development does not require that the meanings and self-other-world understandings of their minority culture be assimilated into a dominant Autonomous culture, since these are not deficits but assets – particularly under conditions of racism, immigration, or poverty (Harrison, Wilson, Pine, Chan, & Buriel, 1990) – that serve as indicators of promise rather than risk.

# REFERENCES

Barna, L. M. (1997). Stumbling blocks in intercultural communication. In L. Samovar and R. Porter (Eds.), *Intercultural communication: A reader* (pp. 370-379). Belmont, CA: Wadsworth.

Bellah, R. N., Madsen, R., Sullivan, W. M., & Tipton, S. M. (1985). *Habits of the heart.* New York: Harper & Row.

Bennet, M. J. (1993). Towards ethnorelativism: A developmental model of intercultural sensitivity. In R. Michael Paige (Ed.), *Education for the intercultural experience.* Yarmouth, ME: Intercultural Press.

Boucher, J. D., Landis, D., & Clark, K. A. (1987). *Ethnic conflict: International perspectives.* Newbury Park, CA: Sage.

Brislin, R. (1993). *Understanding culture's influence on behavior.* For Worth, TX: Harcourt Brace Jovanovich.

Broughton, J. M., & Zahaykevich, M. K. (1988). Ego and ideology: A critical review of Loevinger's theory. In D. K. Lapsley and F. C. Power (Eds.), *Self, ego, and identity: Integrative approaches* (pp. 179-208). New York: Springer-Verlag.

Bruner, J. (1986). *Actual minds, possible worlds.* New York: Plenum Press.

Cantor, N., & Kihlstrom, J. F. (1987). *Personality and social intelligence.* Englewood Cliffs, NJ: Prentice-Hall.

Chao, K. R. (1996). Chinese and European American mothers' beliefs about the role of parenting in children's school success. *Journal of Cross-Cultural Psychology, 27,* 403-423.

Chiu, L. H. (1972). A cross-cultural comparison of cognitive styles in Chinese and American children. *International Journal of Psychology, 7,* 235-242.

Cooper, C. R. (1999). Multiple selves, multiple worlds: Cultural perspectives on individuality and connectedness in adolescent development. In A. S. Masten (Ed.), *Cultural processes in child development: The Minnesota symposium on child psychology* (Vol. 29, pp. 25-57). Mahwah, NJ: Lawrence Erlbaum.

Damon, W. (1995). *Greater expectations: Overcoming the culture of indulgence in America's homes and schools.* New York: Free Press.

Erikson, E. (1968). *Identity: Youth and crisis.* New York: Norton.

Erikson, E. (1982). *The life cycle completed.* New York: Norton.

Ferrante, J. (1992). *Sociology: A global perspective.* Belmont, CA: Wadsworth.

Frankfurt, H. (1993). On the necessity of ideals. In G. Noam & T. Wren (Eds.), *The moral self* (pp. 16-27). Cambridge, MA: The MIT Press.

Gardner, H., & Hatch, T. (1989). Multiple intelligences go to school: Educational implications of the theory of multiple intelligences. *Educational Researcher, 18,* 4-10.

Geertz, C. (1973). *The interpretation of cultures.* New York, NY: Basic Books.

Giesbrecht, N. (1998a). Gender patterns of psychosocial development. *Sex Roles, 39*(5-6), 463-478.

Giesbrecht, N. (1998b). *Liberal decisions and moral reasoning in the Defining Issues Test*. Paper presented at the annual convention for the Association for Moral Education, Dartmouth College, Hanover, NH.

Giesbrecht, N., & Sevcik, I. (2000). The process of recovery and rebuilding among abused women in the conservative evangelical subculture. *Journal of Family Violence, 15*(3), 229-248.

Giesbrecht, N. (2000). *Ego development, religious tradition, and spiritual reflection*. Paper presented at the International Conference Search for Meaning in the New Millenium. Vancouver, BC.

Giesbrecht, N., & Walker, L. (2000). Ego development and the construction of a moral self. *Journal of College Student Development, 41*(2), 157-171.

Gilligan, C. (1982). *In a different voice*. Cambridge, MA: Harvard University Press.

Greenwald, A. G., & Pratkanis, A. R. (1984). The self. In R. S. Wyer & T. Srulll (Eds.), *Handbook of social cognition* (Vol. 3, pp. 129-178). Hillsdale, NJ: Lawrence Erlbaum.

Hall, E. T. (1976). *Beyond culture*. New York: Anchor.

Harrison, A. O., Wilson, M. N., Pine, C. J., Chan, S. Q., & Buriel, R. (1990). Family ecologies of ethnic minority children. *Child Development, 61*, 347-362.

Hauser, S. T. (1993). Loevinger's model and measure of ego development: A critical review, II. *Psychological Inquiry, 4*, 23-30.

Hunter, J. D. (1991). *Culture wars: The struggle to define America*. New York: Basic Books.

Hunter, J. D. (1994). *Before the shooting begins: Searching for democracy in America's culture war*. New York: Free Press.

Hy, X. L., & Loevinger, J. (1996). *Measuring ego development* (2nd ed.). Mahwah, NJ: Erlbaum.

Jensen, L. A. (1997). Different worldviews, different morals: America's culture war divide. *Human Development, 40*, 325-244.

Josselson, R. (1987). *Finding herself: Pathways to identity development in women*. San Francisco: Jossey-Bass.

Kashima, Y. (2000). Conceptions of culture and person for psychology. *Journal of Cross-Cultural Psychology, 31*, 14-32.

Kitiyama, S., Takagi, H., & Matsumoto, H. (1995). Causal attributions of success and failure: Cultural psychology of the Japanese self. *Japanese Psychological Review, 38*, 247-280.

Kitiyama, S., & Wakabayashi, T. (1996). *Script for self-improvement in Japan*. Unpublished manuscript, Kyoto University, Kyoto, Japan.

Kohlberg, L. (1981). *The philosophy of moral development*. San Francisco, CA: Harper & Row.

Liu, I. (1986). Chinese cognition. In M. H. Bond (Ed.), *The psychology of the Chinese people* (pp. 73-105). New York: Oxford University Press.

Loevinger, J. (1976). *Ego development: Conceptions and theories*. San Francisco: Jossey-Bass.

Loevinger, J. (1987). *Paradigms of personality*. New York: Freeman.

Markus, H. R., Mullally, P. R., & Kitiyama, S. (1997). Selfways: Diversity in modes of cultural participation. In U. Neisser & D. A. Jopling (Eds.), *The contextual self in context: Culture, experience, self-understanding* (pp. 13-61). Cambridge, MA: Cambridge University Press.

Markus, H. R., & Kitayama, S. (1991). The cultural psychology of personality. *Journal of Cross-Cultural Psychology, 29*, 63-87.

Markus, H. R., & Kitayama, S. (1998). Culture and the self: Implications for cognition, emotion, and motivation. *Psychological Review, 98*, 224-253.

Maslow, A. H. (1954). *Motivation and personality*. New York: Harper.

Matsumoto, D. (2000). *Culture and psychology: People around the world* (2nd ed.). Stamford, CT: Thomson Learning.

Mead, G. H. (1934). *Mind, self, and society*. Chicago, IL: University of Chicago Press.

Morris, R. W. (1994). *Values in sexuality education: A philosophical study*. New York: University Press of America.

Niedenthal, P. M., & Beike, D. R. (1997). Interrelated and isolated self-concepts. *Personality and Social Psychology Review, 1*, 106-128.

Noam, G. (1993). "Normative vulnerabilities" of self and their transformations in moral action. In G. Noam & T. Wren (Eds.), *The moral self* (pp. 209-238). Cambridge, MA: MIT Press.

Ogbu, J. U. (1990). Cultural model, identity, and literacy. In J. W. Stigler, R. A. Shweder, & G. Herdt (Eds.), *Cultural psychology: essays on comparative human development* (pp. 520-541). Cambridge, MA: Cambridge University Press.

Oyserman, D., Gant, L., & Ager, J. (1995). A socially contextualized model of African American identity: Possible selves and school persistence. *Journal of Personality and Social Psychology, 69*, 1216-1232.

Phelan, P., Davidson, A. L., & Yu, H. C. (1991). "Students' multiple worlds: Navigating the borders of family, peer, and school cultures". In P. Phelan & A. L. Davidson (Eds.), *Renegotiating cultural diversity in American schools* (pp. 52-58). New York: Teachers College Press.

Phinney, J. S. (1993). Multiple group identities: Differentiation, conflict, and integration. In J. Kroeger (Ed.), *Discussions on ego identity*. Hillsdale, NJ: Lawrence Erlbaum Associates.

Ross, L. D. (1977). The intuitive psychologist and his shortcomings: Distortions in the attribution process. In L. Berkowitz (Ed.), *Advances in experimental social psychology* (Vol. 10, pp. 173-220). New York: Academic Press.

Shweder, R. (1991). *Thinking through cultures*. Cambridge, MA: Harvard University Press.

Shweder, R. A., Much, N. C., Mahapatra, M., & Park, L. (1997). The "big three" of morality (Autonomy, Community, Divinity) and the "big three" explanations of suffering. In A. M. Brandt & P. Rozin (Eds.), *Morality and health* (pp. 119-169). New York: Routledge.

Shweder, R. A., & Sullivan, M. A. (1993). Cultural psychology: Who needs it? *Annual review of Psychology, 44*, 497-523.

Smith-Lovin, L., & Robison, D. T. (1992). Gender and conversational dynamics. In C. Ridgeway (Ed.), *Gender, interaction and inequality* (pp. 122-156). New York: Springer-Verlag.

Sternberg, R. J. (1986). *Intelligence applied: Understanding and increasing your intellectual skills*. New York: Harcourt Brace Jovanovitch.

Sternberg, R. J. (1997). *Successful intelligence*. New York: Plume.

Tafarodi, R. W., & Swann, W. B. Jr. (1996). Individualism-collectivism and global self-esteem: Evidence for a cultural trade-off. *Journal of Cross-Cultural Psychology, 27*, 651-672.

Takata, T. (1987). Self-deprecative tendencies in self-evaluation through social comparison. *Japanese Journal of Experimental Social Psychology, 27*, 27-36.

Ting-Toomey, S. (1991). Intimacy expressions in three cultures: France, Japan, and the United States. *International Journal of Intercultural Relations, 15*, 29-46.

Triandis, H. C. (1989). The self and social behavior in differing social contexts. *Psychological review, 96*, 506-520.

Triandis, H. C. (1995). *Individualism and collectivism*. Boulder, CO: Westview Press.

Vaillant, G. E. (1977). *Adaptation to life*. Boston, MA: Little and Brown.

Vygotsky, L. S. (1978). *Mind in society*. Cambridge, MA: MIT Press.

Weisz, J. R., Rothbaum, F. M., & Blackburn, T. C. (1984). Standing out and standing in: The psychology of control in America and Japan. *American Psychologist, 39*, 955-969.

Wells, L. E., & Stryker, S. (1988). Stability and change in self over the life course. In P. B. Baltes & D. L. Featherman, *Life-span development and behavior*, (Vol. 8, pp. 191-229). Hillsdale, NJ, USA: Lawrence Erlbaum.

White, G. M., & Kirkpatrick, J. (Eds.). (1985). *Person, self, and experience: Exploring Pacific ethnopsychologies*. Berkeley: University of California Press.

Whiting, B. (1976). The problem of the packaged variable. In K. Riegel & J. Meachem (Eds.), *The developing individual in a changing world: Historical and cultural issues* (Vol. 1, pp. 303-309). The Hague, Netherlands: Mouton.

Willians, J., & Best, D. (1990). *Measuring sex stereotypes: A multination study*. Beverly Hills, CA: Sage.

Worell, J. (1981). Life-span sex roles: Development, continuity, and change. In R. M. Lerner & N. A. Busch-Rossnagel (Eds.), *Individuals as producers of their development: A life-span perspective* (pp. 313-347). New York: Academic Press.

Wren, T. (1993). The open-textured concepts of morality and the self. In G. Noam & T. Wren (Eds.), *The moral self* (pp. 78-95). Cambridge, MA: MIT Press.

Yan, W., & Gaier, L. E. (1994). Causal attributions for college success and failure: An Asian-American comparison. *Journal of Cross-Cultural Psychology, 25*, 146-158.

Yao, L. E. (1985). A comparison of family characteristics of Asian American and Anglo American high achievers. *International Journal of Comparative Sociology, 26*, 198-206.

Yoshida, T., Kojo, K., & Kaku, H. (1982). A study on the development of self-presentation in children. *Japanese Journal of Educational Psychology, 30*, 30-37.

Yu, A. B. (1992, July). The self and life goals of traditional Chinese: A philosophical and cultural analysis. Paper presented at the meeting of the International Congress of Cross-Cultural Psychology, Liege, Belgium.

# INDEX